POLITICAL PHILOSOPHY
IN A PANDEMIC

POLITICAL PHILOSOPHY IN A PANDEMIC

ROUTES TO A MORE JUST FUTURE

edited by
Fay Niker and Aveek Bhattacharya

BLOOMSBURY ACADEMIC
LONDON • NEW YORK • OXFORD • NEW DELHI • SYDNEY

BLOOMSBURY ACADEMIC
Bloomsbury Publishing Plc
50 Bedford Square, London, WC1B 3DP, UK
1385 Broadway, New York, NY 10018, USA
29 Earlsfort Terrace, Dublin 2, Ireland

BLOOMSBURY, BLOOMSBURY ACADEMIC and the Diana logo are trademarks
of Bloomsbury Publishing Plc

First published in Great Britain 2021

Cover design by Ben Anslow

A catalogue record for this book is available from the British Library.

Library of Congress Cataloging-in-Publication Data
Names: Niker, Fay, editor. | Bhattacharya, Aveek, editor.
Title: Political philosophy in a pandemic : routes to a more just future / [edited by]
Fay Niker and Aveek Bhattacharya.
Description: London ; New York : Bloomsbury Academic, 2021. |
Includes bibliographical references and index. |
Identifiers: LCCN 2021007662 (print) | LCCN 2021007663 (ebook) |
ISBN 9781350225893 (hardback) | ISBN 9781350225909 (paperback) |
ISBN 9781350225916 (ebook) | ISBN 9781350225923 (epub)
Subjects: LCSH: COVID-19 (Disease)–Philosophy. |
COVID-19 (Disease)–Political aspects. | Epidemics–Philosophy.
Classification: LCC RA644.C67 P65 2021 (print) | LCC RA644.C67 (ebook) |
DDC 362.1962/414—dc23
LC record available at https://lccn.loc.gov/2021007662
LC ebook record available at https://lccn.loc.gov/2021007663

ISBN: HB: 9781-3502-2589-3
        PB: 9781-3502-2590-9
        ePDF: 9781-3502-2591-6
        eBook: 9781-3502-2592-3

Typeset by RefineCatch Limited, Bungay, Suffolk
Printed and bound in Great Britain

To find out more about our authors and books visit www.bloomsbury.com
and sign up for our newsletters.

Dedicated to James Towey

CONTENTS

Contents

CONTRIBUTORS

Matthew Adams is Assistant Professor in Philosophy at the University of Indiana, Bloomington. His research interests are in political philosophy, ethical theory and applied ethics. He has published several articles in these areas, as well as co-editing *Methods in Bioethics: The Way We Reason Now* (2017).

Christian Baatz is Professor of Climate Ethics, Sustainability and Global Justice at Kiel University, where he is leading a research project on the just distribution of climate change adaptation finance. His current work also focuses on the justification and application of human rights norms.

Katharina Bauer is Assistant Professor of Practical Philosophy at Erasmus School of Philosophy. Her areas of specialisation are moral philosophy, self-optimisation and enhancement, theories of practical necessity, and theories of personal identity and character.

Aveek Bhattacharya is Chief Economist at the Social Market Foundation, a non-partisan think tank based in London. He holds an MPhil in Political Theory from the University of Oxford and a PhD in Social Policy from the London School of Economics and Political Science. He is one of the editors of *Justice Everywhere*, a blog about philosophy in public affairs.

Paul Billingham is Associate Professor of Political Theory and a Fellow of Magdalen College at the University of Oxford. Most of his research focuses on debates within political liberalism and concerning the place of religion in public life.

Nicolás Brando is Newton International Fellow (British Academy) at the Centre for Children's Rights at Queen's University Belfast. His research focuses on justice, education and children's rights. He is co-editor of the volume *Philosophy and Child Poverty: Reflections on the Ethics and Politics of Poor Children and their Families* (2019).

Kimberley Brownlee is Professor of Philosophy at the University of British Columbia. Her current work focuses on the ethics of sociability, social rights, human rights and freedom of association. Most recently, she has been leading a project entitled 'Investigating the Ethics and Politics of Sociability', which has produced – among other things – a monograph called *Being Sure of Each Other* (2020).

Rowan Cruft is Professor of Philosophy at the University of Stirling. His research examines the nature and justification of rights and duties, and their role in shaping a democratic public sphere. Most recently, he has published a monograph entitled *Human Rights, Ownership, and the Individual* (2019). His research is guided by the aim of demonstrating how philosophical positions bear on the justification of public policies and law and, to this end, he has participated in policy development and public inquiries, including as an invited witness at the Leveson Inquiry and as co-author of a submission to the Commission on a Bill of Rights for the UK.

Avner de-Shalit is a political philosopher and Max Kampelman Chair of Democracy and Human Rights at the Hebrew University of Jerusalem. His research and teaching interests lie in equality, democracy and human rights, environmental politics and urban politics. His current research focuses on political theory and cities, about which he has published two books: *The Spirit of Cities: Why the Identity of a City Matters in a Global Age* (with Daniel Bell, 2013) and *Cities and Immigration: Political and Moral Dilemmas in the New Era of Immigration* (2018).

Katarina Pitasse Fragoso is a postdoctoral research fellow in the Political Science department at São Paulo University, where her research is attached to the Centre for Metropolitan Studies. Her work focuses on issues of relational inequalities, poverty and public policy.

Anca Gheaus is Assistant Professor in Political Theory at the Central European University in Vienna. Her research centres on justice and the normative significance of personal relationships. She is the co-editor of the *Routledge Handbook of the Philosophy of Childhood and Children* (with Gideon Calder and Jurgen De Wispelaere, 2018) and is currently writing a monograph on child-centred child-rearing.

Julia Hermann is Assistant Professor in Philosophy and Ethics of Technology at the University of Twente. Her current research is embedded in the ten-year research programme 'The Ethics of Socially Disruptive Technologies', funded by the Dutch Organisation for Scientific Research (NWO). She is the author of the book *On Moral Certainty, Justification and Practice: A Wittgensteinian Perspective* (2015).

Lisa Herzog is Associate Professor and Rosalind Franklin-Fellow in the Faculty of Philosophy and the Centre for Philosophy, Politics and Economics at the University of Groningen. Her research lies at the intersection of political philosophy and economic thought. She is the author of *Inventing the Market* (2013) and *Reclaiming the System: Moral Responsibility, Divided Labour, and the Role of Organizations in Society* (2018).

Jeffrey Howard is Associate Professor of Political Theory at University College London. He works on topics in contemporary political and legal philosophy, focusing on freedom of speech, criminal punishment and democracy.

Viktor Ivanković is a research assistant at the Institute of Philosophy in Zagreb, Croatia. He holds a PhD in Political Theory from Central European University. His current research focuses on the ethics of nudging, namely the institutional requirements for nudge permissibility. His other interests are in distributive justice and bioethics.

David Jenkins is Lecturer in Political Theory at the University of Otago. His current work focuses on sociality within urban experiences, the concept of partisanship (with an emphasis on the Communist Party India (Marxist) in Kerala) and homelessness and housing rights. He is co-editor, together with Kimberley Brownlee and Adam Neal, of *Being Social: The Philosophy of Social Human Rights* (2021).

Rebecca Lowe is a doctoral researcher at King's College London, and research director at an investment company. Her current research is on Lockean justifications for private property. She is the former (and inaugural) director of FREER, a small think tank promoting economically and socially liberal ideas housed at the Institute of Economic Affairs, where she was also a research fellow.

Fay Niker is Lecturer in Philosophy at the University of Stirling. Her main research and teaching interests lie in social and political philosophy and practical ethics. Within this, her current research focuses on the ethics of influence broadly understood, including topics such as autonomy, paternalism, nudging and trust. She also co-edits a collaborative blog about philosophy in public affairs, *Justice Everywhere*.

Onora O'Neill is Emeritus Honorary Professor at the University of Cambridge and a cross-bench Member of the House of Lords. Baroness O'Neill has written widely on political philosophy and ethics, international justice and bioethics. In addition to serving as a member of the House of

Lords since 2000, she has also served as President of the British Academy (2005–9), chaired the Nuffield Foundation (1998–2010) and chaired the Equality and Human Rights Commission (2012–16).

Tom Parr is Associate Professor in Political Theory at the University of Warwick and a Marie Skłodowska-Curie Individual Fellow at Universitat Pompeu Fabra, Barcelona. He is currently completing a project on 'Social Justice and the Future of Work'. His first book is *Introducing Political Philosophy: A Policy-Driven Approach* (with Will Abel, Elizabeth Kahn and Andrew Walton, 2021).

Felix Pinkert is Assistant Professor of Philosophy and Economics at the University of Vienna, working on contemporary moral, political and social philosophy. His research is motivated by an interest in ethical puzzles that arise when we can make the world better only by working together, in climate ethics, and in how to justly live together in an ideologically, religiously and culturally diverse society.

Diana Popescu is a teaching fellow at King's College London. She works on distributive justice, recognition theory and the relation between the two with respect to recognition struggles, disability rights, minority discrimination and social exclusion.

Lovro Savić is a doctoral researcher at the Ethox Centre, Wellcome Centre for Ethics and Humanities, and Green Templeton College, University of Oxford. His research interests include public health ethics, bioethics and philosophy of medicine and psychiatry.

Marc Stears is the Director of the Sydney Policy Lab at the University of Sydney. Before this, he was Professor of Political Theory at the University of Oxford and Chief Executive of the New Economics Foundation. He has also been Chief Speechwriter to the UK Labour Party, a co-author of the party's 2015 election manifesto and a member of the Party's general election steering committee (2012–15). In his academic work, Professor Stears is an expert in democratic theory and the history of ideologies and social movements. His most recent book is *Out of the Ordinary: How Everyday Life Inspired a Nation and How It Can Again* (2020).

Adam Swift is Professor of Political Theory at University College London. He works on a wide range of issues in political theory, and with a wide range of collaborators. In recent years he has come to specialise in debates around equality of opportunity, education and the family. His most recent books are

Educational Goods: Values, Evidence and Decision Making (with Harry Brighouse, Helen F. Ladd and Susanna Loeb, 2018) and *Family Values: The Ethics of Parent–Child Relationships* (with Harry Brighouse, 2014).

Sara Van Goozen is Associate Lecturer in Political Philosophy at the University of York. Her research focuses on topics in contemporary just war theory and the ethics of killing, but she also works on issues relating to migration, animals and political obligations.

Alexandru Volacu is Associate Professor in the Faculty of Business and Administration at the University of Bucharest, and Director of the Bucharest Centre for Political Theory. He is currently the director of a national research grant titled 'Electoral Rights: a Relational Approach', and is a member of the REDEM Horizon 2020 project consortium. His research focuses on the ethics of voting, justice and the ideal/non-ideal theory debate. His most recent book is *Do We Have a Duty to Vote [Avem datoria de a vota?]* (2019), published in Romanian.

Katy Wells is Assistant Professor in Political Theory at the University of Warwick. Her research focusses on property and justice and, specifically, on the topics of housing and renting. She is currently writing a book about renting.

Jonathan Wolff is the Alfred Landecker Professor of Values and Public Policy at the Blavatnik School of Government at the University of Oxford. He is the author of several books in ethics and political philosophy, including *An Introduction to Political Philosophy* (1996, third edition 2016), *Disadvantage* (with Avner de-Shalit, 2007), *Ethics and Public Policy: A Philosophical Inquiry* (2011, second edition 2019), *The Human Right to Health* (2012) and *An Introduction to Moral Philosophy* (2018, second edition 2020). He is currently developing a new research programme on revitalising democracy and civil society, in accordance with the aims of the Alfred Landecker Professorship.

David Yarrow is Lecturer in International Political Economy at the University of Edinburgh. His research focuses on how economic ideas and expertise are used in public administration and democratic discourse. Specifically, he explores how economic ideas and expertise serve to naturalise contestable assumptions about human nature, work, money, ethics and the environment, and the implications of this for contemporary economic policy debates.

FOREWORD
Onora O'Neill, Baroness O'Neill of Bengarve

Many crises are followed by a return to normality. That has been a standard pattern for natural and social crises within and beyond living memory: storms were followed by calmer, normal weather; floods eventually ebbed and water levels returned to normal; wars were followed by normal peace time; economic slumps gave way to normal, ordinary levels of prosperity. But there have also been inflection points when events did not confirm these comforting expectations, and there was no return to the *status quo ante*. The pandemic that began in 2019 may be one of those points of transition where a return to what used to be, and to be seen as, normal may neither be feasible nor desirable. There is constant and understandable discussion of how life will improve when the schools can open, when we can see our friends, when we can go on holiday, when everyday interactions are once again possible. But some changes that have been introduced to deal with the pandemic may last after it has ended, and other changes may turn out to be necessary or desirable.

The essays in this volume look at some of the possibilities for seeking and building a better future after the pandemic through the lens of political philosophy, broadly understood. They have been written mid-pandemic, hence with no certainty about how long it may last, no tally of the total deaths, no certainty about the extent of longer-lasting morbidity, about the duration of the immunity produced by the new vaccines, about the cumulative economic damage, or about feasible or likely futures. Many of the authors hope that it will be possible to shape futures that are better than a 'return to normality', and explore possibilities for reshaping aspects of the world as it has been in recent times to make it fairer and more just.

Philosophers are not in the business of predicting the future, but they are rather used to looking at hypothetical scenarios, at possibilities as well as certainties, at the way things ought to be as well as at the way things actually are. Many of the essays in this collection take one or another, or several, of these approaches. The questions addressed are forward-looking. Rather than trying to chronicle what has happened, or asking who was to blame for the way things turned out, or trying to predict how things will turn out, they take a more practical approach and ask what aims, which action and which policies could or should be implemented after the pandemic.

Possibilities are not certainties. Both the duration and the severity of the pandemic and the extent and distribution of its human and economic consequences are still incompletely known. However, it is already evident that the effects of contracting the virus vary greatly for differing individuals, differing communities and differing societies. Some of these differences are correlated with age, some with health status and some with housing type or type of employment, while others are correlated with income and ethnicity. These correlations raise questions which the post-pandemic world will need to address, even if many of them cannot yet be answered. It is evident that clear thinking about possible futures will matter in selecting and implementing future policies that bear not only on public health, but on wider aspects of social and economic life. It is time to start considering which policies and which changes could help shape a more just future.

Clear thinking is not a matter of simple thinking, and any attempt to sketch how the post-pandemic world could and should be different must take account of the fact that the pandemic is not the only challenge with global implications that is currently disrupting established social and political practices and expectations. Other challenges include the pace of global warming and its urgent implications for climate change; the growth of economic inequality; the mushrooming use of digital technologies, including their frequent misuse to spread misinformation and disinformation, and the resulting proliferation of conspiracy theories and polarisation of public opinion. They also include intense challenges to democratic governance in some parts of the world, and an increase in the number of authoritarian regimes.

The essays collected here discuss many of these large and looming challenges. They ask what could be done post-pandemic to lessen inequalities, including unequal access to medical care and to education. They ask who should carry how much of the burden of meeting the economic costs of the pandemic. They investigate some of the damage that democratic processes have suffered, including those which have been exacerbated by responses to the pandemic. They discuss ways in which communication and interaction have changed in a world that uses digital technologies, but has yet to work out how to limit their misuse by disinformation campaigners and those who peddle conspiracy theories.

The COVID-19 pandemic has seen some of the world's most developed societies faltering in various ways. Some had been negligent about ensuring that they had the right structures and policies for addressing large-scale threats to public health. Some had come to rely on distant but potentially unreliable supply chains and just-in-time delivery systems for medical supplies. Others had failed to ensure that their medical services had the necessary surge capacity, or that they were training enough doctors or nurses. Despite serious (but much smaller) epidemics in the recent past—including SARS, MERS and Ebola—many societies lacked robust ways of securing equipment or facilities for testing, tracing and isolating suspected cases, for treating all who were infected, and even for ramping up supplies of oxygen.

In the wake of crises of all sorts it is conventional to say that lessons must be learned. The cliché has great relevance in this case. Much that has gone wrong in some societies and in some health care systems could have been avoided or averted. Responses to the pandemic in some countries were effective, but in all too many they were slow or ineffective. So, there are rather a lot of lessons to be learned, and this collection contributes some of the underlying considerations that will be relevant in working out what must be done.

CHAPTER 1
INTRODUCTION
Aveek Bhattacharya and Fay Niker

This book started its life in what we now, in hindsight, refer to as the first lockdown. In April 2020, we collected some early reflections from philosophers and political theorists on the ethical dimensions of the developing COVID-19 pandemic and published them on *Justice Everywhere*, the blog we help to run (Bhattacharya and Niker 2020). We soon noticed a few common themes running through the contributions. One was the idea that although the pandemic itself was unprecedented, many of the issues it has raised link to long-running questions of justice and political contestation. A second was the impulse to draw on these moral ideas and political debates to try to create a better society as we attempt to overcome the current crisis and to envisage the world beyond it.

It is common to note that crisis and opportunity often go together. There is something a little uncomfortable about this idea, in one sense. This discomfort perhaps comes from the thought that we shouldn't be thinking about the opportunities that a crisis like the COVID-19 pandemic offers; something about this forward-looking orientation seems not to pay due attention to the human tragedy currently being lived through. And this can certainly be the case when it comes to certain kinds of opportunism. For example, Naomi Klein opens her book *The Shock Doctrine* (2008) by describing how entrepreneurs viewed the devastation wrought by Hurricane Katrina in 2005 as an opportunity for property development and remaking the city's school system. One of New Orleans' wealthiest developers, Joseph C. Canizaro, epitomised the attitude behind what Klein has called 'disaster capitalism' when he said: 'I think we have a clean sheet to start again. And with that clean sheet we have some very big opportunities' (Rivlin 2005; cited in Klein 2008: 4).

There is clearly a different attitude motivating the 'build back better' impulse, which has been animating efforts across societies at framing what the pandemic recovery should involve and what our post-pandemic world should look like. The dramatic rupture to 'business as usual' that crises produce opens up space for collective reflection, political contestation and policy change.

There are at least two reasons for this. First, in dramatically disrupting the *status quo*, crises invite us – individually and collectively – to take stock, to reflect on and assess our existing situation. By exposing our vulnerabilities and highlighting deep social problems (often through exacerbating them), they summon us to consider how to redress, repair and rebuild our societies. Second, crises require that we take drastic steps. Such actions either remind us or demonstrate to us what we are capable of and what is politically possible. By showing that other worlds are possible, crises can inject more agency back into political discourse, since it is much more difficult for politicians to mobilise a sense of inevitability around the *status quo*.

Clearly, the current pandemic has the two features outlined above. First, the virus has picked at societal wounds, opening them for all to see. As many of the chapters in this collection detail, several forms of injustice that pre-dated the crisis have contributed to the damage caused by the virus, been worsened by it, or both – for example, educational inequalities, intergenerational inequity or inadequacy of housing. And it has also increased the spotlight on other ethical and political questions, such as how to address the problem of misinformation and disinformation being proliferated on social media. Second, we have seen fundamental changes and monumental achievements that could barely have been envisaged pre-pandemic. Individuals have made significant sacrifices and dramatically altered their behaviour – consuming less, travelling less and working from home. At a societal level, we have seen an outpouring of solidarity and appreciation for 'key workers' previously taken for granted. And governments have quickly produced bold and far-reaching policies, on a scale rarely seen outside of wartime, to guarantee economic security and temporarily end homelessness. A natural question, explored in a number of chapters, is whether these positive trends will continue beyond the crisis. And if not, why not – since we have already seen what is achievable?

The contributions to this volume explore the relationship between crisis and opportunity in an effort to set out routes to a more just world after the pandemic. In so doing, the volume examines a set of distinctively political-philosophical issues raised by the COVID-19 crisis. Some of these are obvious (e.g. the issue of what to do about elections scheduled during a pandemic); some are less obvious, but not necessarily any less important for that (e.g. how public health measures undermine our democratic culture). So, while the book touches upon important issues in medical and public health ethics, it is primarily a collection of essays in political theory. It is comprised of five parts, each picking out a major theme in the social and political fallout of the pandemic. The first is **social welfare and vulnerability**, which includes essays on the social determinants of health and the corrosive nature of disadvantage, the vulnerability of children during school closures, and the right to adequate housing. The second theme is **economic justice** and includes discussions of precarity, universal basic income, and intergenerational justice. The third part discusses questions relating to **democratic relations**, such as the two mentioned above – whether and how we should hold elections during a pandemic and the pandemic's effects on the democratic way of life – and others relating to the discriminatory assumptions underlying lockdown measures and whose voices should (and should not) count in legitimating pandemic-responsive policy. The fourth theme is **speech and (mis)information**, which examines issues such as whether efforts to repress misinformation about COVID-19 on social media violate freedom of speech, and the moral permissibility of shaming those who flout social distancing guidelines. Lastly, the essays in the fifth part examine the relationship between **crisis and justice**, including essays on the pandemic as an experiment in egalitarian living for the middle classes and on the lessons that we might take from the COVID-19 crisis for climate justice. This focus on the political-theoretical questions makes this book a valuable complement to other, vital collections that have concentrated on questions of public health ethics (e.g. Schwartz 2020).

Since we first began working on this book, many of those with whom we have discussed it have asked us if it will cover some or other significant aspect of pandemic: the ethics of vaccination and vaccine distribution, the legitimacy of restricting freedom of movement to slow the spread of the virus, and individuals' duties to inform themselves regarding the virus and restrictions, to name a few. In several such cases, we have, with regret, informed them that it does not. COVID-19 has been an all-consuming phenomenon, touching on almost every aspect of our lives and societies. This book does not make any claim to comprehensiveness in its coverage of the moral and political philosophy of the pandemic, even despite the wide range of pressing and interesting topics included here. There are certainly many worthy issues we have not addressed. As Onora O'Neill notes in her Foreword, these essays have been written 'mid-pandemic', most before we went into the second lockdown in the UK. We are now in 'Lockdown 3.0' – something that we couldn't have foreseen at the start of this project – and even with the vaccine rollout under way, there is still no certainty about how much longer this pandemic will last. And once the virus itself is under control, the hard work of rebuilding will only be beginning. Thus, this collection of essays is offered as the start of a crucial and ongoing conversation, and certainly not as the final word.

In the spirit of *Justice Everywhere*, the essays in this volume are academically rigorous but accessibly written attempts to apply insights from moral and political philosophy to contribute to our understanding of the pandemic – of what has happened and what should come next. They do not assume background knowledge; we hope, therefore, that they will be understandable and interesting not only to academic political theorists, but also to students (e.g. of politics, philosophy, public policy) and to anyone with a general interest in the questions we raise. The authors have also included some suggestions for further reading with their chapter, for those who may want to explore the ideas in more depth.

Overview of the chapters

One of the most significant aspects of the pandemic in terms of its impact on political culture may prove to be the vivid way that it has demonstrated the harms wrought by social inequality. As many of our contributors observe, among the most insidious aspects of COVID-19 is the way that it's effects have disproportionately hit some of the worst off in society. That is the phenomenon explored by **Jonathan Wolff and Avner de-Shalit** in Chapter 2. Drawing on some of the concepts developed in their book *Disadvantage*, they describe how COVID-19 demonstrates the harm of 'corrosive disadvantage', where deficits in one domain (e.g. lack of money) lead to deficits in another (e.g. worsened health), as well as 'inverse cross-category risk', where disadvantaged people are forced to trade off important goods (e.g. having to choose between financial and physical security). In the case of the pandemic, they argue that these dynamics have proved particularly acute for ethnic minorities in the US and UK.

The COVID-19 pandemic has, then, brought questions of distribution to the fore. Nowhere have they been so significant as in the healthcare system, where tough decisions have had to be made as to how to prioritise and allocate treatment. In Chapter 3, **Sara Van Goozen** reviews some of the decision rules that philosophers have proposed and medics have used in the past. In light of the experience of the current pandemic, she argues that these should be amended so that people with instrumental value in terms of fighting the virus, such as doctors, research scientists and perhaps even delivery drivers, should be fast-tracked towards the front of the queue.

Of course, the pandemic has not just had negative consequences for people's health and financial welfare, but its impact has also been felt in education and housing as well. In both of these domains, too, there has been a clear social gradient in the harms suffered. In Chapter 4, **Nicolás Brando and Katarina Pitasse Fragoso** consider the impact of school closures, as occurred in many countries around the world. They argue that the shift to online teaching failed the most vulnerable children in two major ways: compounding their educational disadvantage and putting their mental, emotional and physical well-being at greater risk. Beyond the current crisis, their article suggests that the move towards online schooling (a source of great enthusiasm in the educational community) is likely to widen rather than narrow inequalities. In Chapter 5, **David Jenkins, Katy Wells and Kimberley Brownlee** explore how government lockdowns should inform our understanding of adequate housing. They show that living in inadequate dwellings entails greater harm when confined to that dwelling under lockdown. They also show that housing that would be considered adequate under normal circumstances can become inadequate when the inhabitants are required to spend most of their time there. They argue that governments should respond by showing greater urgency in securing the right to adequate housing for all and by addressing some of the issues highlighted by the pandemic, such as many people's lack of access to outside space.

A key theme uniting many of the contributions to the book, and particularly those in Part I, is the idea that the negative impact of the COVID-19 pandemic has been mediated through economic inequalities and vulnerabilities. Part II therefore focuses on questions of economic justice raised by the pandemic. All three chapters argue that while the economic challenges we have faced and continue to face, and the responses they have generated, are on a larger scale than what we have seen before, the fundamental issues that gave rise to them long pre-date the current crisis. In different ways, each makes the case for a fundamental reset of our economic settlement and infrastructure.

David Yarrow begins in Chapter 6 with the question of how governments should go about paying off the huge public debts that have been amassed because of the pandemic. His chapter considers the claim that older people should bear more of the cost, either because they have received greater health benefits or because they have suffered less economic difficulty as a result of measures to control the virus. He argues that such notions have their basis in a luck egalitarian intuition but apply that normative framework too narrowly. He calls for governments to take a broader perspective and recognise that the economic vulnerability of younger generations is the consequence of a longer-term trend of privatisation and individualisation of the welfare state – a trend that must be reversed for fundamental intergenerational injustices to be righted.

In Chapter 7, **Lisa Herzog** picks up where Yarrow leaves off, describing in more detail 'the great risk shift' of recent decades that saw governments and businesses (especially in English-speaking countries) divest themselves of their obligations to their citizens and workers, leaving individuals more exposed to reversals of fortune. This has led, she observes, to an increase in 'economic precarity', which has contributed to the harm caused by measures to control the spread of COVID-19. In response, she advocates a return to the principle of social insurance, with a stronger safety net guaranteeing greater economic security against future downturns.

Diana Popescu shares a similar diagnosis to Yarrow and Herzog, seeing existing welfare states as deeply inadequate for the challenges faced by modern societies. However, she is dissatisfied with Herzog's proposal for a system oriented around social insurance. Instead of seeing social protection as a way of sharing individual risks across society, in Chapter 8 Popescu argues that a better reflection of the values and moral motivations demonstrated in our response to the COVID-19 crisis would be a regime based on social solidarity, recognising our common concern for one another. Such a regime, in her view, would involve a universal basic income for every citizen.

The pandemic has prompted governments to take dramatic, often unprecedented actions such as issuing stay-at-home orders to citizens and forcing businesses to close their doors for prolonged periods. This raises several deep political questions about legitimacy and democracy, which are the focus of Part III. In Chapter 9, **Rowan Cruft** takes on the question of how public support for a policy, for instance relating to the imposition or lifting of lockdown measures, contributes to the democratic legitimation of that policy's imposition. Specifically, he considers a largely neglected aspect of this issue: whose voices count in legitimating pandemic-responsive policy, and when? Cruft argues that the force of arguments – say, in favour of reopening the economy or schools – varies depending on who makes them, and on how these arguments treat the views and interests of others within their society. His chapter offers a new way of thinking about why some kinds of public support for a policy often do little to confer legitimacy on it.

Chapter 10 also engages with pandemic-responsive policy, and lockdown restrictions in particular, but raises questions about justifiability from the perspective of the design of these measures and what this reveals about governments' discriminatory assumptions about our social lives. **Felix Pinkert** contends that the 'household model' assumes a particular picture of social life that is outdated and has had harmful and discriminatory consequences for people – non-cohabiting couples and single people, for example – who do not fit this model. Governmental attempts to address this problem in an *ad hoc* fashion have revealed further discriminatory assumptions – in this case, of the elevated significance given to sexual relationships relative to other relationships. As a result, Pinkert argues that policymakers should better interrogate their social biases and seek out more neutral measures, for example, giving people a 'contact budget' that can be used to see any nominated others, regardless of one's relationship to them.

The two other chapters in Part III focus on democracy, in its formal and informal modes, respectively. In Chapter 11, **Alexandru Volacu** describes the 'pandemic electoral trilemma' facing polities with elections due during the coronavirus crisis. The three broad options on the table are to go ahead as usual with in-person voting, to switch to convenience voting mechanisms, or to postpone elections. Volacu argues that each of these options is bound to violate some plausible principle of electoral justice, but that depending on the context these concerns can be at least partially defused. The threat to formal democracy, described by Volacu, has received a lot of attention. What has gone largely unnoticed is the way in which COVID-19 has impacted on democracy as a lived practice by blocking everyday social connections. **Marc Stears** draws attention to and explains this danger in Chapter 12, before outlining three ways in which our collective response to COVID-19 needs to change if we are to protect and sustain our democratic way of life in this (and any future) pandemic moment: prioritising social contact alongside health and the economy, investing in socially distanced forms of social organisation, and deepening our commitment to social infrastructure that encourages serendipitous interactions.

Public communication plays a critical role in addressing a public health emergency such as COVID-19. In itself, this raises several political-theoretical questions around transparency and expertise. But added issues arise when this communication is taking place within our current social media landscape, in which misinformation and disinformation are widespread and our virtual social interactions can be vicious (double meaning intended). Part IV tackles pressing issues under this heading of speech and (mis)information. **Jeffrey Howard** kicks us off in Chapter 13 with his analysis of whether repression of rampant misinformation about

COVID-19 on social media networks violates freedom of speech. Such dangerous speech, Howard argues, is not protected by the moral right to free speech, and this opens up the possibility of justifying restrictions against it. The chapter then explores what such restrictions might look like.

Chapter 14 shifts our attention to governmental speech and in particular the issue of whether, as some believe, the democratic state's obligation to transparency is lessened in times of crisis, such as that posed by COVID-19. **Rebecca Lowe** argues that this view is mistaken, developing a framework for determining the justifiability of instances of state non-transparency generally, and then applying this to a COVID-related scenario relating to governmental speech about mask-wearing. But what about what we, as laypersons, can say concerning COVID-19? In their own ways, the other two chapters in this part explore this question. In Chapter 15, **Viktor Ivanković and Lovro Savić** argue that, when we're in a public health emergency, laypersons should practice restraint in their public speech and deliberation, especially with respect to empirical matters about the virus. But the need for restraint goes further, according to these authors. It extends to experts, too, who should abide by certain standards – set out by Ivanković and Savić – when communicating evidence and recommendations to laypersons. Chapter 16 addresses this question from a different angle. It asks whether we should use our speech to shame those who flout social distancing and mask-wearing guidelines. Public shaming has been a common feature in recent months, especially online, as new (and previously unthinkable) norms have been established; but is this practice ethically justifiable? While recognising the distinctive appeal of public shaming given the various roles it plays, **Paul Billingham and Tom Parr** distinguish several reasons for caution, including epistemic concerns, considerations of proportionality, and the dangers of privacy violations. The chapter concludes by making the more general point that social distancing shaming, even if justifiable, might be the wrong kind of speech; more specifically, it may be a distraction from the crucial democratic work of holding our governments to account by scrutinising their decisions and conduct through a crisis.

The final part of the book, Part V, takes up a related set of questions about the nature and value of crises such as the coronavirus crisis and the ways in which they might indirectly contribute to the development of a more just society. As we mentioned earlier, there is an impulse to hope for renewal, for a better world after this deep fracture. But this hope is nested within, or perhaps springs from, the despair wrought by this fracture and the destruction to people's lives, livelihoods and liberties that it has brought in its wake. The contributions in Part V seek to make sense of and to capture the hope, without falling prey to unrealistic optimism – but this is not an easy tightrope to walk.

In Chapter 17, **Matthew Adams and Fay Niker** locate the grounds for hope in the fact that crises transform people's understanding of the world in significant ways. But this revelatory potential, despite being a force of political and policy change, is limited in its reach. What might we do to enhance the epistemic function of a crisis, then? Adams and Niker explore different ways in which the social facts and injustices (further) revealed by the COVID-19 crisis might be made more salient to others, so as to prompt or even steer these people's personal reflection on the crisis. They raise an empirical concern for direct salience-raising measures, in the form of 'backfire effects', and then explore and defend an indirect means called 'epistemic nudging'.

Chapter 18 also reflects on how the experience of living through COVID-19 might have a silver lining. **Anca Gheaus** focuses her attention on the middle classes, and specifically those who are committed to some ideal of living in an egalitarian society but who, through a motivational shortfall, fail to make some of the necessary lifestyle changes required to bring this about. Gheaus charts the ways in which the enforced changes to our lifestyles under lockdown might help us to overcome these shortfalls by modelling to us what it means to live in a just world. But her analysis also highlights two dystopian features of these enforced changes: social disconnection and a denial of children's right to access to multiple sources of care.

One aspect of Gheaus's blueprint for a just world is climate justice. This theme is picked up and explored in Chapter 19. **Julia Hermann, Katharina Bauer and Christian Baatz** draw out the similarities and differences between the COVID-19 crisis and the climate change crisis, contending that this analysis gives us reasons both for concern and for hope. In this spirit of cautious optimism, the authors then offer some ways in which our response to the climate crisis might learn from the experiences of the current pandemic.

The final chapter, Chapter 20, takes a step back to consider what the COVID-19 crisis reveals about the nature of politics and political theory *in general*. **Adam Swift** suggests that the pandemic has, in large part, simply provided more vivid evidence of something we already knew – that we live in societies where people are subject to unjust laws made in unjust ways. But, slightly more optimistically, Swift considers the possibility that the pandemic might function as a wake-up call, alerting us to just how bad things have become and giving us evidence that big changes are politically possible. For that reason, he speculates, it may prove to be more effective in altering societal values than political theorists have managed to be.

References

Bhattacharya, A. and F. Niker (eds) (2020), 'Philosophers' Rundown on the Coronavirus Crisis', *Justice Everywhere*. Available online: http://justice-everywhere.org/international/philosophers-rundown-on-the-coronavirus-crisis/ (accessed 11 November 2020).

Klein, N. (2008), *The Shock Doctrine: The Rise of Disaster Capitalism*, London: Penguin.

Rivlin, G. (2005), 'A Mogul Who Would Rebuild New Orleans', *The New York Times* (29 September). Available online: https://www.nytimes.com/2005/09/29/business/a-mogul-who-would-rebuild-new-orleans.html (accessed 25 January 2021).

Schwartz, M.C. (ed) (2020), *The Ethics of Pandemics*, Peterborough, Ontario: Broadview Press.

PART I
SOCIAL WELFARE AND VULNERABILITY

CHAPTER 2
RISK, DISADVANTAGE AND THE COVID-19 CRISIS
Jonathan Wolff and Avner de-Shalit

Introduction: the unequal burden of COVID-19

The purpose of this chapter is to apply the framework set out in our earlier work *Disadvantage* (2007) to aspects of the COVID-19 crisis. By doing this we aim to highlight some key social vulnerabilities in a stark light, in order to aid thinking about how to prevent or remedy some of the worst inequalities that have been magnified in these most difficult times. In addition, it allows us to present a detailed case study to illustrate our earlier analysis and supplement the more general accounts we have presented before.

In our previous work we proposed that disadvantage has multiple dimensions, and that it is quite possible, conceptually, to be relatively disadvantaged on one or more dimensions but not necessarily in others. Yet a key idea from our work is that a number of empirical mechanisms tend to 'cluster' different dimensions of disadvantage together. The COVID-19 pandemic intensively illustrates this point, as if society has been hit by a gale-force wind, amplifying cracks into full-scale fractures. The concentration of disadvantage was not completely obvious at first, as the initial indications of heightened risk from the pandemic, at least in Europe, did not fall unambiguously into established patterns of disadvantage. For instance, while on the one hand there was a very stark age gradient in fatality, with older people being much more likely to die, and infection especially dangerous for those with co-morbidities, such as diabetes or heart conditions, on the other hand the percentage of deaths among men significantly exceeded those of women.

Since then, three more high-risk categories have been identified: those in low-paid or low-skilled occupations, those living in deprived areas, and those from black and ethnic minority communities (Harrison et al. 2020; Booth and Barr 2020). In this chapter we focus on these additional risk groups, especially the last one, and ask what can explain their vulnerability, drawing on our previous theoretical analysis of risk, vulnerability and corrosive disadvantage.

The figures regarding minority populations are highly alarming. In the United States, Latinos and African Americans are more likely to be infected than White Americans across all age groups. More specifically, in the 40–59 age range, Latino people are five times more likely to be infected than White people (Oppel et al. 2020). More troubling still is the percentage of deaths of those infected among African Americans, which became apparent early on and has not changed. According to a report issued on 17 May 2020 and based on racial details on the deceased for 93 per cent of all American deaths to that point, African Americans were 2.4 times more likely to die from COVID-19 if infected than White Americans, and 2.2 times more likely to die than Asians and Latinos. In some parts of the country the African American/White death rate ratio was extraordinary, such as that of 5.7 in the District of Columbia (APM Research Lab 2020). Figures in London and throughout the United Kingdom were not very different (Platt and Warwick 2020).

There could be various explanations for these gaps. Some will look first for genetic or other biological factors. Another obvious possibility is racism, either in discrimination in the provision of medical care, or in a deeper sense, in that being a victim of long-standing racism may take a biological toll and render a person more vulnerable. Environmental (socio-economic) explanations are also plausible. It is probable that several different factors all play a role.

Scholars of health inequality and the social determinants of health (that is, how our health is strongly influenced by the conditions in which we live and work) will not be surprised to see environmental factors affecting health. The social gradient in health is a long-observed trend (CSDH 2008; Marmot 2015). However, the effects of the social determinants appear to have intensified with the COVID-19 virus. The crisis has opened up fissures that have long afflicted many of the today's wealthy countries. The affluent, largely White middle classes have the assets and privileges that give them the best possible chance of riding through comfortably and coming out the other side relatively unscathed. Those in the risk groups mentioned above are more likely to struggle and suffer. And note that, unlike age and co-morbidity – at least as far as we know, at the time of completing this chapter (October 2020) – there is no purely medical reason why this should be so.

A theory of disadvantage

To put the issues in context, we draw on the analysis we presented in *Disadvantage* (2007), in which we attempted to tie questions of justice and equality to certain risk factors to life and health, drawing on the social determinants of health and other sources. At the heart of the analysis is a conception of human well-being, not as a deep philosophical theory but as an operational concept that should be taken into account by governments and other policymakers. We understand it as a political conception of well-being, which we defined as *genuine opportunities for secure functionings* (Wolff and de-Shalit 2007: 80).

The notion of functioning is taken from the capability literature, following Amartya Sen (1993) and Martha Nussbaum (2000). They argue that well-being is not a matter of wealth, or even happiness, alone, but rather is to be understood in terms of how well people can function. Hence they suggest the term *functionings*, which stands for what people have good reason to want to be or do. There are endless functionings: to love, to be loved, to read, to enjoy music, to run, to walk, to drive, to be healthy, and so on. Sen and Nussbaum differ in many details, including their accounts of which functionings are most important, and how to determine these questions, but they both agree that governments should not directly be concerned with functionings. Instead governments should act on capabilities, which are opportunities for (or freedoms to achieve) these functionings, and should evaluate policies by examining whether they offer these opportunities. For example, if reading and driving are functionings, literacy is a capability that can help enable them.

Our own research, which follows this track, enhances the analysis through interviews with many disadvantaged people – the poor, disabled, chronically unemployed, women in shelters, homeless people and so on – as well as those who provide services to them. Based on these interviews we argue that in order to profoundly understand well-being we must modify the capability approach to emphasise *secure* functionings and *genuine* opportunities for secure functionings (Wolff and de-Shalit 2007: 36–88).

Consider the contrast between someone with a permanent job, and someone with a job ostensibly on the same terms and conditions but on a fixed-term contract, and with uncertain prospects of renewal. This second person will have a completely different experience of life. They may postpone important life decisions, such as buying a house, getting married or having children, as they may be worried about what would happen if they suffer a dramatic fall in income. Our argument was that this aspect of vulnerability had not been sufficiently taken into account in contemporary philosophical accounts of well-being.

Furthermore, once it is understood that this type of vulnerability or insecurity is part of the lived experience of many people, and a critical aspect of disadvantage, it is possible to trace out its further effects. In fact, we distinguished two ways in which risk in one functioning spreads to another. The first is straightforward. Risks to one functioning can create risks to other functionings. If you lose income you might also lose your housing and your health, and in the worst case even find that your children are taken into care. In our terminology some lack of (or risk to) functionings creates *corrosive* disadvantages in that they are disadvantages that cause further disadvantages (i.e. risks to other functionings). And it is very easy to see how exactly the same reasoning applies to the pandemic. For example, a shop worker on low pay put on short hours, or even laid off, because of reduced opening hours and custom, is likely to suffer a series of other significant losses as a result.

The second way in which risk to one functioning spreads to another is when people 'trade' risks, putting one functioning at risk in order to protect another, because the other is more urgent, even if not more important. A good example is the reason why children below the poverty line are twice as likely to suffer from diabetes than children above it. Their parents want to secure the children's functioning of satiation, by means of cheap food, which is rich in carbohydrates (bread, pasta, rice, potatoes) that turn to sugar in the children's bodies. Because being hungry is unbearable, the parents act urgently to secure the functioning of being free from the feeling of hunger. In doing so, they put the functioning of being healthy at risk. In similar ways, people take risky jobs to protect their functioning of providing food and shelter for their families. In these ways, then, attempts to protect against one risk to functioning lead to increased risk to other functionings.

Note that this differs from the previous type, in which a risk to one's income leads directly to risks to different functionings. In these further examples, the risk comes from trying to protect income or health. Hence we call it 'inverse cross-category risk'. Consider someone who is aware that they are in a high-risk group regarding COVID-19 infection, for example because they are an ethnic minority or have diabetes. In order to protect their health from fellow travellers and workers they do not wish to travel on public transport for work that cannot be done at home, and so they resign from their job. They will thereby suffer both a loss of income and the adverse consequences of greatly reduced social contact. Attempting to secure what is immediately their highest priority – reduced risk of infection in this case – makes them highly vulnerable in many other respects. Therefore, we regard people in such situations as lacking *genuine* opportunities for secure functionings. To take another example, if a poor person is offered an opportunity to earn a decent salary only provided they commit to working regular lengthy night shifts – with the implication that they risk giving up going out with friends (the functioning of friendship), having a partner and a sex life (the functioning of intimacy), and so on – it rings hollow to say that they have an opportunity for a decent salary, although strictly speaking it is accurate to say this. But it is not a *genuine* opportunity in the sense in which we intend that phrase, because the costs of exercising it are too high.

This may seem mundane and obvious. But there is a further twist. A relatively modest increase in risk can have dramatic consequences when conditions turn extreme. A habit of staying at home with closed windows is bad for health in normal times, but in a heatwave leads to tragic deaths of elderly people. Furthermore, it has also been documented that in the Chicago heatwave of 1995 there was a clear divide on racial grounds, with African Americans affected to a much higher degree than, for example, Italian Americans in an adjacent neighbourhood because within the African American community the fear of harm to bodily integrity was much higher (Klinenberg 2002). The COVID crisis forces people to trade risks in a similar way.

COVID-19 and clustering of disadvantage

We noted above that on a multi-dimensional analysis of well-being it is possible for those who do poorly in one respect to do adequately on another. Our hypothesis, however, is that when we start to look for patterns, different factors of disadvantage will tend to cluster together, in that those who do badly in one respect will tend to do badly in others. And we have also postulated two possible mechanisms. One is where doing badly in one respect leads to problems elsewhere (corrosive disadvantage), and the other is where an attempt to secure one functioning puts others at risk (inverse cross-category risk). Before we can explore these possible mechanisms, however, we need to confirm that there is something to explain. In other words, we need to see whether COVID-19 has in fact clustered together different dimensions of disadvantage. To do this we have collated data from a number of sources. While we accept that there are always limits to the accuracy of data, the broad patterns are highly revealing.

We analysed the rate of morbidity and of deaths from COVID-19 among different ethnic groups in London and New York City. These cities have detailed data for each zip code (New York) or borough (London – albeit much larger in size than New York zip codes), both about COVID-19 victims and about the income, ethnicity and age of residents in each unit. The analysis was undertaken four times in 2020: in mid-April, mid-May, mid-June and late August. The results were consistent, with only very marginal differences between the four rounds.

We first noticed that poverty alone is not a very good predictor for the rate of morbidity or death. In fact, in London boroughs there was a negative (inverse) correlation between poverty and morbidity and even more so with death (see Figure 2.1). Nor could we find any clear association in New York between the percentage of people below the poverty line and official records of confirmed COVID-19 cases as of 15 June 2020. For example, in Long Island, North Queens and South East Queens morbidity is relatively high despite these being relatively affluent areas, whereas the poorest areas in the Bronx have lower rates of infection. This is somewhat counter-intuitive. For example, those on low pay designated as doing non-essential work may have lost their jobs or been furloughed and had to rely on state benefits often well below the level they are used to. This may have led to difficulties feeding families, or paying rent, and may therefore have led people to look for opportunities to earn money in the informal economy, which again may mean increasing contact with others outside the home and thus increased risk of infection. Yet the statistics do not show that such mechanisms alone have played a decisive role in determining infection and death.

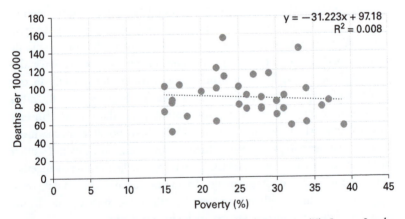

Figure 2.1 London boroughs. Death/100,000 (Y) for poverty (X). *Source: London Datastore (2020a; 2020b); Trust for London (2020); BBC News (2020); authors' calculations.*

The lack of association between poverty and death appears to run counter to our theory that disadvantage tends to cluster. However, further analysis is needed. What appears to be much more significant is that in both New York and London the percentage of non-White people and the percentage of African Americans or Black Britons were good predictors for morbidity and death, alongside different measures of age (both average age and percentage of those in the area older than 65). Different characteristics may well be more salient in different types of cases (see Appendix: figures 2.2–2.5 for London; figures 2.6–2.7 for NYC).

Explaining COVID-19 and clustering of disadvantage

The correlations between race and morbidity and between race and mortality are clear. What, then, can explain these phenomena? One obvious thought is that it has to do with the cost of health insurance and patterns of non-insurance. If this is right then it would be an explanation that fits well with our theory: lack of health insurance would be a type of corrosive disadvantage. In the UK, of course, it could not apply, but in the US it could. Compared to White Americans, African Americans are almost twice as likely to be uninsured (Bartel et al. 2019), and in all age groups African Americans are more likely than White Americans to have avoided seeing a doctor in the past year because of cost (Cunningham et al. 2017). But this does not give us the full picture. First of all, while healthcare is relevant to the progression of disease and death, it has little or no effect on who becomes infected. Second, compared to White Americans, Hispanic Americans are almost *three* times as likely to be uninsured (more than African Americans), and yet their share among deaths is disproportionally smaller than that of the African Americans. Hence lack of medical insurance alone does not seem to be a determining factor.

An alternative approach can be taken from our theory, according to which disadvantaged people often risk some functioning to secure another; what we called an inverse cross-category risk. Therefore, we need to ask whether there is a special reason why Black Britons and African Americans risk infection with the COVID-19 virus in order to secure other functionings. We suggested above that it could often be due to an attempt to secure the functioning of work and having consistent income. We noted that there was not a general correlation between poverty and high infection, but if working patterns vary by racial classification then associations may appear at a finer level of detail. Consequently, we need to look at employment patterns, and whether the work of Black Britons and African Americans puts them at special risk. This would be so if, for example, they are more likely to be employed in 'essential' or 'key' work sectors and so cannot isolate at home but must risk public transport and other social contact. And of course the danger is even higher if they work in sectors, such as health and social care, that put them at heightened risk. This is exactly what we find.

African Americans are 12 per cent of the American population, but they account for 30 per cent of licensed practical and licensed vocational nurses (Berchick, Barnett and Upton 2019). Nurses, of course, are in the front line of infection. The most dangerous occupations, other than health and social care, are likely to be forms of manual work that cannot be done from home, which are designated essential, and bring the worker into close contact with many others, also raising their chance of infection. Indeed, 27 per cent of the USA's bus drivers and 25 per cent of transport security workers are African Americans. Why, though, continue to work when one's health is put at extreme risk? Some, of course, will decide that they cannot take the risk, and thereby may lose their job and suffer further hardship. Others may not be fully aware of the risk, or may have a sense of personal invulnerability, or may feel it is their duty to remain, or believe they simply cannot afford to stop working. Most, surely, fall into this last category, even if they fall into others too. If so, we can advance the hypothesis that one reason for a higher death rate among African Americans is they are more likely to be placed in a situation that forces an inverse cross-category risk on them: the need to bring in an income forces them to risk their health, with inevitable visible effects at a population level.

In addition, living in a deprived area may well correlate with being regularly dependent on public transportation, and so those who live there are more likely to find it difficult to keep social distance. Indeed 20 per cent of African American households lack access to a car, compared to 6.5 per cent of White households. Moreover, those who decide to avoid the rush hour by starting their journey to work much earlier 'trade' securing their health by risking other functionings, such as being a good parent, as they would often start the journey before their children wake up or return home too late to be able to play with the children or read them a bedtime story. Although in some sense they are able to secure their health by these measures, we do not regard them as having a genuine opportunity for the secure functioning of health. It is not genuine because it involves risking other very important functionings.

Furthermore, poor-quality housing and overcrowding have always been understood to be corrosive disadvantages, associated with increased spread of infection, for obvious reasons. The latter could be yet another reason why African Americans die disproportionally to their share in the population. One aspect of such overcrowding is that, probably through a combination of cultural and economic factors, much more than White Americans, 25 per cent of African Americans reside in intergenerational housing (Loftquist 2017). If family members become infected at work or school, the grandparents who live with them are likely to be infected as well, and will be very vulnerable if they belong to other risk groups.

At this point it is hard to determine whether the attempt to secure other functionings by risking health is sufficient to explain the large racial disparities in health we have presented. We suspect that much more needs to be said. Earlier we suggested that biological issues might play a role too. For example, we understand that 26 per cent of those who have died from COVID-19 in the UK had diabetes (Diabetes UK 2020). Similar or even more extreme figures are reported in the US (Bode et al. 2020). This is very important because in the US diabetes is much more common among African Americans than among White Americans. The age-adjusted percentage of persons 18 years of age and over with diabetes in 2018 is 13 per cent for African Americans and 8 per cent for non-Hispanic Whites (OMH 2019)

Table 2.1

	White	African American	Asian	Hispanic	Total
Asthma hospitalizations per 10,000 population, age-adjusted (2012–2014)	7.8	44.1	5.6	33.8	27.6
Diseases of the heart hospitalizations per 10,000 population, age-adjusted (2012–2014)	70.4	106.8	36.1	73.6	94.0
Diabetes (primary diagnosis) hospitalizations per 10,000 population, age-adjusted (2012–2014)	10.0	37.3	5.0	22.6	22.4

Source: New York State Department of Health (2020)

and the gap in pre-COVID-19 death rates per 100,000 due to diabetes in 2017 is even worse: 38.7 for African Americans and 18.8 for non-Hispanic Whites (CDC 2019). Other illnesses that increase the likelihood of death associated with COVID-19 are asthma and heart disease. Table 2.1 shows the figures from New York.

These gaps are simply huge. We are not claiming to be medical experts, but on the basis of the evidence we have, it is likely that immediate environmental issues such as work and housing cannot explain everything. The statistics we see are consistent with various biological theories, including genetic predisposition. But we should be careful to distinguish 'biological' from 'natural'. If it turns out that there is a biological explanation, the degree to which such differences relate to longer-standing environmental causes, or even to the effects on the body of long exposure to racism, requires careful investigation as a matter of research priority. Any such research must be carried out with extreme sensitivity, so as to avoid stigma and the reinforcement of prejudice.

Similar considerations apply to body weight. One hospital manager told us that 'nearly all who died in my hospital were overweight.' Figures from the US indicate that, for example, about four out of five African American women are overweight or obese, and in the period 2013–2016, non-Hispanic black females were 2.3 times more likely to be overweight as compared to non-Hispanic white females (OMH 2020). These differences may well have multiple complex causes, combining genetic factors with lifestyle and diet, and the effects of low income on food choice and availability. Again, it is clear that further research is needed concerning how environmental and biological factors determine one's likelihood to become ill or even die due to COVID-19.

Conclusion

In our work *Disadvantage* (2007) we presented the hypothesis that different disadvantages 'cluster' together, and proposed two explanations for why this occurs. One possible mechanism is corrosive disadvantage, where one disadvantage leads to others, and the other is inverse cross-category risk, where the attempt to secure one functioning puts others at risk. As we hope to have demonstrated, the COVID-19 pandemic provides a critically important case study for our analysis, demonstrating how vulnerability intensifies risk. This, in turn, can aid policy development. In 2008 the WHO

Commission on the Social Determinants of Health announced that 'Social injustice is killing people on a grand scale' (CSDH 2008). The pandemic must concentrate minds on the fact that these death statistics are not merely misfortunes, but the result of policy choices that reflect and transmit injustice.[1]

Suggestions for further reading

- Marmot, M. (2015), *The Health Gap*, London: Bloomsbury.
- Klinenberg, E. (2002), *Heat Wave*, Chicago: Chicago University Press.
- Nussbaum, M. (2013), *Creating Capabilities*, Cambridge, MA.: Harvard University Press.

Notes

1. We would like to thank Aveek Bhattacharya, Fay Niker and Katarina Pitasse Fragoso for exceptionally helpful written comments on earlier drafts as well as the participants at the online workshop where this and other draft chapters were discussed.

References

APM Research Lab (2020), 'Color of Coronavirus'. Available online: https://www.apmresearchlab.org/covid/deaths-by-race (accessed 9 November 2020).

Bartel A.P., S. Kim, J. Nam et al. (2019), 'Racial and ethnic disparities in access to and use of paid family and medical leave: evidence from four nationally representative datasets', *Monthly Labor Review*, U.S. Bureau of Labor Statistics, January 2019.

BBC News (2020), 'Covid-19 in the UK: how many coronavirus cases are there in your area.' Available online: https://www.bbc.co.uk/news/uk-51768274 (accessed 22 July 2020).

Berchick, E.R., J.C. Barnett and R.D. Upton (2019), *Health Insurance Coverage in the United States: 2018. Current Population Reports, P60–267(RV)*, Washington DC: U.S. Government Printing Office.

Bode, B, V. Garret, J. Messler et al. (2020), 'Glycemic characteristics and clinical outcomes of COVID-19 patients hospitalized in the United States', *Journal of Diabetes Science and Technology*, 14 (4): 1–9.

Booth, R. and C. Barr (2020), 'Black people four times more likely to die from COVID-19 ONS finds', *The Guardian*, 7 May. Available online: https://www.

theguardian.com/world/2020/may/07/black-people-four-times-more-likely-to-die-from-covid-19-ons-finds (accessed 9 November 2020).

CDC (2019), *National Vital Statistics Report*, 68 (9): Table 10. Available online: https://www.cdc.gov/nchs/data/nvsr/nvsr68/nvsr68_09-508.pdf (accessed 9 November 2020).

CSDH (2008), 'Closing the gap in a generation: health equity through action on the social determinants of health' (WHO). Available online: https://www.who.int/social_determinants/thecommission/finalreport/en/ (accessed 9 November 2020).

Cunningham, T.J., J.B. Croft, Y. Liu, et al. (2017), 'Vital signs: racial disparities in age-specific mortality among blacks or African Americans – United States, 1999–2015', *MMWR: Morbidity and Mortality Weekly Report*, 66 (17): 444.

Diabetes UK (2020), 'NHSE statistics on coronavirus deaths in people with diabetes'. Available online: https://www.diabetes.org.uk/about_us/news/coronavirus-statistics (accessed 9 November 2020).

Gothamist/WNYC (2020), 'COVID-19 Deaths in NYC'. Available online: https://covidinteractivesny.s3.us-east-2.amazonaws.com/deaths-map.html (accessed 30 June 2020).

Harrison, E.M., A.B. Docherty, B. Barr et al. (2020). 'Ethnicity and outcomes from COVID-19: the ISARIC CCP-UK prospective observational cohort study of hospitalised patients', *The Lancet* pre-prints. Available online: https://papers.ssrn.com/sol3/papers.cfm?abstract_id=3618215 (accessed 9 November 2020).

Klinenberg, E. (2002), *Heat Wave*, Chicago: Chicago University Press.

Loftquist D. (2012), 'Multigenerational Households: 2009–2011', *Current Population Reports, P60–267(RV)*, Washington DC: U.S Census Bureau.

London Datastore (2020a), 'Coronavirus (COVID-19) cases'. Available online: https://data.london.gov.uk/dataset/coronavirus--covid-19--cases (accessed 22 July 2020).

London Datastore (2020b), 'Focus on London – Poverty'. Available online: https://data.london.gov.uk/dataset/focus-on-london-poverty (accessed 21 July 2020).

London Datastore (2020c), 'Ethnic Groups by Borough'. Available online: https://data.london.gov.uk/dataset/ethnic-groups-borough (accessed 23 June 2020).

Marmot, M. (2015), *The Health Gap*, London: Bloomsbury.

New York State Department of Health (2020), 'New York City Health Indicators by Race/Ethnicity 2015–2017'. Available online: https://www.health.ny.gov/statistics/community/minority/county/newyorkcity.htm (accessed 19 June 2020).

Nussbaum, M. (2000), *Women and Human Development*. Cambridge: Cambridge University Press.

OMH (2019), 'Diabetes and African Americans'. Available online: https://minorityhealth.hhs.gov/omh/browse.aspx?lvl=4&lvlid=18 (accessed 9 November 2020).

OMH (2020), 'Obesity and African Americans'. Available online: https://www.minorityhealth.hhs.gov/omh/browse.aspx?lvl=4&lvlID=25 (accessed 9 November 2020).

Oppel, R.A., Jr, R. Gebeloff, K.K.R. Lai, W. Wright and M. Smith. (2020), 'The fullest look yet at the racial inequity of coronavirus', *New York Times*, 6 July. Available online: https://www.nytimes.com/interactive/2020/07/05/us/coronavirus-latinos-african-americans-cdc-data.html (accessed 9 November 2020).

Platt, L. and R. Warwick (2020), *Are Some Ethnic Groups More Vulnerable to COVID-19 Than Others?* London: The Institute for Fiscal Studies.

Sen, A. (1993), 'Capability and well-being', in M. Nussbaum and A. Sen (eds), *The Quality of Life*, Oxford: Clarendon Press.

Trust for London (2020), 'Overview of London Boroughs'. Available online: https://www.trustforlondon.org.uk/data/boroughs/overview-of-london-boroughs/ (accessed 22 July 2020).

Wolff, J. and A. de-Shalit (2007), *Disadvantage*, Oxford: Oxford University Press.

Zipatlas (2020), 'Zip codes with the highest percentage of population below poverty level in New York'. Available online: http://zipatlas.com/us/ny/zip-code-comparison/population-below-poverty-level.htm (accessed 30 June 2020).

Appendix

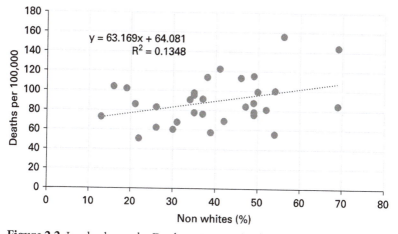

Figure 2.2 London boroughs. Death per 100,000 (Y) for % non whites (X). *Source: London Datastore (2020a; 2020c); authors' calculations.*

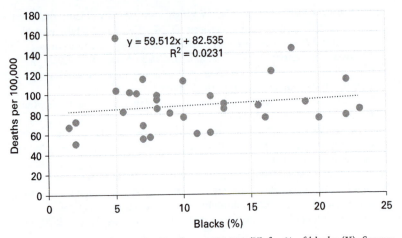

Figure 2.3 London boroughs. Death per 100,000 (Y) for % of blacks (X). *Source: London Datastore (2020a; 2020c); authors' calculations.*

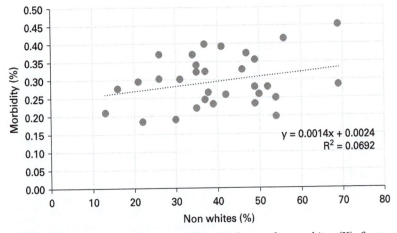

Figure 2.4 London boroughs. Morbidity (Y) for % of non whites (X). *Source: London Datastore (2020a; 2020c); authors' calculations.*

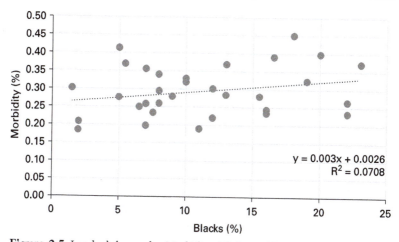

Figure 2.5 London's boroughs. Morbidity (Y) for % blacks (X). *Source: London Datastore (2020a; 2020c); authors' calculations.*

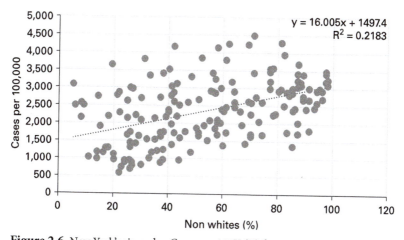

Figure 2.6 New York's zip codes. Cases per 100K (Y) for percentage of non whites (X). *Source: Gothamist/WNYC (2020); Zipatlas (2020); authors' calculations.*

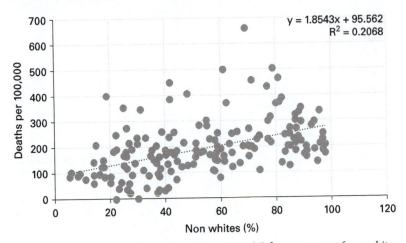

Figure 2.7 New York's zip codes. Deaths per 100K (Y) for percentage of non whites (X). *Source: Gothamist/WNYC (2020); Zipatlas (2020); authors' calculations.*

CHAPTER 3
HOW SHOULD WE DISTRIBUTE SCARCE MEDICAL RESOURCES IN A PANDEMIC?
Sara Van Goozen

Introduction

The question of how to allocate scarce, life-saving medical resources is unavoidable in healthcare. Even under non-emergency conditions, hospitals and health officials have to deal with scarcity of many essential resources, such as donor organs. Sudden, largely unpredictable increases in scarcity of essential resources due to natural events (such as hurricanes, earthquakes or tsunamis) are a recurring reality in many places across the world. A global pandemic like COVID-19 further highlights the need to decide on fair and practicable methods of allocating scarce life-saving resources.

In this chapter, I will first explain some of the key principles that need to be considered when deciding on a system for allocating extremely scarce medical resources in the context of a pandemic. I will focus on the allocation of resources necessary for treating the pandemic disease, such as ventilators, though much of what I say will also be applicable to other scarce medical resources. Subsequently, I will address one particularly controversial issue: should we give priority to those whose instrumental value is greater? I will suggest that in the context of pandemic disease, especially a disease such as COVID-19, it is appropriate to prioritise certain individuals on account of the roles they play in combating the disease.

General overview

When considering the allocation of scarce resources in emergency conditions, the relevant framework is that of medical triage. When more people arrive at a hospital than can be taken care of, a set of clear triage rules makes it possible for medical professionals to prioritise or de-prioritise patients, and to allocate to each the most appropriate – under the conditions – level of care. A simple, and fairly standard, approach to triage is based on the principle of maximising lives saved given the available resources. It divides patients arriving at a hospital into four categories:

1. those who are unlikely to survive even with treatment;
2. those who are likely to survive if they receive treatment urgently;
3. those who need treatment to survive but do not need treatment urgently (or who only need relatively uncomplicated or inexpensive treatment);
4. those who are likely to survive even without treatment.

The requirement to maximise lives saved then dictates that those in group 1 should not be treated (or only receive palliative care, depending on availability), and that those in group 2 should receive priority over those in groups 3 and 4 (Holm 2007).

However, such a simple approach, based on a single consequentialist principle, is open to serious objections. For instance, it ignores long-term prospects: it does not distinguish between someone who will die from a pre-existing condition within a year and someone who will go on to live for many healthy, happy years. A range of additional principles, which can be used to devise allocation strategies, have been proposed in the literature. I summarise the candidate principles in Table 3.1, drawing on a range of different sources (e.g. Cookson and Dolan 1999; Persad, Wertheimer and Emanuel 2009; Vawter et al. 2010a; White et al. 2009).

Relying on any one principle to determine allocation is likely to lead to unpalatable results (cf. Persad et al. 2009; Vawter et al. 2010a; White et al. 2009). For instance, focusing only on life-years saved does not account for the quality of those life-years, and may inadvertently exacerbate existing injustice: in the US, a healthy forty-year-old white woman from an affluent neighbourhood and a healthy forty-year-old man of colour from a low-income neighbourhood have very different life expectancies as a result of social inequality and racism. An approach focused solely on maximising life-years saved will prioritise white middle-class women, thus exacerbating the inequality (Vawter et al. 2010b). An approach focused on maximising QALYs (quality-adjusted life years) saved obscures the distribution of those QALYs – an outcome in which ten people get one additional QALY looks the same as an outcome in which one person gets ten additional QALYs (cf. Persad et al. 2009) – and may discriminate against people with disabilities. In addition, a single-principle approach does not enable us to choose between similarly situated people. It is therefore necessary to combine principles in

Table 3.1 Summary and explanation of possible triage principles

Principle	Underlying ethical principle	Summary
Maximising lives saved	Consequentialism (maximising a desirable outcome)	Maximise the total number of lives saved with the available resources
Maximising life-years saved		Maximise the total number of life-years saved with the available resources
Maximising QALYs[a]/DALYs[b] saved		Maximise the total number of QALYs/DALYs saved with the available resources
Lottery	Egalitarianism (chiefly equality of opportunity and/or luck egalitarianism)	Use a lottery to allocate life-saving resources
First come, first served		Help those that arrive at the hospital first
Priority for those not responsible for their condition		Help those that are not to blame for their condition first/de-prioritise those whose own choices led to their ill-health
Sickest-first	Prioritarianism (prioritising the worst-off)	Prioritise those who are currently the most ill
Youngest-first (Life-cycle principle)		Prioritise those who are the youngest (and have "the most to lose")
Adolescents/ young-adults first		Prioritise adolescents/young adults (for whom the misfortune of death is the most severe (cf McMahan 2002))
Reciprocity	Rewarding/ promoting social value	Prioritise those who have provided a valuable service to society (e.g. organ donors)
Instrumental value		Prioritise those who play an important (instrumental) role in society (e.g. doctors)

[a] Quality Adjusted Life Years: A measure of the state of a person's health in which the benefits, in terms of length of life, are adjusted to reflect the quality of life. Thus, one year of perfect health is assigned a value of 1, whereas a year of life with an illness is assigned a value of less than 1, for instance 0.75 or 0.5, depending on the severity of the illness.

[b] Disability Adjusted Life Years: as QALYs, but instead this measure adjusts for *disability*. For instance, a year of life with minor hearing loss might be assigned a value of 0.8, whereas a year of life with significant hearing loss is assigned a lower value.

such a way that the undesirable consequences of each principle are cancelled out or at least mitigated.

One attempt to combine principles into a single multi-principle system for allocating medical resources is worth mentioning briefly here. Persad and colleagues defend what they call the 'Complete lives system' (Persad et al. 2009, and for this model applied to COVID-19, see Emanuel et al. 2020). This system combines the two consequentialist principles ('maximising lives', 'maximising life-years') with 'adolescents/young adults first', and the lottery principle to decide between otherwise equal cases. It also allows a place for 'instrumental value', in specific kinds of public health emergencies. A virtue of this approach is that it provides a fine-grained system, which incorporates a range of plausible principles.

However, there are also issues with this approach. Most notably, Persad et al.'s model combines *too many* principles, including some which are likely to pull in different directions. For example, in the case of COVID-19, which largely affects older people, 'maximising lives saved' and 'maximising life-years saved' are likely to conflict. Consider the choice between saving a small number of people in their thirties, who are likely to live for forty or more years if saved, and saving a considerably larger number of people in their seventies, who are unlikely to live for more than ten years if saved. Here, the former principle suggests we need to save the people in their seventies whereas the latter principle – especially if it is combined, as Persad et al. do, with a young-adults-first principle – suggests we need to save the people in their thirties. This means that a complex approach such as Persad et al.'s is very difficult to operationalise (see Kerstein and Bognar 2010) and, as noted previously, it is incredibly important that triage rules are easy to use given the kind of situations in which they are used.

This issue could be resolved by using a ranking system. For instance, White et al. (2009) combine the two consequentialist principles (maximising lives saved and maximising life-years saved) with the youngest-first principle. Their ranking system allows clinicians to assign points to incoming patients based on where they fall on each of the three scales. This makes it more straightforward to operationalise this approach because it makes it easier to reach a decision in cases where two principles conflict.

The point of this discussion is not to defend a specific approach or combination of principles. However, it should be clear that the issue of how to combine different principles to arrive at a morally sound *and* easy-to-use approach is both serious and difficult to resolve. Some principles are less controversial than others – most models include one or more of the consequentialist principles. One question, then, is whether we should only use uncontroversial principles, or whether there is value in including some of the more controversial ones. In the next section, I want to develop an argument for the inclusion of a principle which is often considered one of the more controversial – instrumental value.

Should we include instrumental value?

The principle of instrumental value says that certain people should receive priority treatment because they play an important role in society. It is not strictly speaking an independent principle (cf. Persad et al. 2009), but it derives its justification from the consequentialist principle of maximising lives saved. Thus, as instrumental value is ultimately rooted in saving the most lives, it simply says that those who have an important role to play in maximising lives saved, such as doctors and nurses, should receive priority. The idea is that prioritising these people will ultimately enable us to save the most lives.

As the COVID-19 pandemic and the associated lockdowns across the globe have shown, there are many people who are instrumental in saving lives. This group, most obviously, includes doctors, nurses, others working in hospitals (including cleaners, for example), workers in care homes (especially in the case of the COVID-19 pandemic, which disproportionally affects the elderly), as well as research scientists working to develop a cure or vaccine. However, the category of 'essential workers' plausibly also includes others who save lives in a more indirect way. For instance, in order to limit the spread of the disease, it is critical that those who have been infected self-isolate. However, maintaining self-isolation for an extended period of time is difficult if you also need to go out and buy food. Thus, supermarket delivery drivers enable those who need to self-isolate to do so, playing a crucial role in limiting the spread of the disease. Similarly, the ability to work effectively from home whenever possible reduces the risk of infecting others, and so engineers working for internet service providers and IT support staff contribute to fighting the disease.

In what follows, I want to defend the inclusion of the principle of instrumental value as one of the principles that need to be used to guide allocation of scarce resources such as ventilators. Points could be given to patients arriving at hospital on the basis of their degree of instrumental value: those who are directly involved in combating the disease (and therefore maximising lives saved) would receive more points than those indirectly involved (such as delivery drivers). Those who receive a higher score overall are to be prioritised over those who receive a lower score. When forced to choose between multiple people with the same score, a lottery (or similarly fair decision-making procedure) should be used. For an example of what such a system would look like, consider Table 3.2 (adapted from White et al. 2009).

However, instrumental value is a controversial principle. Although some have endorsed it in the context of public health emergencies such as the COVID-19 pandemic (Emanuel et al. 2020), many have rejected it. I will now discuss three objections to the inclusion of the instrumental value principle.

Objection 1: Prioritising those who are involved in combating the disease is unlikely to contribute to saving the most lives

White et al. (2009) suggest that, given the average lifespan of a pandemic viral disease, and given the time it takes to recover fully from needing to be put on a mechanical ventilator, it is unlikely that those who present at hospital will be well enough to return to work in time to make a meaningful contribution to combating the disease. As such, it might be suggested, including instrumental value just makes the decision-making procedure more complicated, without any clear benefit.

In response, first, the claim that frontline medical workers are unlikely to be able to return to work quickly enough even if they are prioritised is highly contingent on a) the kind of disease and b) other measures taken to control the disease. For instance, in the case of COVID-19, many countries in Europe and elsewhere faced a 'second wave' with significant spikes in cases about six months after the initial burst of infections (Reynolds 2020). In such cases, it is likely that some doctors and nurses would have been well enough to return to work in time to treat the second wave. Because the reason for including the instrumental value principle is ultimately to maximise lives saved, whether it is included in a particular case is dependent on whether it would in fact contribute to maximising lives saved. In the case of a pandemic disease that is not likely to last more than a couple of months, there is therefore little reason to include it. However, where the effects of the pandemic are expected to last for several months, it should be included. Moreover, even when the worst of the pandemic is over, hospitals are still likely to be dealing with a backlog of serious cases, including delayed cancer treatments and so on. 'Maximising lives saved' does not simply concern lives

Table 3.2 Example of a multi-principle allocation system incorporating instrumental value

Principle	Specification	Points system			
		4	3	2	1
Maximising lives saved	Prognosis for short-term survival (e.g. SOFA[a] score)	SOFA score <6	SOFA score 6–9	SOFA score 10–12	SOFA score >12
Maximising life-years saved	Prognosis for long-term survival[b]	No comorbid conditions that limit long-term survival	Minor comorbid conditions with small impact on long-term survival	Major comorbid conditions with substantial impact on long-term survival	Severe comorbid conditions: death likely within 1 year
Life-cycle principle[c]	Prioritise those who have had the least chance to live through life's stages (age in years)	Age 12–40 y	Age 41–60 y	Age 61–70 y	Age > 70 y
Instrumental value	Prioritise those who play an instrumental role in combating the disease and maximising the total number of lives saved	Direct frontline involvement in combating the disease (doctors, nurses, other hospital workers)	Direct non-frontline involvement in combating the disease (e.g. medical researchers working on a vaccine)	Indirect involvement in combating the disease (e.g. delivery drivers, cleaners of public spaces)	No involvement in combating the disease

[a] Sequential Organ Failure Assessment.

[b] White et al. (2009) do not account for *quality* of life-years. If desirable (or feasible), allowance could be made for quality of life-years saved by using a measure such as QALYs instead of a simple assessment of the presence of comorbid conditions.

[c] As White et al. point out, in many situations paediatric patients may need to be considered separately with regards to e.g. the distribution of ventilators because their small size may require the use of different machines.

saved *from the pandemic disease*, but lives saved *overall*. Thus, even if there are few new cases coming in, doctors and nurses will still be working harder than usual to clear the backlog.

One might concede that it would be apt to include some priority measure for medical personnel, but question whether it is necessary to prioritise those indirectly involved. Medical personnel are difficult to replace, because of their extensive training. However, many of those who are indirectly involved in fighting the disease, such as delivery drivers, are relatively low-skilled and therefore easy to replace if they fall ill. There are two possible responses to this. On the one hand, we might concede that many low-skilled essential workers should not receive priority. This still leaves, however, a non-negligible group of higher-skilled essential workers which should receive priority, such as IT service workers.

On the other hand, we might want to assign a limited role to *reciprocity* as well as instrumental value. The reciprocity principle says that those who have provided valuable services in the past should be given priority. For instance, those who have donated kidneys or bone marrow in the past could be moved to the front of the queue if they themselves require an organ donation. Many essential workers often carry out their roles at significant risk of getting ill themselves. In these cases, assigning some priority to these people would serve as a recognition of this fact and could moreover serve as an incentive to take on these kinds of jobs, thus ensuring there is an adequate number of, for example, delivery drivers and cleaners throughout the pandemic, despite the risks associated with these jobs.[1] Regardless of whether we take the first or second approach – reducing the number of essential workers who receive priority, or incorporating reciprocity – some essential workers who play (or have played) an indirect but instrumental role in fighting the disease should be prioritised.

Objection 2: Prioritising those who contribute to fighting the disease introduces a slippery slope

Some might worry that allowing instrumental value to play a role in allocation opens the door to a much more dangerous and flawed principle: the 'broad social value' principle (cf. White et al. 2009). This principle suggests that those who contribute more to society should receive priority. This principle is obviously problematic: it is not clear who is in a position to decide what social value actually *is*, and people should not be penalised for their choice to pursue a career which happens to be valued as less worthy.

'Instrumental value' in the context of a pandemic is liable to be politically contested and difficult to define. As a result, its meaning could be stretched until it is ultimately not very different from broad social value.

However, this does not invalidate the instrumental value principle. The fact that instrumental value is justified by its link to the maximising lives saved principle limits its applicability to cases in which prioritising people on the basis of their role in society does actually contribute to maximising the total number of lives saved. This is true even if we decide to incorporate the principle of reciprocity, as suggested under Objection 1 above. The incentive-justification for the inclusion of reciprocity is a forward-looking instrumental justification. The claim was not simply that we should reward those who have provided valuable services, but more narrowly that we should prioritise those who contribute to fighting the disease in order to ensure that sufficient numbers of people will be available to fight the disease, for instance because including a priority measure might have an incentivising effect.[2] This closes off the possibility of a slippery slope towards assigning priority based on broad social value more generally.

Second, the specification that those who receive priority must be directly or indirectly involved in combating the disease serves to delineate those who may be prioritised according to this principle from the broader category of essential workers. The latter is a considerably larger group of people whose work is deemed essential for keeping the country (or the economy) 'going', and may include for instance police officers, postal workers and so on. Although it is certainly important to keep the country (and the economy) going during a pandemic, not least because doing so will enable a quicker recovery, these people are not involved in actually combating the disease. Since the instrumental value principle is derived from the principle of maximising lives saved, the instrumental value principle cannot justify giving priority to this broader group of essential workers, because prioritising them will not obviously result in an overall increase in the number of lives saved.[3] In other words, the instrumental value principle is actually quite narrow and less open to political manipulation than the broader category of essential workers. There is therefore little need to worry that it may lead us to embrace the implausible and dangerous 'broad social worth' principle.

Objection 3: Any kind of priority rule is unfair

The third objection is that it would be unfair to operate any kind of priority rule, but especially one that rewards or punishes people based on their choice of work. Martin Peterson (2008) argues that vaccines against pandemic influenza should be distributed by lottery. He does not address the distribution of other kinds of treatment, but his argument is not obviously limited to vaccines. He suggests that we owe it to everyone to give them an equal opportunity to receive required medical treatment. All priority rules, including principles such as 'maximise lives saved', are in violation of this principle of equality of opportunity (see also Taurek 1977).

The first thing to notice here is that this argument appeals to a very specific, and controversial, understanding of fairness. Consequentialists – the main target of Peterson's argument – will of course disagree fundamentally with this conception of fairness and offer their own version of fairness in response. After all, consequentialist approaches also appeal to fairness: the consequentialist approach to fairness is that each person should be given equal weight in determining the goodness of an outcome (Hirose 2010). This disagreement between consequentialists and non-consequentialists is fundamental and difficult to resolve, though one reason why a multi-principle approach is so attractive is that it enables us to combine consequentialist and non-consequentialist principles (for instance by using the consequentialist principles to make an initial priority ordering, and using a lottery to decide between otherwise equal cases).

It should also be noted that this objection misconstrues the argument for instrumental value. The claim is not that those who play an instrumental role in combating the disease are *entitled* to special treatment (and thus have a special moral status). As I have noted throughout this chapter, the argument for including instrumental value is more limited than that: it is simply that, in certain circumstances, giving priority to certain people may help us maximise the overall number of lives saved. Peterson's argument goes awry because he seems to assume that once a vaccine has been distributed to prioritised groups, there will be nothing left for anyone else. However, more vaccines can be produced, so it is not true to say that some people have *no* chance of receiving a vaccine – they might just have to wait a little longer (Hirose 2010). Of course, some individuals may end up not receiving a vaccine if they die before they receive it. But *ex ante* everyone does have a chance of receiving a vaccine, and this is also what matters for Peterson – after all, once the lottery has played out, it is no longer true that everyone has an equal chance of receiving a vaccine, as some will and others won't receive a vaccine. In a similar vein, prioritising certain individuals in a pandemic that lasts for several months does not mean others have no chance of receiving care. In fact, it might increase their chances of not only receiving care but having the care administered by a trained medical professional. In other words, by prioritising certain people so they are able to return to work as quickly as possible, we are actually ensuring that more people get an opportunity to be helped.

Conclusion

Pandemics and similar crises can cause medical resources to become scarce, raising the difficult question of how to prioritise care and treatment. I have suggested that the best approach is one that combines multiple principles – for example, considering both the number of lives saved and also the number of life-years saved among other things. In particular, I have made the case that instrumental value should be one of the principles we take into account when allocating medical resources: people who play a role in combating the disease and saving lives should be given priority over the rest of the population.

Suggestions for further reading

- Emanuel, E.J., G. Persad, R. Upshur, B. Thome, M. Parker, A. Glickman, C. Zhang, C. Boyle, M. Smith, and J.P. Philips (2020), 'Fair Allocation of Scarce Medical Resources in the Time of Covid-19', *The New England Journal of Medicine*, 382 (21): 2049–55.

- Gamlund, E. and C.T. Sollberg (eds) (2019), *Saving People from the Harm of Death*, Oxford: Oxford University Press.

- Rhodes, R., M. Battin and A. Silvers (eds) (2012), *Medicine and Social Justice: Essays on the Distribution of Health Care*, 2nd ed., Oxford: Oxford University Press.

- Vawter, D.E., J.E Garrett, K.G Gervais, A. Witt Prehn, D.A. DeBruin, C.A. Tauer, E. Parilla, J. Liaschenko and M.F. Marshall (2010), *For the Good of Us All: Ethically Rationing Health Resources in Minnesota in a Severe Influenza Pandemic*, St. Paul, MN: Minnesota Center for Health Care Ethics and University of Minnesota Center for Bioethics. This can be accessed at: https://www.health.state.mn.us/communities/ep/surge/crisis/ethics.pdf.

Notes

1. Alternatively, this priority rule could be thought of as a kind of risk-pooling scheme: those who are performing societally important tasks are often given certain kinds of special permissions which impose costs on others – e.g.

ambulance drivers are allowed to exceed the speed limit, inconveniencing and potentially imposing some risks on other road users – because these permissions make it easier for them to perform their societally important roles, and so everyone will ultimately benefit (cf. Fried 1970: 189). In the same way, giving some priority to essential workers imposes a small cost on others, but ultimately has the overall beneficial outcome of reducing the spread and impact of the pandemic disease.

2. Not everyone treats the reciprocity principle as a forward-looking principle. For instance, Persad et al. (2009: 426) refer to it as a backward-looking principle. The key point here is that it can be used in a limited and forward-looking way.

3. In a way, of course, many 'essential workers' do contribute to saving lives – for instance, by maintaining food supplies or lessening the impact of economic recession. However, those directly and indirectly involved in combating the pandemic disease contribute to maintaining food supplies and lessening the impact of economic recession, too: the people they save will be able to return to work more quickly if there are a sufficient number of doctors and nurses, and those engaged in essential work will be able to do their jobs more effectively and safely if those who need to self-isolate are able to do so. Thus, prioritising those directly and indirectly involved in combating the disease has a multiplier effect and this justifies prioritising them over the rest of the essential workers. In some cases it may be appropriate to prioritise certain other essential workers as well, but this will be highly context-dependent. For instance, if a very large number of HGV drivers or farmers fall ill, threatening the country's food supplies, they too may need to be prioritised. However, again, whether this is appropriate will depend on the specific case. Prioritising too many categories of essential workers when this is not clearly required in order to save more lives will undermine the whole approach.

References

Cookson, R. and P. Dolan (1999), 'Public views on healthcare rationing: a group discussion study', *Health Policy*, 49 (1–2): 63–74.

Emanuel, E.J., G. Persad, R. Upshur et al. (2020), 'Fair allocation of scarce medical resources in the time of Covid-19', *The New England Journal of Medicine*, 382 (21): 2049–55.

Fried, C. (1970), *An Anatomy of Values*, Cambridge, MA.: Harvard University Press.

Hirose, I. (2010), 'Should we select people randomly?', *Bioethics*, 24 (1): 45–6.

Holm, S. (2007), 'Medical aid in disaster relief', in R.E. Ashcroft, A. Dawson, H. Draper et al. (eds) *Principles of Healthcare Ethics*, 2nd ed., Chichester: Wiley: 671–7.

Kerstein, S.J., and G. Bognar (2010), 'Complete lives in the balance', *The American Journal of Bioethics*, 10 (4): 37–45.

McMahan, J. (2002), *The Ethics of Killing: Problems at the Margin of Life*, Oxford: Oxford University Press.

Persad, G., A. Wertheimer and E.J. Emanuel (2009), 'Principles for allocation of scarce medical interventions', *Lancet*, 373: 423–31.

Peterson, M. (2008), 'The moral importance of selecting people randomly', *Bioethics*, 22 (6): 321–27.

Reynolds, E. (2020), 'How it all went wrong (again) in Europe as second wave grips continent' *CNN.com*, 20 September. Available online: https://edition.cnn.com/2020/09/19/europe/europe-second-wave-coronavirus-intl/index.html (accessed 22 September 2020).

Taurek, J.M. (1977), 'Should the numbers count?', *Philosophy & Public Affairs*, 6 (4): 293–316.

Vawter, D.E., J.E. Garrett, K.G. Gervais et al. (2010a), *For the Good of Us All: Ethically Rationing Health Resources in Minnesota in a Severe Influenza Pandemic*, St. Paul, MN.: Minnesota Center for Health Care Ethics and University of Minnesota Center for Bioethics

Vawter, D.E., J.E. Garrett, K.G. Gervais et al. (2010b), 'Dueling ethical frameworks for allocating health resources', *The American Journal of Bioethics*, 10 (4): 54–56.

White, D.B., M.H. Katz, J.M. Luce et al. (2009), 'Who should receive life support during a public health emergency? Using ethical principles to improve allocation decisions', *Annals of Internal Medicine*, 150 (2): 132–8.

CHAPTER 4
ASSESSING THE IMPACT OF SCHOOL CLOSURES ON CHILDREN THROUGH A VULNERABILITY LENS

Nicolás Brando and Katarina Pitasse Fragoso

Introduction

At the height of the lockdowns introduced in response to the COVID-19 pandemic in 2020, school closures affected 90 per cent of the global student population – 1.5 billion school-aged children according to UNESCO's statistics (UNESCO 2020). This unexpected shift in the way education had to be delivered led the global schooling system to devise creative solutions to ensure children kept learning during lockdown.

The forced closure of schools was seen as an invaluable test case for exploring the move towards a more digitalised educational system. Andreas Schleicher, head of education at the OECD, considered the situation 'a great moment' for education, as it allowed exploration of the potential for digitalisation of the educational system (Anderson 2020). According to Schleicher, digital education is a tool capable of offering individualised learning plans, adapting to children's specific needs and increasing their productivity.

While recognising its potential benefits, this chapter provides a word of caution concerning the digitalisation of education by exploring the risks of such a process, particularly as these disproportionally affect the least advantaged children. Drawing from the conceptual framework provided by the literature on the ethics of vulnerability, we explore two fundamental issues that should be addressed in order to ensure that school closures do not unduly threaten children's lives. First, digitalisation can have a grave impact on *equality of opportunity*, as different socio-economic groups have radically differing access to the fundamental resources required to make the most out of digital education. Second, school closures may put *children's well-being* at risk, depriving them of a fundamental source of support and protection from many threats and harms. In the next section, we introduce the concept of 'vulnerability' as we will be using it in this chapter. We then explore how vulnerability frames our understanding of equality of opportunity and illuminates the threats that affect children's well-being.

Forms of vulnerability

The concept of 'vulnerability' is a valuable tool for evaluating the ways in which social circumstances and political decisions may create threats to particular sections of society. Following theorists of the ethics of care (Rogers, Mackenzie and Dodds 2012; Mackenzie, Rogers and Dodds 2014), we consider that applying a vulnerability lens to assess the threat of harm or loss of educational opportunities that affect different sections of the child population is required to evaluate the full impact caused by school closures during a pandemic crisis.

Childhood is considered a particularly vulnerable stage of human life. Children tend to be physically weaker than adults, easier to manipulate and to control, and, importantly, the disadvantages and harms that affect a child during childhood may have corrosive and long-term effects on the individual's life as a whole (Brighouse 2002; Schweiger and Graf 2015). Vulnerability tends to be understood as one trait that all children have in common due to their developmental stage, and their dependence on others for protection and care (Ben Porath 2003). In short, children are vulnerable because they are children (Gheaus 2015; Macleod 2015).

Beyond this vulnerability inherent to their condition *as children*, the social, economic and cultural situation particular to each child either increases or reduces the ways in which they are vulnerable. In this sense, to understand how external factors can affect an individual's susceptibility to harm and to being wronged, we must go beyond an embodied understanding of children's vulnerability, to analyse the sources from whence these vulnerabilities arise (Lotz 2018). Mackenzie et al. (2014) argue that, in order to understand what vulnerability is, and to develop principles of justice that address the plights of vulnerable populations, we must understand the different sources of vulnerability and various ways in which they may affect an individual.

Mackenzie et al. (2014) distinguish between three forms of vulnerability: inherent, situational and pathogenic. *Inherent vulnerability* is that which comes with human embodiment and our dependent nature – we are inherently vulnerable to others, to hunger, physical harm, death and so on. While all humans are inherently vulnerable in a generic sense, an individual's particular embodiment could make her more or less inherently vulnerable (Rogers et al.

2012: 24). *Situational vulnerability* is a context-specific condition 'caused or exacerbated by the personal, social, political, economic, or environmental situations of individuals' (Mackenzie et al. 2014: 7). Situational vulnerability highlights the factors external to a person which may create or increase our susceptibility to harm: losing one's job, a natural disaster or a pandemic, for example, can all be sources of situational vulnerability. Finally, there is *pathogenic vulnerability* (Rogers et al. 2012: 25). Pathogenic vulnerability is like situational vulnerability in that it derives from an external source. The difference is that pathogenic vulnerability has a systemic or all-encompassing effect, which tends to intensify existing threats or create new ones. Pathogenic forms of vulnerability are conditioned by the social norms, cultural practices and political decisions that frame an individual's life. A pandemic, for example, could be understood as a source of situational vulnerability, in the sense that it creates exceptional and temporary threats to our life options. However, depending on how a political system responds to it – to whom it gives priority, how it provides economic or social support, what policies it puts in place to address it, and so on – this temporary vulnerability may become pathogenic, by creating corrosive and long-term consequences which could have been avoided through alternative measures (Mackenzie et al. 2014: 9).

During school closures, two areas of children's lives may be negatively affected: their educational opportunities and their physical and mental well-being. In what follows, we evaluate the ways in which school closure during times of pandemic (or other crises where such action might be taken) can have a long-term and corrosive impact on children's lives. That is, how the situational vulnerabilities formed due to an exceptional event can turn into pathogenic vulnerabilities which may affect many children's lives beyond those exceptional times. Though the COVID-19 pandemic has made the existence of these harms and threats very explicit and salient, the forms of vulnerability explored in this chapter are systemic and affect many children's lives even in normal circumstances. The vulnerabilities created by school closures on children are ever-present; the issues caused by lockdowns during the pandemic merely highlight the normative issues at stake with the expansion of online schooling even in 'normal' times (Armitage and Nellums 2020).

Vulnerability and equality of opportunity

All children are affected by school closures, in the sense that all miss out on direct contact with teachers and the educational support that being in school provides. In theory, digitalisation can level the educational playing field. Children lacking the best material resources in their schools could have access to the best possible education online without having to leave their homes. Yet the experience of school closures during the COVID-19 pandemic shows consistently that it has failed to reduce inequality of opportunity. Even if the best educational online platforms, pedagogical online tools and courses were developed and available to all children, access to basic technological resources is a precondition for the system to work. Some 45 per cent of the global population does not have internet access at home, with the figure rising to more than 80 per cent for the least developed countries (ITU-UNESCO 2019). Children are not affected equally by school closures, and they do not benefit equally from digitalisation.

Exceptional circumstances lead to an exceptional risk of missing out on education, and unequal access to the material and human resources required to keep learning at home means that children of different socio-economic status have widely differing digital learning experiences.[1] If anything, what the COVID-19 test run for digitalisation of schooling has shown is that current disadvantages in educational opportunities among the well off and the least advantaged children will widen to insurmountable levels if nothing is done to alleviate the inequality of access to digital technologies and learning resources.

Researchers at Harvard and Brown are comparing American students' performance in mathematics via digital education before and after the pandemic. Early results show that, in late April 2020, the performance of students located in low-income zip code areas declined 50 per cent, while the performance of students located in high-income zip code areas did not change at all (Chetty et al. 2020). Additionally, an empirical analysis by McKinsey and Company highlighted that Black and Hispanic students might lose between three to four months more in the learning process in comparison with the national average (Dorn et al. 2020).

In Brazil, where socio-economic disparities are even higher than in the US, a very small fraction of children have access to digital technologies and to the resources required to make effective use of remote learning. Thirty-three per cent of Brazilian families do not have internet access, and 58 per cent do not have computers. At least eight million children between the ages of six and fourteen have not received any school activities to do at home during the pandemic (CGI 2020).

Translating these numbers into real experiences, schoolteachers from a public school in Sapopemba, a city in the State of São Paulo, said that out of thirty students enrolled in their online class, only five students participate in the activities (Schneider 2020). Moreover, girls like four-year-old Raphaela dos Santos, living in a favela in Brazil, do not even have basic resources such as notebooks, pens or pencils with which to write and draw (ibid.). A survey conducted by the Centre for Global Development found that almost 85 per cent of children in Senegal are in a similar situation to Raphaela's, receiving no instruction from their teachers during lockdown (Le Nestour and Moscoviz 2020). This means that school closures intensify social class divisions between children who have access to remote education and those who will not receive a proper instruction.

The issue, of course, goes beyond unequal access to resources. A fundamental requirement of online learning is having the support necessary to make effective use of it at home. First of all, many students from low-income families live under unstable circumstances lacking either educational supervision, supportive parental relationships, or even a quiet place to study.[2] This is partially explained by the fact that many jobs done by parents in low-income households are essential during the pandemic, leaving children without learning instruction or supervision at home. Yet, even if children have their parents at home, they may be unable to help with digital technologies or school lessons (UNICEF 2020).

As mentioned before, pathogenic vulnerabilities arise when institutional structures and social norms transform exceptional threats into systemic ones. Digitalisation of education can have this effect on the least advantaged children if equalisation of educational resources is not achieved prior to digitalisation. Education is a positional good; that is, its value is conditioned by one's access to this good in comparison to others'; thus, any inequality in access to this good will inevitably lead to stable and widening disadvantages throughout the life-course (Brando 2016). In this sense, it can be understood how the problems of exceptional school closures can create pathogenic vulnerabilities in children: while inequality existed prior to school closures, the added disadvantages created by lack of support to children who cannot make the most out of digital schooling means that they will be in an even worse position once they return to school (if they do return). Ensuring equal and inclusive educational opportunities is a foundation of an egalitarian account of justice, since it can bring about socio-economic benefits (Brighouse 2003; Brighouse and Swift 2006). Education is necessary as a tool which enables better opportunities later in life, enabling social mobility and helping to break the poverty cycle; in Wolff and de-Shalit's terminology, education is a fertile functioning if well provided, and its absence can be understood as a corrosive disadvantage, as it perpetuates the existence of other long-term harms (Wolff and de-Shalit 2007: 121; Wolff and de-Shalit, this volume).

The least advantaged children should be a priority when it comes to educational access. The experience of online schooling has shown that the worse off will be in an even more precarious situation if the resources and supports required for them to make use of digital education are not available. Vulnerabilities caused by not having access to quality education are always pathogenic, as they reflect faulty political decisions in the distribution of resources. Unless we can ensure that children who have most to lose from the changes are provided with substantive access to the resources and support needed to make the most out of digital education, inequalities in educational opportunities will widen rather than narrow.

Vulnerability and well-being

Access to school, beyond its pedagogical benefits, plays a huge role in many aspects of children's lives. Schools can be safe spaces, providing supervision, sanitation, nourishment and protection. School closures thus intensify children's situational vulnerability in ways that not only affect their learning prospects; closures make children more susceptible to malnutrition, violence at home, or being compelled to work in order to supplement their family's income. As before, the risks to children's well-being due to school lockdowns, while situational, may turn pathogenic in the absence of appropriate social, economic and political safeguards, due to the nature of the risks involved.

Data from previous large-scale school closures, as well as recent data on the human development impact of COVID-19, show that the harms to which children are exposed during school closures could be lasting, and can have corrosive and irremediable long-term effects on their lives (Doctors Without Borders 2020). The closure of schools creates alarming risks to the well-being of children that depend on them for a supportive and protective environment.

For example, many children depend on schools to have at least one healthy meal a day. In times of school closure, not only do they miss the meal they relied on, but the quality of nutrition they receive at home may fall as well. A recent analysis using economic growth data from the International Monetary Fund suggests that in 2020 the number of undernourished people around the world may increase by 14 to 80 million (UNDP 2020). Research carried out by Data Favela in Brazil found that in 269 favelas, 72 per cent of families ran out of food in the first week of the COVID-19 lockdown (Schneider 2020). In Latin America, 85 million children have been cut off from school food programmes, and many young girls have lost a place of safety (Lancet 2020).

Besides nutrition, vulnerability to physical and sexual violence increases with school closures, with a concerning gendered impact. In 2020, there has been an increase in cases of physical and sexual violence towards women at home of more than 25 per cent (Fragoso and Sanglard 2020; UN Women 2020). Empirical findings from past viral pandemics, such as Ebola in Sierra Leone, demonstrated that teenage pregnancies increased by 10.7 per cent (UNDP 2015). In Malawi, early analysis of the impact of COVID-19 estimated that forced marriages of children rose 83 per cent between March and May of 2020 compared to the same period in the previous year. Girls also are more likely to be abused and sexually exploited when not at school: cases of rape are estimated to increase 151 per cent in 2020 (Grant 2020; UN Women 2020).

Due to the nature of some of these gendered threats, their intersection with certain inherent vulnerabilities of different stages of childhood, and the inevitable long-term psychological traumas they create, it is impossible not to think of these vulnerabilities as pathogenic. Doctors Without Borders has warned of the fact that during a humanitarian crisis many girls are at high risk of dying or being severely hurt. This is worsened by limited access to care services and hospitals (Doctors Without Borders 2020). The threats that come with traumas, rape, unwanted pregnancy and early marriage can potentially bring about irreversible damage to girls' lives; many will not return to school, will become ill, or will be forced to enrol in precarious work, therefore being trapped in a corrosive cycle of risk (Grant 2020).

For many children, school closure had a limited impact on their basic well-being. Others have suffered situational threats from it. However, there is an important part of the child population who may never recover from the threats posed by these temporary school closures. When policies do not account for the irreversible collateral damage caused, the exceptional vulnerabilities that children suffer during lockdown may become permanent and pathogenic. It is crucial to be aware of this possibility, and to take it into consideration when making decisions like closing schools, in order to avoid situational problems becoming pathogenic. This requires both measures prior to imposing closures (such as ensuring that children still have access to adequate nourishment or safe spaces) and measures during and after closures (with social services checking in with at-risk children and developing special programmes for children who may have had their well-being affected during closures).

Conclusion

Seemingly exceptional and short-term circumstances (such as those caused by a lockdown during a pandemic) can generate or perpetuate dangers to children's long-term well-being or their interest in having equal educational opportunities. Our intention in this chapter was to highlight some collateral issues that arise from school closures, how they may create long-lasting vulnerabilities to the child population, and how, in particular, they affect the least advantaged children (with a concerning gendered dimension). While online schooling seems at the moment to be gaining more traction, governments must find ways to ensure that children have access to the appropriate resources, support and goods necessary to make the most out of this change. Of particular importance is ensuring that the fundamental interests that schools provide to students besides their education (nourishment, safety from violence, mental and physical well-being) are secured.[3]

Suggestions for further reading

- Brighouse, H. and A. Swift (2006), 'Equality, priority, and positional goods', *Ethics*, 116: 471–97.
- The Lancet (2020), 'Redefining Vulnerability in the era of COVID-19', *The Lancet*, 395: 1089–1166.
- Mackenzie, C., W. Rogers and S. Dodds (2014), 'What is vulnerability and why does it matter for moral theory?' In C. Mackenzie, W. Rogers and S. Dodds (eds), *Vulnerability: New Essays in Ethics and Feminist Philosophy*, Oxford: Oxford University Press.
- UNESCO (2020), 'COVID-19 Impact on Education', UNESCO DATA.
- UN Women (2020), *The Impact of COVID-19 on Women*, https://www.unwomen.org/-/media/headquarters/attachments/sections/library/publications/2020/policy-brief-the-impact-of-covid-19-on-women-en.pdf.

Notes

1. Different digital pedagogical tools can benefit some children and disadvantage others. Indeed, inequality may increase not only because of unequal distribution of resources, but because of the pedagogical method adopted, which will require different skills and talents from the students. We think this is an important issue, and should be further explored; however, our focus here is on injustice that comes from external forms of vulnerability.

2. This may also be an issue for children living in upper and high-income families, limiting their ability to learn during school closures.

3. We are very grateful to Aveek Bhattacharya and Fay Niker for their attentive readings and comments that led to major improvement of this chapter. We are also grateful for the excellent discussion of our chapter during the workshop organised by the editors, and would like to thank Avner de-Shalit, Jo Wolff and Sara Van Goozen for their insightful comments and suggestions.

References

Anderson, J. (2020), 'The coronavirus is reshaping education', *Quartz. Brave New World Series*, 30 March. Available online: https://qz.com/1826369/how-coronavirus-is-changing-education/ (accessed 28 September 2020).

Armitage, R. and L.B. Nellums (2020), 'Considering the inequalities in the school closure response to COVID-19', *The Lancet*, 8 (5): E644.

Ben Porath, S.R. (2003), 'Autonomy and vulnerability: on just relations between adults and children', *Journal of Philosophy of Education*, 37 (1): 127–45.

Brando, N. (2016), 'Distributing educational opportunities: positionality, equality and responsibility', *International Journal of Children's Rights*, 24: 575–98.

Brighouse, H. (2002), 'What rights (if any) do children have?' in D. Archard and C.M. Macleod (eds), *The Moral and Political Status of Children*, Oxford: Oxford University Press.

Brighouse, H. (2003), 'Educational equality and justice', in R. Curren (ed), *A Companion to the Philosophy of Education*, Oxford: Blackwell Publishing.

Brighouse, H. and A. Swift (2006), 'Equality, priority, and positional goods', *Ethics* 116: 471–97.

Chetty, R., J.N. Friedman, N. Henderen et al. (2020), 'The economic impacts of COVID-19: evidence from new public database built from private sector data', *Working Paper: Opportunity Insights Economic Tracker*: Available online: https://opportunityinsights.org/wp-content/uploads/2020/05/tracker_paper.pdf (accessed 28 September 2020).

CGI (2020), *Relatório Internet, Desinformação e Democracia*: Available online: https://www.cgi.br/publicacao/relatorio-internet-desinformacao-e-democracia/ (accessed 5 July 2020).

Doctors Without Borders (2020), 'Women and girls face greater dangers during COVID-19 pandemic', *Médecins Sans Frontières News Stories.* Available online: https://www.doctorswithoutborders.org/what-we-do/news-stories/news/women-and-girls-face-greater-dangers-during-covid-19-pandemic (accessed 28 September 2020).

Dorn, E., B. Hancock, J. Sarakatsannis et al. (2020), 'COVID-19 and student learning in the United States: the hurt could last a lifetime', *McKinsey & Company Working Brief.* Available online: https://www.mckinsey.com/industries/public-and-social-sector/our-insights/covid-19-and-student-learning-in-the-united-states-the-hurt-could-last-a-lifetime (accessed 28 September 2020).

Gheaus, A. (2015), 'Unfinished adults and defective children: on the nature and value of childhood', *Journal of Ethics and Social Philosophy,* 9 (1): 1–21.

Grant, H. (2020), 'Why Covid school closures are making girls marry early', *The Guardian,* 7 September. Available online: https://www.theguardian.com/global-development/2020/sep/07/why-covid-school-closures-are-making-girls-marry-early (accessed 28 September 2020).

Fragoso, K. and N. Sanglard (2020), 'A new virus an old problem: why lessons from poverty and gender inequality in Brazil matter', *Justice Everywhere*, 1 May. Available online: http://justice-everywhere.org/general/a-new-virus-an-old-problem-why-lessons-from-poverty-and-gender-inequality-in-brazil-matter/ (accessed 1 May 2020).

ITU-UNESCO (2019), *The State of Broadband 2019.* ITU/UNESCO Broadband Commission for Sustainable Development. Available online: https://www.itu.int/dms_pub/itu-s/opb/pol/S-POL-BROADBAND.20-2019-PDF-E.pdf (accessed 28 September 2020).

The Lancet (2020), 'Redefining vulnerability in the era of COVID-19', *The Lancet,* 395: 1089–1166.

Le Nestour, A. and L. Moscoviz (2020), 'Five findings from a new phone survey in Senegal', *Centre for Global Development Analyses,* 24 April. Available online: https://www.cgdev.org/blog/five-findings-new-phone-survey-senegal (accessed 28 September 2020).

Lotz, M. (2018), 'The vulnerable child', in A. Gheaus, G. Calder and J. De Wispelaere (eds), *The Routledge Handbook of Philosophy of Childhood and Children,* London: Routledge.

Mackenzie, C., W. Rogers and S. Dodds (2014), 'What is vulnerability and why does it matter for moral theory?' in C. Mackenzie, W. Rogers and S. Dodds (eds), *Vulnerability: New Essays in Ethics and Feminist Philosophy,* Oxford: Oxford University Press.

Macleod, C. (2015), 'Agency, authority and the vulnerability of children', in A. Bagattini and C. Macleod (eds), *The Nature of Children's Well-Being: Theory and Practice,* Dordrecht: Springer.

Rogers, W., C. Mackenzie and S. Dodds (2012), 'Why bioethics needs a concept of vulnerability', *International Journal of Feminist Approaches to Bioethics,* 5 (2): 11–38.

Schneider, A. (2020), 'Coronavírus terá efeito collateral de ampliar desigualdade na educação', *Folha de São Paulo*, 13 June. Availble online: https://www1.folha.uol.com.br/educacao/2020/06/coronavirus-tera-efeito-colateral-de-ampliar-desigualdade-na-educacao.shtml (accessed 28 September 2020).

Schweiger, G. and G. Graf (2015), *A Philosophical Examination of Social Justice and Child Poverty*, Houndsmills: Palgrave Macmillan.

UNESCO (2020), 'COVID-19 impact on education', UNESCO DATA. Available online: https://en.unesco.org/covid19/educationresponse (accessed 9 November 2020).

UNICEF (2020), 'Parental engagement in children's learning', *Innocenti Research Brief*. Available online: https://www.unicef-irc.org/publications/pdf/IRB%20 2020-09%20CL.pdf (accessed 5 July 2020).

UNDP (2020), *COVID-19 and Human Development: Assessing the Crises, Envisioning the Recovery*. Available online: http://hdr.undp.org/sites/default/files/covid-19_and_human_development_0.pdf (accessed 5 July 2020).

UNDP (2015), 'UNDP Africa policy note: confronting the gender impact of Ebola virus disease in Guinea, Liberia, and Sierra Leone'. Available online: https://reliefweb.int/sites/reliefweb.int/files/resources/RBA%20Policy%20Note%20 Vol%202%20No%201%202015_Gender.pdf (accessed 3 July 2020).

UN Women (2020), *The Impact of COVID-19 on Women*. Available online: https://www.unwomen.org/-/media/headquarters/attachments/sections/library/publications/2020/policy-brief-the-impact-of-covid-19-on-women-en.pdf (accessed 3 July 2020).

Wolff, J. and de-Shalit, A. (2007), *Disadvantage*, Oxford: Oxford University Press.

CHAPTER 5
ADEQUATE HOUSING IN A PANDEMIC
David Jenkins, Katy Wells and Kimberley Brownlee

Introduction

When a state imposes a lockdown during a pandemic, its residents are going to have to spend an awful lot of time in their homes. The text that was sent to all residents in New Zealand on 25 March 2020 framed it this way: 'Where you stay tonight is where you must stay from now on. You must only be in physical contact with those you are living with.'[1] Four weeks spent in one's housing where that is *the only place where one is allowed to be* is a very different experience to living in that housing under normal circumstances. To ensure that lockdowns have their intended effect of slowing the transmission of a disease, it is crucial for people to obey government guidelines. But obedience to those guidelines translates into substantially different burdens for people depending on their housing circumstances (see also Pinkert, this volume).

In some respects, different governments have recognised these different burdens. New Zealand has managed to reduce homelessness to practically nil, and $100m has been pledged to keep 1,200 motel rooms available for homeless people until April 2021 (Graham-McLay 2020). In the Indian state of Kerala, which, like New Zealand, has received considerable praise for its handling of the pandemic, substantial numbers of migrant workers have been provided with housing during lockdown (Jenkins and Ram 2020). In the UK, though less highly praised, rough-sleeping homeless people who fall outside legal definitions of 'priority need' have received temporary accommodation to which they otherwise would not have access.[2] Both private renters and mortgagees who would struggle to meet payments due to economic hardship brought on by the crisis have received assistance in the form of moratoriums on evictions. However, other people's housing situations, which also fall below the threshold of adequacy, have received less attention. Also, not enough consideration has been given to the issue of whether our understanding of housing adequacy requires re-configuring for a lockdown context and, specifically, to the following question: in what ways does housing that is adequate in the absence of a lockdown become inadequate during one?

We take up these issues in the present chapter. Taking the UK as our central example, we highlight the additional burdens placed on those who, in the context of lockdown, and an ongoing pandemic more broadly, find themselves without adequate housing, where adequacy in housing is understood along the lines of the definition of *housing adequacy* provided by the United Nations. We also argue, however, that the lockdown context is transformative, with respect to housing adequacy: housing that is adequate outside a lockdown may become inadequate during one. Governments need to be cognisant of this when imposing lockdowns on their populations, and take steps to preserve housing adequacy. The chapter concludes with a number of proposals for governments in the UK and beyond that would ensure comprehensive housing adequacy sensitive to the challenges of lockdown and whatever 'new normal' we, eventually, find ourselves in.

Understanding adequacy

We start by defining *housing adequacy* and explaining the importance of adequate housing. Before proceeding, however, let's address the possible objection that, since lockdowns are rare events, the effect they have on the adequacy of people's housing is immaterial. In reply, first, pandemics (and multiple waves of a single pandemic) and other catastrophes may become more common in the future as increasing numbers of coronaviruses make the jump from non-human animals to humans and as we face the increasingly devastating effects of the climate crisis. Second, even if pandemics and lockdowns are rare events, the potential severity of their impact on people makes them morally significant, especially as they interact with and exacerbate already existing disadvantages and inequalities. By way of analogy, torture is an egregious act, against which we have an absolute right. The fact that a person subjected to it may experience it only once and only briefly does nothing to diminish its gravity.

In both the *Universal Declaration of Human Rights* and the *International Covenant on Economic, Social and Cultural Rights*, the UN warns against understanding the right to adequate housing too narrowly. The UN Committee on Economic, Social, and Cultural Rights argues in its General Comment No. 4 that this right should be understood in terms of having 'a right to live somewhere in security, peace and dignity' (UN Committee on

Economic, Social, and Cultural Rights 1991). UN-Habitat's factsheet on adequate housing is explicit that adequate housing 'must provide more than four walls and a roof' and lists a further seven criteria, all of which must be fulfilled to some minimal degree if housing is to be deemed adequate. These criteria are: 1) security of tenure; 2) availability of services, materials, facilities and infrastructure; 3) affordability; 4) habitability; 5) accessibility; 6) location; and 7) cultural adequacy (UN-Habitat 2014).

When people's housing meets all of these criteria, it will protect them from arbitrary interference from landlords such as forced evictions and harassment; it will have energy for cooking, heating and light as well as safe drinking water and sanitation; it will ensure that meeting the costs of occupancy will not compromise occupants' enjoyment of other rights; it will guarantee occupants' safety and protect them from the elements; it will be suitable to the needs of occupants who have disabilities or might otherwise be disadvantaged; it will be located near to healthcare facilities, schools and places of employment and far from polluted or dangerous areas; and it will be consistent with occupants' cultural identities.

Presently, over a billion people live in slums that fall grievously short of the above conditions in a clear, ongoing and systematic violation of the human right to adequate housing (Davis 2017: 26–7). And even in the affluent, industrialised West, the standard of 'security, peace and dignity' in housing is not always met. In her preliminary statement on the UK's housing, UN Special Rapporteur Raquel Rolnik noted 'signs of retrogression in the enjoyment of the right to adequate housing' (Rolnik 2013). She also criticised the UK government for not making every effort 'to protect the most vulnerable from the impacts of retrogression' (ibid.). Across many of the above criteria, she argued 'people appear to be facing difficulties to access adequate, affordable, well-located and secure housing.' (ibid.).

Adequate housing is a basic right, not an optional extra. Minimally decent housing provides us with the shelter necessary for survival and basic health. In order to do so, it must not be too hot or too cold, must not be mouldy or damp and must not be overcrowded. In giving us a retreat from the world, housing also protects our privacy, gives us space for family life and intimate relationships, and protects our physical safety. Housing provides us with an important measure of social control (or, put differently, protects our freedom of association), allowing us to withdraw from those people whom we do not wish to encounter. Housing with secure tenure offers us important stability, allowing our housing situation to fade into the background, so that we can focus on pursuing what is important to us. Additionally, in many contexts, access to decent housing is a condition of respectability and, therefore, of basic self-respect. In many contexts, too, our ability to act in the world is limited if we lack housing: for example, often, if we lack a fixed address, we cannot get a bank account.

Inadequacy during lockdown

During the height of their respective coronavirus outbreaks in 2020, many countries imposed a lockdown. In the UK, lockdown meant that citizens were not to leave their homes except for certain limited purposes such as food shopping and daily exercise. This lockdown was less harsh than in places such as Italy, Spain and parts of China, where inhabitants were only allowed outside for essential business and not even for exercise. In what follows, we consider a number of different aspects of housing adequacy during a lockdown. We argue, first, that those in housing that was, prior to lockdown, considered inadequate face additional burdens in the lockdown context; and, second, that housing that was considered adequate prior to lockdown can be transformed into inadequate housing in a lockdown context.

One question raised by the present discussion is whether the housing-related burdens that lockdowns impose on people could be so great that this would cast doubt on the all-things-considered justifiability of lockdowns as a policy. When, for instance, sufficient numbers of people would be confined to dangerous accommodation, or would be placed in situations in which they are at significant risk of domestic abuse, or else lack access to the services, food and water that would make lockdown survivable, does this mean governments should not impose lockdowns?[3] One way of answering this question requires the weighing-up of a range of competing considerations, including the effectiveness of lockdowns as a way of addressing the spread of a disease like COVID-19 as compared to other measures that could be taken. Another involves arguing that the housing situation in particular settings could be so bad that no government would be justified in restricting people to their homes under those circumstances. Given the limited space we have to do justice to such an exploration, we cannot further consider either of these lines of argument. However, what we argue below certainly has a bearing on the question of the all-things-considered justifiability of lockdowns, and in particular may form a basis for arguing that certain *kinds* of lockdown are unacceptable as responses to a pandemic, for instance lockdowns in which people are not allowed outside for exercise, or lockdowns which force some into complete social isolation.

Homelessness

If someone is homeless, they lack adequate housing by definition. Those who are homeless in the sense of sleeping rough already face very significant burdens, among other things the burdens of lacking shelter, basic personal security and a basic ability to control their social environment. In the context of a pandemic, these burdens are added to considerably. Those who sleep rough cannot participate in a lockdown without assistance, which leaves them exposed to catching the virus and without a sheltered, secure space in which to be ill should they contract it. In addition, public space more generally will not be available to rough sleepers, which will negatively impact their relationships and their ability to make the money on which they might otherwise rely.

In some respects, the pandemic has heightened public recognition of the vulnerabilities that street-homeless people face. In the UK – and elsewhere – homelessness is an issue that rarely tops government agendas. Indeed, 2019 saw a 23 per cent rise in the number of homeless persons, but no significant uptick in parliamentary concern (Busby 2019). In 2020, however, as a result of the pandemic, the government has begun to address the issue of homelessness. Street-homeless people have been moved from the streets into temporary accommodation. However, although getting people off the streets is a good thing, this has not meant these individuals now have *adequate* accommodation. They do not, for instance, have tenancy rights over their accommodation. Once the pandemic is under some kind of control, there is every chance these people – at least those who do not meet the threshold of 'priority need' – will find themselves back on the street.

In addition, it is important to distinguish between rough sleeping homelessness and the scores of homeless people who are *not* sleeping on the streets. This latter category includes people who are (i) living in housing where they lack access to their own room, (ii) 'couch surfing' and (iii) living in temporary accommodation, whose housing needs might have triggered statutory duties of the state but exist in a kind of bureaucratic limbo. In the UK, such people enjoy access to shelter, but are often living in overcrowded accommodation, lack property rights, and are not to be even *legally* categorised as 'homed'. These individuals lack adequate housing in the sense of enjoying any basic *stability*, an issue that can affect even people who *are* housed.

Insecure tenure

A central element of *housing adequacy*, as we have defined it, is security of tenure for a decent minimum period. This protects our interest in stability with respect to our place of residence. As noted above, people with insecure tenancies may well be preoccupied by their housing situation, making it harder to pursue the things that are important to them (Wells 2019). A pandemic is likely to place greater burdens on such people. Personal stability, already important, takes on increased importance in times of great societal instability, such as a global pandemic. Losing access to one's housing during a pandemic, when there is little other housing available, is particularly problematic.

In the UK, some measures were taken to address insecurity of tenure during the lockdown. Renters and mortgagees received some government assistance in the form of moratoriums. Lodgers (i.e. those living with their landlord), however, received no special protection during lockdown, and so continued to face eviction. Nor were any measures taken to ensure that those 'couch surfing' have stable accommodation. In addition, travelling communities were still being moved on from roadside encampments during lockdown (Vickers 2020).

The threat of unemployment, whether in the short, medium or long term, could push tenants into rent arrears and the eventual loss of their homes, irrespective of whatever moratoriums were in place for the duration of the lockdown. As moratoriums come to an end, landlords will be free to begin eviction procedures in order to sell their properties – a process made considerably quicker when there are arrears. At the time of writing, the UK Conservative Government has promised to reform tenancy law via the abolishment of 'no fault' evictions amongst other policies, but this will come too late for many people, if it arrives at all (Taylor 2020).

Overcrowding

In the UK, overcrowding can be measured by the 'bedroom standard', which sets out the number of bedrooms required to 'avoid undesirable sharing', given the occupants of the property in question. For example, if parents must share bedrooms with children, this housing counts as inadequate (Ministry of Housing, Communities & Local Government 2020: 21). Prior to the 2020 lockdown in England, 8 per cent of social renters and 6 per cent of private renters lived in overcrowded accommodation on this definition (ibid.: 2). However, housing can also be understood as overcrowded if there is not enough space, regardless of whether the bedroom standard is met. In the UK, for instance, if there are two people in a given dwelling, there must be one room and this must be a minimum of 110 square feet (UK Housing Act 1985).

Housing that is overcrowded in either of these senses is inadequate for life outside lockdown, but becomes deeply inadequate for life during it, when all household members spend the majority of time indoors together. In addition, living in overcrowded housing endangers residents, since there is evidence that such residents are more likely to contract COVID-19 (Kenway and Holden 2020).

Consideration of overcrowding also highlights that whether we view housing as adequate or not will change in the context of lockdown. Consider, for instance, a couple living in a studio or one-bedroom flat with no garden. This space may be minimally adequate under normal circumstances, on the assumption that a range of facilities outside the home – workplaces, cafes, restaurants, the homes of friends and family – are available to the couple. During a lockdown, however, these facilities are unavailable and only limited time can be spent outside the home. Consequently, one has to do *everything* at home and housing must perform a multiplicity of functions – the living rooms and/or bedroom double up as offices, classrooms and playgrounds. Constant confinement within a cramped space is very different from periodically inhabiting it; constant confinement within a cramped space that must be *shared* with another person or several persons is, again, very different from periodically inhabiting that space with them. In the lockdown case, each person sees their ability to control their social environment and to disassociate from each other, if only for a brief spell, drastically reduced.

This implies that governments should be careful to take measures during lockdowns to *preserve* the adequacy of people's housing. In the present context, this means trying to ensure that homes do not become inadequate with respect to space. The lack of a garden, or more broadly safe access to outdoor space, may not typically feature in definitions of *adequacy*. In the context of a lockdown, however, wherever such access cannot be secured, wherever public space cannot be managed in ways that permit people time outside of cramped settings, then those people's housing will fall below a threshold of adequacy.

Poor-quality housing

For those who must live in poor-quality housing, there are considerable additional burdens to remaining in the house all the time. The effects of living in accommodation that is below minimally decent standards can, in ordinary circumstances, be mitigated to some degree by, for instance, finding other places to be for part of the day. During lockdowns, this exit option and the coping strategies it enables are eliminated. Consequently, inhabitants find themselves constantly confined to housing that may be too hot, too cold, damp, mouldy or dangerous.

Housing location and relationships

In the UN definition of *adequacy*, location is a key feature of adequate housing. While the UN definition focuses on employment and education opportunities, how we are located vis-à-vis our meaningful relationships, and the economic, social and emotional support we derive from them, is also important. This is perhaps especially significant to people living under the threat of domestic violence: in such cases, access to friends, family or state services will be crucial. More generally, whenever people must sacrifice such connections to access secure housing, we can still describe their housing situation as inadequate. For example, people whom the state recognises as homeless and in priority need, but who must nevertheless leave friends and family in order to access that secure housing, are forced into compromises that reduce the adequacy of that housing.

During pandemics, social contact and the preservation of existing relationships must go online.[4] It is arguably the case (although we do not commit very firmly to this claim) that in certain non-lockdown contexts, it is not necessary for everyone to have this kind of internet access at home.[5] People can (depending on their context) rely on libraries, cafes, their workplaces and their phones. In other words, adequacy during ordinary times need not include reference to internet access. What does seem clear, however, is that during lockdown our understanding of what adequate housing involves ought to include fast and reliable internet access. During the COVID-19 crisis, many came to rely on the internet as a means of maintaining social connections, education, and employment. Without it, there is a greater risk of social isolation and poor mental health, missed schooling, and affected work. Where the internet facilitates connections of a virtual sort, those who live alone will be unable to meet with others in offline environments. Where work and public places are out of bounds, those who might otherwise prefer to live alone might change this preference, without having any possibility to satisfy it.

How should governments act?

We will now consider how governments should act to address the housing-related vulnerabilities that have been exposed or exacerbated by the pandemic, and how the impact of people's being confined to their houses, or of lacking homes altogether, might be better mitigated in advance of future possible lockdowns. To do this, we make the following six proposals:

1. House street-homeless people. Governments must ensure access to adequate housing for all. Finland, which adopted a 'Housing First' approach, where people sleeping rough are granted independent housing with normal leases rather than having to work from night shelters, through hostels and transitional housing units, has seen its levels of homelessness drop significantly (Housing First Europe Hub 2020). Government action to provide street-homeless people with accommodation in hotels during the lockdown should be understood as an opportunity to provide more permanent housing to those people.

2. Provide protections for those at risk of losing their housing, particularly private renters. Security should also be increased for members of travelling communities. Governments must put in place long-term protections for renters, to prevent the loss of housing not just during, but after lockdown. The government's proposal to abolish no-fault evictions – to match protections already available in Scotland – should be implemented as soon as possible. These protections should include continued protection from eviction, more generous housing benefits, and the covering or waiving of back rent.

3. Universal rollout of the internet into people's houses to ensure uninterrupted access to important social relationships, work and virtual classrooms.

4. Stronger enforcement against landlords who fail to maintain minimally decent properties. The introduction of compulsory licensing schemes to regulate landlord quality should also be

considered. As part of this, support can be made available to landlords
– in the form of low-interest loans perhaps – but landlords who
repeatedly fail to maintain properties eventually should be banned
from renting out property.

5. Review any restrictions in place on access to public outdoor spaces.
Where decisions are made to restrict access to outdoor public space
as part of lockdowns, governments must consider how access to this
space can be regulated, to ensure low-risk access for all or for those
most severely affected by overcrowding or having to live in
substandard accommodation. The blanket closure of all public space
might not be justifiable, especially if the overall impositions of
lockdown are not fairly distributed.

6. Reduce problems of overcrowding in rental and social housing by
increasing the amount of social housing available to rent. Where this
is not feasible in the short term, councils should seek other solutions
to mitigate overcrowding during the lockdown. For example,
councils can establish incentive schemes, rather than punitive
schemes like the 'bedroom tax', to encourage tenants in under-
occupied property to move, and thereby maximise the use of social
housing stock. During lockdown, another alternative is to give
households more time to join with other household bubbles in
order to escape inadequate housing and access more adequate
housing.

Conclusion

Adequate housing is something to which we are all entitled. Where governments
have failed to secure this entitlement for citizens, they have exposed them to
additional burdens during the COVID-19 pandemic. Such burdens include
rough sleepers being exposed to the virus and losing public spaces on which
they were dependent; people in insecure tenancies lacking stability when it
matters most; and residents having to endure lockdown in overcrowded
housing with scant opportunity to escape it. Moreover, housing that we may
count as adequate in more ordinary circumstances may become inadequate
in a lockdown – for instance housing that lacks a high-quality internet
connection, or outdoor space. To ensure adequate housing for all, in the
pandemic context and beyond it, governments must do at least six things: house

street-homeless people, protect those with insecure tenure, secure internet connection for all, take tougher action to ensure landlords maintain minimally decent properties, protect access to public outdoor spaces and reduce overcrowding.

Suggestions for further reading

- Hohmann, J. (2013), *The Right to Housing: Law, Concepts, Possibilities*, Oxford: Hart Publishing.
- Young, I.M. (2015), 'House and Home: Feminist Variations on a Theme', in her *On Female Body Experience: 'Throwing Like a Girl' and other essays*, Oxford: Oxford University Press.
- Desmond, M. (2016), *Evicted: Poverty and Profit in the American City*, New York: Crown Publishing.
- Boughton, J. (2018), *Municipal Dreams*. London: Verso.

Notes

1. As of January 2021, New Zealand had recorded 2,188 confirmed and probable cases, with 25 deaths (New Zealand Ministry of Health 2021; Dong, Du and Gardner 2020).
2. A rough-sleeping person is entitled to state assistance only if they are pregnant, under a certain age (usually 18, but 21 for those who have lived in care), have responsibilities for children, or are vulnerable as a result of infirmity, age, domestic violence or drug abuse. See Shelter's definition of priority need in the UK (Shelter 2020).
3. Thanks to Avner de-Shalit for raising this issue.
4. Of course, this might benefit rather than disadvantage some, for instance those now able to access their work remotely, who no longer have to undertake a long commute. When it comes to housing, online working may allow more flexibility around one's location, and therefore the opportunity to live in areas with more affordable housing.
5. For a recent discussion of justice and internet access, see Reglitz (2020).

References

Busby, M. (2019), 'Homeless households in England rise by 23% in a year', *The Guardian*, 18 December. Available online: https://www.theguardian.com/

society/2019/dec/18/homeless-households-in-england-up-by-23-in-a-year-official-figures (accessed 16 July 2020).

Davis, M. (2017), *Planet of Slums*, London: Verso.

Dong, E., H. Du, and L. Gardner (2020), 'An interactive web-based dashboard to track COVID-19 in real time', *The Lancet*, 20 (5): 533–4.

Graham-McLay, C. (2020), 'New Zealand sheltered its homeless during Covid-19 – but can it last?' *The Guardian,* 27 May. Available online: https://www.theguardian.com/world/2020/may/27/new-zealand-sheltered-its-homeless-during-covid-19-but-can-it-last (accessed 21 October 2020).

Housing First Europe Hub (2020), *Finland*. Available online: https://housingfirsteurope.eu/countries/finland/#:~:text=The%20Finnish%20Housing%20First%20approach,solution%20for%20each%20homeless%20person (accessed 19 October 2020).

Jenkins, D. and L. Ram, (2020), 'Kerala's pandemic response owes its success to participatory politics', *Novara Media*, 7 August. Available online: https://novaramedia.com/2020/08/07/keralas-pandemic-response-owes-its-success-to-participatory-politics/ (accessed 21 October 2020).

Kenway, P. and J. Holden (2020), *Accounting for the Variation in the Confirmed Covid-19 Caseload across England: An analysis of the role of multi-generation households, London and time*, London: New Policy Institute.

Ministry of Housing, Communities & Local Government (2020), *English Housing Survey Headline Report 2018–19*. Available online: https://www.gov.uk/government/statistics/english-housing-survey-2018-to-2019-headline-report (accessed 7 January 2021).

New Zealand Ministry of Health (2021), *Covid 19: Current Cases*. Available online: https://www.health.govt.nz/our-work/diseases-and-conditions/covid-19-novel-coronavirus/covid-19-data-and-statistics/covid-19-current-cases (accessed 7 January 2021).

Reglitz, M. (2020), 'The Human Right to Free Internet Access', *Journal of Applied Philosophy*, 37 (2): 314–31.

Rolnik, R. (2013), *Press Statement by the United Nations Special Rapporteur on Adequate Housing: End Mission to the United Kingdom of Great Britain and Northern Ireland, 29 August to 11 September 2013* [Press Release], 11 September. Available online: https://newsarchive.ohchr.org/EN/NewsEvents/Pages/DisplayNews.aspx?NewsID=13706&LangID=E (accessed 16 July 2020).

Shelter (2020), *Priority Need*. Available online: https://england.shelter.org.uk/housing_advice/homelessness/rules/priority_need (accessed 16 July 2020).

Taylor, D. (2020), '230,000 could lose homes as eviction ban ends in England and Wales', *The Guardian*, 19 August. Available online: https://www.theguardian.com/society/2020/aug/19/230000-could-lose-homes-as-eviction-ban-ends-in-england-and-wales (accessed 21 October 2020)

UK Housing Act 1985, Part X. Overcrowding. Available online: https://www.legislation.gov.uk/ukpga/1985/68/contents (accessed 19 October 2020).

UN Committee on Economic, Social, and Cultural Rights (1991), *General Comment No. 4: The Right to Adequate Housing (Art. 11 (1) of the Covenant)*. Available online: https://www.refworld.org/docid/47a7079a1.html (accessed 19 October 2020).

UN-Habitat (2014), *The Right to Adequate Housing: Fact Sheet No. 21/Rev.1.* Available online: https://unhabitat.org/the-right-to-adequate-housing-fact-sheet-no-21rev1 (accessed 19 October 2020).

Vickers, H. (2020), 'A National Disgrace', *New Internationalist*, 21 August: 11–12.

Wells, K. (2019), 'The Right to Housing', *Political Studies*, 67 (2): 406–21.

PART II
ECONOMIC JUSTICE

CHAPTER 6
SHOULD THE OLDER GENERATION PAY MORE OF THE COVID-19 DEBT?
David Yarrow

Introduction

The COVID-19 pandemic has slashed government revenues whilst simultaneously necessitating welfare programmes of unprecedented scale to protect firms, workers and public institutions from the economic impacts of containing the virus. Governments around the world – many only just emerging from harsh austerity programmes imposed in the wake of the 2008 financial crisis – have, almost overnight, incurred a vast amount of additional public debt. In the UK, government borrowing for the fiscal year of 2020–21 rose to a peacetime high of £355 billion, and is forecast to remain elevated for years (OBR, 2021).

During the onset and initial peak of the epidemic, discussions of the mounting public debt understandably took a back seat. But as countries grapple with the health crisis, vital fiscal policy questions are coming to the fore. Broadly, these questions can be divided into two categories. First, questions over *how much* and *how fast* deficits and debt ratios need to be reduced in advanced economies, given the historically low interest rate climate. Second, questions over how post-COVID stimulus measures and/or fiscal contraction should be *distributed* between generations, classes and regions. The former are largely questions of macroeconomic policy, at a hugely important moment in the ongoing debate between Keynesians, New Classical macroeconomists and Modern Monetary Theorists over the merits of government-financed stimulus in times of low aggregate demand (Fullbrook and Morgan 2019). The latter questions concern distributional justice and the model of risk-sharing that should underpin the post-COVID welfare settlement. The two are intimately related but distinct.

This chapter focuses on a question that falls into the second category: *who should pay* for the debt incurred as a result of fighting the pandemic and the financing of any stimulus spending undertaken in its wake? In particular, it will analyse one of the most distinctive distributional dilemmas of this crisis: that the economic impacts of the lockdown measures have fallen disproportionately on younger generations, while the health risks they were designed to mitigate have fallen overwhelmingly on older generations. This feature of the crisis raises an important question: should the asymmetric intergenerational features of the pandemic inform the design of post-COVID stimulus, welfare and tax policy? Several media commentators and civil society actors have called for such post hoc intergenerational redistribution (Resolution Foundation 2020a; Intergenerational Foundation 2020a; Cunliffe 2020). However, there is little clarity about the different ways in which this claim could be conceptualised and their differential implications for the design of post-pandemic welfare, social security and taxation systems.

To address this, the first section outlines the intergenerational features of the crisis that urgently raise this question. The second will examine the way this has informed calls for post-COVID intergenerational redistribution, distinguishing between narrow *compensatory* and broad *universalist* versions of this claim. The third section will contextualise these claims within broader debates on neoliberal political economy. I argue that the compensatory version of the claim – that the intergenerational injustices of the pandemic alone should be corrected through the design of post-COVID fiscal and welfare policy – rests on an implicit but inconsistently applied luck egalitarianism, and risks legitimising ongoing shifts towards the individualisation and privatisation of social risk. The universalist claim – that COVID has revealed and amplified broader intergenerational inequities created by financialised neoliberal welfare systems – is both more defensible on luck egalitarian grounds and more radical in its implications, when situated in the history of welfare policy in the neoliberal age.

COVID-19 debt and intergenerational justice

The health risks of the COVID-19 virus and the economic impact of the drastic public health interventions imposed to contain it are asymmetrically distributed across age groups. Put simply, *the economic costs of fighting the pandemic have fallen disproportionately on those least at risk from it.*

Regarding the immediate health risks posed by the virus, it is clear from meta-analyses that these are heavily skewed towards the older generations (Bonanad et al. 2020). While there are other significant risk factors –

including co-morbidities, gender, ethnicity and obesity – age is the single biggest predictor of risk of dying from contracting the virus. Moreover, risk of mortality has an exponential, rather than linear, relationship to age. The UK Office for National Statistics (ONS) reports that, per 100,000 COVID-19 cases, the mortality rate for those under 65 is 17, compared with 134 for those aged 65–69, 452 for those aged 75–79 and 2,068 for those over 85 (ONS 2020c). However, in terms of the distribution of the economic and social costs incurred by interventions to limit transmission of the virus – including job losses, reduced earnings and career prospects and the lived experience of lockdown – the reverse is true. These costs have fallen disproportionally on the young.[1]

Firstly, job losses have impacted younger workers most severely since they are disproportionately likely to work in more precarious employment, and in the sectors hardest hit by the lockdown measures such as retail and hospitality (Intergenerational Foundation 2020b). By the end of May 2020 in the UK, 9 per cent of all employees under 24 had lost their jobs, compared with 3 per cent of workers overall. One-third of 18–24 year-old employees (excluding students) have either lost jobs or been furloughed, compared to one-in-six prime-age adults (Resolution Foundation 2020a). Though subject to considerable uncertainty (and contingent upon the policy response), at the time of writing youth unemployment in the UK is forecast to have risen to between 11 per cent and 17 per cent by the end of 2020 and is likely to remain elevated for years (Resolution Foundation 2020b: 10). While there is in fact evidence of a 'U-shaped' impact on employment, with older workers near retirement also more likely to be laid off during lockdown, the longer-term 'scarring' effects on skill formation and future earnings of a significant period of unemployment are higher for those at the beginning of their career (ibid.). This is compounded by disruption to the learning activities of younger people in education and training (Brando and Fragoso, this volume).

Secondly, in terms of income and consumption, it has been easier for older people to cut back spending during lockdowns to cover reduced income, as more of their consumption is discretionary. ONS data has shown that:

> in households where the reference person is under 30 years old, 58% of the weekly budget goes on essentials (including rent and housing costs) and 19% on goods and services that have been unavailable during lockdown. On the other hand, older households where the reference person is aged between 65 and 74 years spend far less of

their budget on essentials (43%) and considerably more (29%) on activities that have been prevented.

ONS 2020a

Consequently, young people have been less able to adjust their spending by cutting back on non-essential consumption during the lockdown. They also have, on average, fewer assets and savings, more debt, and fewer non-labour sources of income such as pensions or property income to manage through a period of reduced or wages (ONS 2020b; Resolution Foundation 2020b: 17). Moreover, furlough and self-employment support schemes were designed for those in secure salaried positions or with a stable earnings history. Since younger people undergo more frequent labour market transitions (or, if self-employed, were more likely to have recently set up their business), they have disproportionately fallen through the cracks.

Finally, younger people tend to live in smaller (often shared) accommodation, of worse quality and with less access to green space; hence the lived experience of lockdown itself has an uneven intergenerational profile (Jenkins, Wells and Brownlee, this volume). One study has found that homes are twice as spacious (50m square/person) for those aged 65+ than for 16–24-year-olds (26m square/person). Furthermore, young people (aged 16–24) in England are three times more likely to live in a damp home than older age groups (aged 65+), and more than one-and-a-half times as likely to have no garden (Judge and Rahman 2020). These factors impact the way in which lockdown has disproportionately affected the mental health of the younger generation compared with the family-age population, which again potentially feed through into longer-term economic outcomes (Resolution Foundation 2020b).

The unprecedented public health interventions implemented in response to COVID-19 have thus impacted different generations in deeply asymmetric ways. Moreover, these asymmetries are inversely rather than positively correlated with the health risks posed by the virus itself.

Narrow and broad varieties of post-COVID intergenerational justice

These intergenerational features of the pandemic have led to calls from various media commentators and civil society groups for post-COVID fiscal policy to compensate young people for the asymmetric impact of lockdown restrictions. For instance, a report by the Resolution Foundation has argued that:

> at some point soon, the Government will have difficult decisions to make on how to bring the public finances back on a sustainable footing, and, regardless of whether this [is] done by spending cuts or tax rises, those need to be informed by an understanding of the generational impact of the crisis.
>
> *Resolution Foundation 2020b: 149*

Rachel Cunliffe, writing in *City A.M.*, similarly suggested that:

> The vast costs of handling the crisis will need to be paid for ... Any government remotely interested in generational equality or social mobility should be prioritising the 'Covid cohort', ensuring that their life chances are not utterly annihilated and that the high economic and social price they have already paid for their elders is recognised.
>
> *Cunliffe 2020*

These claims are intuitively appealing: an intergenerational *injustice* should be corrected through taxation and welfare/stimulus spending, by allocating more of the costs to the elderly and more of the benefits to the young. Currently, however, there is little precision about how this general principle is arrived at and the scope of its implications. Specifically, the suggestion that the asymmetry between the mortality risk of COVID-19 and the economic impact of fighting it should be reflected in future post-COVID fiscal policy could be read in (at least) two ways. A narrow *compensatory* version would seek intergenerational redistribution to redress the specific impacts of lockdown measures. A broad *universalist* version sees no basis for addressing these impacts in isolation from broader distributional justice questions: the COVID-19 crisis has merely amplified and clarified existing intergenerational injustices in our society and therefore mandates action on these wider injustices.

Before outlining the compensatory version of the claim, we can briefly introduce a hypothetical *premium*-based claim that compensatory models implicitly reject. This position might suggest that those at the most risk of death from COVID-19 should pay *more* in the overall post-COVID fiscal settlement. In other words, because the elderly were most at risk, the way governments recoup the economic costs incurred in containing the virus should have an intergenerational weighting that reflects this. This could be conceptualised as a 'premium' that the elderly should pay the rest of society since the collective costs of containing the virus were undertaken disproportionately for their benefit.

The premium-based approach is vulnerable to a critique founded on luck egalitarianism, which, in turn, sets the scene for the compensatory approach. Luck egalitarianism is an approach to distributive justice that focusses on 'counteracting the distributive effects of luck on people's lives' (Knight 2013: 924). Inequalities of outcome that result from people's choices can be tolerated, but those that result from luck and circumstance should be corrected. Superficially, a premium-based argument about COVID-19 would mimic those found in other areas of health ethics where individual choice and responsibility seem to play a larger role – for example the argument that smokers should pay more tax to cover the increased healthcare costs they incur for society due to that behaviour (see Voigt 2005). However, there is the obvious difference between these two situations in that, in the case of lifestyle diseases there is (on some accounts) a degree of agency and choice (for example, people can choose not to smoke), and thus it is possible to understand this in terms of responsibility. In the case of the COVID-19 pandemic, however, there is clearly nothing that the elderly could have done to avoid incurring these costs; it was simply that they were members of a certain age bracket when the pandemic hit.[2] Thus, according to a luck egalitarian view of distributional justice, this was an instance of 'brute luck' (Dworkin 1981: 293) and a premium-based approach that would make the old pay more than any other age bracket seems prima facie unjust.

Yet, as far as a luck egalitarian conception of justice can be used to demolish the premium-based approach it also seems to necessitate another *compensatory* principle. This is because, just as the elderly cannot possibly be accused of choosing whether to be old when a pandemic struck, the young likewise did not chose to be young when extraordinary public health measures that disproportionately impact the economic prospects of their age bracket were introduced. This luck egalitarian reasoning, however implicit, underpins the calls of journalists such as Cunliffe that 'the high economic and social price [the COVID cohort] have already paid for their elders is recognised' (Cunliffe 2020) in subsequent fiscal policy. If luck egalitarianism exempts the elderly from paying more than their share because of the unequal health outcomes of COVID-19, it also seems to generate a duty to compensate the younger members of society for the misfortune of being young when lockdown measures were needed.

Such a compensatory model would imply that taxation and stimulus policies enacted in the wake of COVID-19 should have an explicit objective of correcting for the disproportionate costs it has imposed upon the unlucky younger generation. This would not try to charge the elderly more for the uneven risks of dying from the virus, but would seek to restore the pre-COVID intergenerational settlement by redressing the asymmetric economic impacts of lockdown. As a simplified example, if it could be shown that on average those under thirty incurred £1,000 more in lost income or wealth due to the lockdown, then the net intergenerational effects of the post-COVID taxation and spending policies should benefit those under thirty by an average of £1,000 more than the elderly.[3] Clearly, achieving this in practice would be impossible given the complexity and incommensurability of the impacts, but it is a heuristic principle that could inform the broad intergenerational profile of such policies.

The problem with this is that if we apply luck egalitarian principles with any consistency there is no basis for restricting ourselves to the intergenerational effects of COVID-19 itself. Thus, a *universalist* version of this claim seeks to correct for the broader weakening of intergenerational solidarity in general that has occurred over the past forty years, rather than limiting intergenerational redistribution to the specific contingencies of lockdown. It would suggest merely that the COVID-19 pandemic has exposed intergenerational inequities that this prior weakening of social insurance and risk-sharing has introduced, since the breakdown of universalist post-war social democratic welfare states, and has therefore made the case for reversing these shifts more urgent. In other words, this claim suggests that *no COVID-specific* intergenerational redistribution is necessary, as this cannot be separated from the reconstruction of intergenerational risk-sharing and solidarity more generally, which COVID has urgently revealed the need for.

The compensatory position, reflected in the quotes above, is thus (I suggest) arrived at by an implicit luck egalitarian position on the intergenerational impact of lockdowns. The problem with this is that if such a position is used to defend such measures in the narrow context of COVID-19, we must logically apply it more generally. When viewed in light of the past four decades of neoliberal welfare policy, luck egalitarianism necessitates going beyond compensatory framings of the intergenerational injustices COVID-19 has highlighted and requires that we place these within the context of broader luck-based inequities that have resulted from the rise of financialised, asset-based welfare systems. Moreover, it is dangerous for progressive voices to fall into the trap of defending narrower compensatory framings in attempting to mobilise support for post-COVID intergenerational redistribution, as they risk legitimising the individualised parameters of the neoliberal welfare settlement. As we explore in the final section, a consistent application of the luck egalitarian principles, on which the calls for a COVID-specific intergenerational redistribution rest, would demand contesting these wider luck-based inequities that asset-based welfare systems have introduced.

Luck, intergenerational justice and neoliberal welfare

Political economy scholarship has shown how, since the 1980s, a model of 'asset-based welfare' has emerged in which citizens are increasingly required to rely, not upon state-provided universal services funded through progressive taxation, but rather upon the financial value of their assets, primarily housing (Doling and Ronald 2010). This has been supported by a deregulation of mortgage lending and housing debt in both Europe and the USA, which caused house prices to rise progressively, far exceeding average earnings (Tooze 2019). This debt-driven rise in housing prices has enabled the state to withdraw welfare provision in the expectation that households will provide for their own needs by selling assets such as their houses, or equity withdrawal. Matthew Watson has argued that this trend has 'turned the focus away from the passive receipt of state-provided welfare services and towards active management of assets through which individuals become personally responsible for releasing future income streams when welfare needs demand they do so' (Watson 2009). The neoliberal model of asset-based welfare has had two notable effects.

The first is to create and exacerbate the intergenerational inequalities and injustices that COVID-19 has so starkly exposed. The problem with this model of welfare is that it was premised on ever-rising housing values making up for the loss of state-funded social insurance. Yet, as Montgomerie and Büdenbender have argued, 'the financialisation of housing in the UK is a unique set of political and economic circumstances that cannot be repeated; therefore, current gains from residential housing are a one-off wealth windfall *to particular (lucky) groups within society*' (Montgomerie and Büdenbender 2015; emphasis added). After the 2008 financial crisis in particular, the housing market has levelled off, locking in the gains of the 'baby boomer' generation who entered the property market at the beginning of this financialisation process and locking out the generation beneath them (those now hit hardest by the effects of COVID lockdown measures) from home ownership and the welfare goods that are now made to depend on it. The second effect has been to increase intra-generational inequality, through inheritance of this windfall housing wealth. Historic gains from financialisation by the lucky few 'insiders' in this asset-based welfare regime are passed down generations, reinforcing inequality as a structural feature of contemporary societies, and making access to public goods and life opportunities dependent on intergenerational gains or losses from the era of financial deregulation.

The fundamental consequence of the individualised and financialised conception of welfare that has arisen over the past four decades is to introduce a fundamental arbitrariness or *luck* to the way in which social welfare and risk are allocated. According to the neoclassical principles on which these theories draw, the value of assets should be a reward for shrewd choices about risk appetite and asset quality made by rational investors ('choice luck' in the language of luck egalitarians (Cohen 1989)). But the practical consequence is that the whim of global financial markets and the year and postcode in which one's parents may have bought a house now determine access to basic welfare goods such as healthcare and education. Consequently, a consistent application of the luck egalitarian perspective, which seems to underpin compensatory claims for post-COVID intergenerational, must in fact go much deeper. Only the broad version of the claim that COVID-19 necessitates a process of intergenerational redistribution would act on these deeper sources of luck and contingency that the financialisation of social policy has introduced into the distribution of welfare goods.

Significantly, this also changes the sorts of economic policies that are advocated to effect this redistribution. It is notable that those advocating narrower, compensatory visions of the post-COVID intergenerational settlement advocate policies such as 'boosting home ownership in younger cohorts … and facilitat[ing] wider asset accumulation (and therefore financial resilience)' (Resolution Foundation 2020b: 149). This may have the effect of correcting some of the specific luck-based inequities the COVID cohort has endured as a result of lockdown. However, by working firmly within the paradigm of neoliberal asset-based welfare models, it is unable to challenge the wider luck-based intergenerational injustices that they have already engendered. Instead, what is required is a shift of taxation from income to wealth (particular property assets) and corporate profits (which have benefited from the reduction in welfare costs and marginal tax rates) in order to fund the reconstruction of a more comprehensive and universalist welfare system. Such policies would have the effect of counteracting the intergenerational inequalities and vulnerabilities that the pandemic and the lockdown have exposed. However, they would *also* counteract broader luck-based inequalities and endemic insecurity that have been generated by asset-based welfare systems.

Conclusion

COVID-19 presents a distinctive problem for intergenerational justice: *the costs of fighting the pandemic have fallen disproportionately on those least at risk from it.* This has informed calls for post-COVID fiscal and welfare policy to have the explicit aim of intergenerational redistribution. We can distinguish two versions of this claim – compensatory and universalist. However, a consistent application of the luck egalitarian principles that ground the former in fact necessitates the latter. Despite the intuitive immediacy and force of the compensatory model of post-COVID intergenerational redistribution, the universalist version of this claim is thus both more defensible and more radical. Moreover, we have seen how the historical political economy dimensions of this problem are inseparable from the normative and ethical questions it raises. It is vital to understand how neoliberal political economy, specifically through its promotion of financialised, asset-based welfare systems, has introduced a fundamental arbitrariness and luck into the intergenerational distribution of public goods, that long pre-dates the pandemic.

A broader, universalist reconstruction of welfare systems in the wake of COVID-19 would have the effect of intergenerational redistribution. However, staking this out explicitly in terms of a distinctive intergenerational justice claim generated by the pandemic itself risks undermining the more fundamental principle of luck-based risk-sharing on which universal social insurance and welfare depend. The public health response to the virus has had dramatically unequal economic impacts on different generations, generating a need for policies to address these disparities. But there is no coherent way of grounding that claim, at least within a luck egalitarian framework, that does not also mandate a broader rethinking of the intergenerational settlement underpinning neoliberal welfare models.

Suggestions for further reading

- Cohen, G.A. (1989), 'On the currency of egalitarian justice', *Ethics*, 99: 906–44.
- Knight, C. (2013), 'Luck egalitarianism', *Philosophy Compass*, 8 (10): 924–34.
- Montgomerie, J. and M. Budenbender (2015), 'Round the houses: homeownership and failures of asset-based welfare in the United Kingdom', *New Political Economy*, 20 (3): 386–405.
- Resolution Foundation (2020b), *An Intergenerational Audit for the UK*.
- Watson, M. (2009), 'Planning for a future of asset-based welfare? New Labour, financialised economic agency and the housing market', *Planning, Practice &Research*, 1: 41–56.

Notes

1. See Resolution Foundation (2020b) for a detailed analysis of data on the intergenerational effects of the lockdown in the UK.

2. A luck egalitarian account would have more complex implications for the treatment of co-morbidities that *do* relate more to choice, such as obesity. This lies outside the scope of the present discussion.

3. There is a further question within this approach as to whether this should aim to correct merely for the costs incurred during the pandemic itself or attempt to estimate lifetime costs that would account for the longer-term after-effects of the lockdown measures.

References

Bonanad, C., S. Garcia-Blas, E. Tarazona-Santabalbina et al. (2020), 'The effect of age on mortality in patients with COVID-19: a meta-analysis with 611,583 subjects', *The Journal of Post-Acute and Long-Term Care Medicine*, 21 (7): 915–18.

Cohen, G.A. (1989), 'On the Currency of Egalitarian Justice', *Ethics* 99: 906–44.

Cunliffe, R. (2020), 'The pensions triple-lock is unjustifiable in normal times – in the Covid era it is utterly unconscionable', *City A.M.*, 9 October. Available online: https://www.cityam.com/the-pensions-triple-lock-is-unjustifiable-in-normal-times-in-the-covid-era-it-is-utterly-unconscionable/ (accessed 9 November 2020).

Doling, J. and R. Ronald, (2010), 'Home ownership and asset-based welfare', *Journal of Housing and the Built Environment*, 25: 165–73.

Dworkin, R. (1981), 'What is equality? Part two: equality of resources', *Philosophy and Public Affairs*, 10: 283–345.

Fullbrook, E., and J. Morgan (eds) (2019), *Modern Monetary Theory and its Critics*, Bristol: World Economics Association Books.

Intergenerational Foundation (2020a), 'COVID-19: this is the moment to scrap student debt'. Available online: http://www.if.org.uk/2020/03/20/covid-19-scrap-student-debt/ (accessed 9 November 2020).

Intergenerational Foundation (2020b), 'COVID-19: young adults' livings standards take biggest hit'. Available online: http://www.if.org.uk/2020/07/20/covid-19-young-adults-living-standards-take-biggest-hit/ (accessed 9 November 2020).

Judge, L. and F. Rahman (2020), *Lockdown Living: Housing Quality Across the Generations*, London: Resolution Foundation. Available online: https://www.resolutionfoundation.org/publications/lockdown-living/ (accessed 9 November 2020).

Knight, C. (2013), 'Luck Egalitarianism', *Philosophy Compass*, 8 (10): 924–34.

Montgomerie, J. and M. Büdenbender (2015), 'Round the houses: homeownership and failures of asset-based welfare in the United Kingdom', *New Political Economy*, 20 (3): 386–405.

OBR (2021), 'Economic and Fiscal Outlook: March 2021'. Available online: https://obr.uk/download/economic-and-fiscal-outlook-march-2021/ (accessed 8 March 2021).

ONS (2020a), 'More than one fifth of usual spending has been largely prevented during lock-down'. Available online: https://www.ons.gov.uk/peoplepopulationandcommunity/personalandhouseholdfinances/expenditure/articles/morethanonefifthofusualhouseholdspendinghasbeenlargely preventedduringlockdown/2020-06-11 (accessed 9 November 2020).

ONS (2020b), 'Financial resilience of households; the extent to which financial assets can cover an income shock'. Available online: https://www.ons.gov.uk/peoplepopulationandcommunity/personalandhouseholdfinances/incomeandwealth/articles/financialresilienceofhouseholdstheextenttowhichfinancialassetscancoveran incomeshock/2020-04-02 (accessed 9 November 2020).

ONS (2020c), 'Deaths due to COVID-19 compared with deaths from influenza and pneumonia, England and Wales'. Available online: https://www.ons.gov.uk/peoplepopulationandcommunity/birthsdeathsandmarriages/deaths/bulletins/deathsduetocoronaviruscovid19comparedwithdeathsfrominfluenza andpneumoniaenglandandwales/deathsoccurringbetween1januaryand 31august2020/pdf (accessed 9 November 2020).

Resolution Foundation (2020a), *Young Workers in the Coronavirus Crisis: Findings from the Resolution Foundation's Coronavirus Survey*. Available online: https://www.resolutionfoundation.org/publications/young-workers-in-the-coronavirus-crisis/ (accessed 9 November 2020).

Resolution Foundation (2020b), *An Intergenerational Audit for the UK*. Available online: https://www.resolutionfoundation.org/publications/intergenerational-audit-uk-2020/ (accessed 9 November 2020).

Tooze, A. (2019), *Crashed: How A Decade of Financial Crises Changed the World*, London: Penguin.

Voigt, K. (2013), 'Appeals to Individual responsibility for health: reconsidering the luck egalitarian perspective', *Cambridge Quarterly of Healthcare Ethics*, 22: 146–58.

Watson, M. (2009), 'Planning for a future of asset-based welfare? New Labour, financialised economic agency and the housing market', *Planning, Practice & Research*, 1: 41–56.

CHAPTER 7
REBUILDING SOCIAL INSURANCE TO END ECONOMIC PRECARITY
Lisa Herzog

Introduction

Imagine two childhood friends in their late twenties, Anna and Barbara, whose lives looked very similar before the COVID-19 crisis. Both had gone to college, both had a middle-class income, both could afford to eat out from time to time and were saving a bit of money for emergencies. But Anna had found a permanent job, while Barbara was working as a freelancer. When the crisis hit, Anna continued to receive wage payments and benefits; in contrast, Barbara's income suddenly dried up and she found herself sleepless at night, worrying about how to pay her bills.

Of course, it also makes a huge difference which country Anna and Barbara live in. Is it one where individuals receive unemployment payments? Is their health insurance tied to their job, or does it also hold in case of unemployment? And how likely is it that someone like Anna, in regular employment, loses her job? Is she employed 'at will', vulnerable to dismissal for any reason, or is there employment protection? Does she even have a formal, legally binding labour contract?

In this chapter, I reflect on what the coronavirus crisis tells us about economic precarity. By economic precarity I mean, broadly speaking, the existential economic insecurity that comes from the lack of stable employment and safety systems. Guy Standing, who coined the term 'precariat' for describing the – internally rather varied – group of individuals who live in economic precarity, notes that 'one shock, mistaken decision or illness could tip them over the edge into the under-class, cut adrift from society and probably condemned to social illness or an early death' (Standing 2016; see also Standing 2011). Economic precarity should not be misunderstood as a phenomenon that hits only the very poor. Many individuals in economically precarious situations have work experience and university degrees; their lives may look 'middle class' even though they may have incurred high debts.

I argue for two related claims in this chapter. First, instead of only looking at the individual level, we need to understand economic precarity as a *systemic* matter reflecting the underlying economic framework of a society. And second, we need to change this framework in ways that revive and improve the social insurance function of welfare systems. Both prudential arguments based on the logic of insurance and solidarity-based arguments can go hand in hand to support this conclusion. The COVID-19 pandemic and its fallout have made abundantly clear that there is an urgent need to repair and expand social insurance, and also to rethink the roles of employers and employees, in order to protect individuals and families against economic precarity.

It's the system (much more than the individual!)

When discussing the economic fate of individuals, there is a widespread cliché that goes like this: individuals can choose between boring but secure nine-to-five jobs, and riskier but more exciting jobs in which they freelance or cobble together different streams of income. Some choose one option, some the other, according to their individual tastes and preferences. What could be wrong with this? Isn't it mutually beneficial for all members of a society if individuals with different skills and preferences fill different roles?

The problem is that such an approach hides the structural conditions that form the background against which individuals make choices. These background structures influence not only how much one can earn in different jobs, but also many other parameters, such as how much incomes fluctuate, what support systems there are, how deep an individual can fall, economically speaking, and how fast this can happen. These factors are beyond individuals' control: they are a matter of political choices about the legal framework within which economic activities take place. Talk about 'individual choice' or 'individual responsibility' is often misplaced, because these structural features often have a much greater impact on the situation a person finds herself in than agential ones. In other words: under certain circumstances, even the most responsible individuals might end up in dire conditions, through no fault of their own (Young 2010: 70–101).

The pandemic has (further) revealed how different countries have organised these background structures. In some countries, there are reasonable safety nets, at least for most groups (very often, there continue to be problems for groups such as undocumented migrants or disabled people, who still fall through the cracks). For example, some European countries such as Denmark and Germany not only have a relatively strong safety net in ordinary times for those who lose their jobs, but have also quickly installed crisis measures. These include 'short-working time' in which employees accept shorter working hours and a reduction in pay, which is partly compensated by government payments – but they can keep their jobs, and companies can keep their employees (see e.g. Widmer 2009). I would certainly not claim that these systems are perfect; for example, individuals often have to go through humiliating processes of means testing, a point I come back to below. And yet there is a stark contrast with other countries, especially those in which the influence of neoliberalism has been very strong (Hall and Soskice 2001), where such safety nets have only ever existed in very thin forms, or have been eroded over time. While there have been some ad hoc emergency measures, such as more generous unemployment insurance and furlough schemes, these were politically controversial and it was unclear whether they would be continued. Instead of having a secure right to receive certain forms of support, individuals depend on the goodwill (or whims) of their governments.

Whether or not countries take measures against economic precarity is not a matter of absolute wealth. It is a matter of political choices and power relations. For example, the US, one of the richest countries on the globe, has in recent decades experienced what political scientist Jacob Hacker has described as 'the great risk shift'. As he writes: 'Instead of pooling risks through social insurance, those with the power to make policy have been offloading them – and they've been doing so with little interruption for more than a generation' (Hacker 2019: xiv). At the same time, the economic situation in large parts of the American population is highly uncertain. In a 2013 paper, Hacker and his co-authors report data about how long American survey participants would be able to get by if their monthly paychecks stopped: 9.1 per cent said 'less than one week', 48.4 per cent said 'less than two months' (this includes the 9.1 per cent), and only 29.8 per cent said 'six months or more' (Hacker, Rehm and Schlesinger. 2013: 27). Imagine the psychological toll this takes, compared with the security of a stronger safety net and the ability to save more money as a buffer for hard times! But these psychological costs cannot be quantified, they do not enter GDP and only few politicians have taken them up as a matter of concern.

The tendency to shift risks to employees also has an impact on the legitimacy of the capitalist system as a whole. After all, one of the central justifications for why capital investments should carry profits is that investors take on risks – including the risks of economic fluctuations. But the more they can shift these risks to employees (or to temporary workers who are not even employees), the less risk there is for capital. Large parts of the US population are employed 'at will', which means that companies can immediately dismiss them when they wish to do so. The risk of economic fluctuations – or of external shocks such as a public health epidemic – is thus carried to a great extent by employees. Why, then, should capital owners continue to earn profits, one might ask? It is indeed noteworthy that, in many countries, capital gains have continued to flow, and incomes to the very rich have often even increased, while the lower and middle classes have experienced declining incomes and growing precarity (see Piketty 2013).

The COVID-19 crisis has brought these background structures of the economic systems of different countries into the spotlight. It has shown who is most vulnerable, and who can protect himself or herself. The economic consequences of the pandemic have hit certain industries particularly hard (e.g. travel or trade fair organisers), but there are also the general consequences of a massive economic downturn on a global scale. At the time of writing, we do not yet know the precise shape of this downturn, but we do already know that an immediate restart of the economy – the 'V-shape' many politicians invoked – looks unlikely.

Like every crisis, this crisis is, at least potentially, a starting point for change. At the beginning of the crisis, many individuals suddenly got a sense of their dependence on others, and of their own vulnerability.[1] This might be an anchor for arguing for reforms that would change the structures of our economic systems in ways that protect all of us better against the kinds of vulnerabilities we cannot protect ourselves against – of which economic precarity is one. While it takes quite a bit of optimism to hope for structural change, this is the kind of optimism without which we are doomed to remain stuck in the *status quo*. Therefore, in the next section I argue that the direction of change should be to reverse this 'risk shift'.

Putting 'social' back into 'social insurance'

Much could be said about the wrongness of economic precarity from a perspective of social justice. But here I want to emphasise an argument that is even simpler, and that might be able to generate a consensus even among individuals who do not agree on what 'social justice' means. This is the argument from insurance. On its own, it provides strong reasons, based on prudence and efficiency, for ending economic precarity. However, below I will also argue that we should combine this argument with arguments that appeal to solidarity.

The basic principle of insurance is this: you have a group of people, and you know that *some* of them will be hit by certain incidents, such as home fires – but you do not know *who* will be hit. Everyone pays a small sum, which flows into a budget from which those who are *actually* hit receive compensation – the risks are 'pooled'. This buys everyone the security that they will not suffer such a loss. Even if you are never hit, and hence never receive compensation, you are better off because you do not have to worry about this risk. The benefits are psychological – you sleep better at night – but they can also be practical, for example because buying insurance for *some* risks allows you to take on *other* risks, such as starting your own business.

The COVID-19 pandemic should have driven home the message that we can all, quite unexpectedly, be hit by external events that are completely beyond our control. Even the most responsible restaurant owner or freelance worker could hardly have foreseen this pandemic and the economic repercussions it would have. Nor *should* we have expected them to anticipate such an event; after all, according to that logic they would also have to anticipate and insure themselves for all other possible crises. If you considered all such risks, you would probably end up never starting a business at all (the next crisis is, after all, going to look different)! And that would be an outcome that would most likely be harmful for our societies, which often benefit from the positive spillovers – job creation, new technologies, etc. – that businesses, at least socially responsible ones, can bring.

It is a better strategy to have *social* insurance systems that can ensure that individuals never fall below a certain floor. Such a system can also help balance out some of the fluctuations that result from the *temporal* dynamics of our economic systems and their effects on individuals' lives. For example, economists have long known that individuals who enter the labour market in a recession have lifelong disadvantages with regard to earnings (Oreopoulos, von Wachter and Heisz 2012). It should be clear that it is beyond individuals' control what age group they belong to, and whether they happen to graduate in one year or the next. Hence, good social insurance systems – not necessarily the ones we have at the moment – might also help to deal with such fluctuations and provide insurance against such risks.

To be sure, by talking about 'insurance' I do not want to imply that we should *only* take into account economistic arguments that could convince self-interested individuals to join a social insurance scheme. Taken by itself, the principle of insurance can also be understood as an invitation to pool together only those individuals whose risks are small, in order to lower the insurance premium, such that others, with higher risks, remain in the pool for other insurances, which then becomes unfeasible ('adverse selection', as economists call it), or as an invitation to use private insurance mechanisms that only the privileged can afford. It might also invite the thought that individuals should continue to carry at least small amounts of risks in order not to incentivise recklessness ('moral hazard', in economics jargon).

This is *not* the approach I envisage for *social* insurance. I certainly grant that we should not design social systems in ways that make them all too easily exploitable by egotists or criminals. But this is a long way from holding that we should always assume the worst in individuals' behaviour and treat all claims with suspicious scrutiny – as some existing social insurance systems do.[2] Instead, we need policies with a good sense of proportion that can filter out unreasonable demands or requests based on wrongful information, but that nonetheless treat individuals as equal citizens, with the dignity and respect they deserve. Understood in this way, a social insurance system is an expression of practical solidarity among the citizens of a country (see Popescu, this volume).

Critics of the welfare state often hold that one of the problematic aspects of social insurance is that it requires means testing. They think that means testing, in and of itself, is in conflict with the equal respect that citizens owe each other.[3] If one accepts this point, this strengthens the case for *unconditional* forms of support, for example through an unconditional minimum income. I agree with these critics that many existing social insurance systems do indeed fall short in this respect. But it is not so clear, in my eyes, that this is a necessary feature of them such that it could not be reformed. These dehumanising forms of scrutiny were based on assumptions about human nature – often dubbed 'neoliberal' – that came from a reductive picture used in economic modelling, but which psychologists and sociologists have long since disproved. It is simply not true that human beings work only in order to earn money, and are, by default, willing to lie and cheat in order to get more subsidies (see e.g. Pink 2011; Rosenbaum, Billinger and Stieglitz 2014). Hence, the degree of control that was introduced in many systems might not be necessary. Transparency with regard to their income situation could simply be required from all individuals, as is the case in some

Scandinavian countries, so there would be no unequal treatment. And with a bit more money spent on social workers, to reduce their case load, many of the most problematic forms of disrespect could probably be prevented. A key advantage, compared to unconditional schemes, is that those who are in need can receive *more* support. If this is understood as a matter of both prudence and solidarity, I take it that there need not be any stigma in receiving support from such a social insurance system. After all, this is what all of us would do if we were hit by bad luck.

A well-designed social insurance system can reduce the risk of economic precarity to a minimum. Hence it even *enables* individuals to take certain risks, such as investing in higher education, that are often beneficial for everyone. To be sure, such a social insurance system needs to work hand in hand with other institutions, such as the education system and the regulation of the labour market. The linkages between these different systems are crucial for making sure that individuals receive meaningful support, like opportunities for further education if they lose a job.[4] On the other hand, if basic social insurance is lacking, individuals might not be able to take advantage of other opportunities, because the economic risks are too high for them.

How exactly social insurance systems need to be rebuilt or reformed depends, of course, on the situation in different countries. The wave of neoliberal thinking, which saw the welfare state as an inefficient bureaucratic monster, has swept over most countries – but the flawed assumptions of this way of thinking have, by now, been sufficiently exposed. The COVID-19 crisis has revealed, once more, why we do need social insurance, and need to rebuild the institutions through which it is realised. To some extent, countries can learn from one another and take on institutional solutions that have been successful elsewhere. One example, which I have already mentioned above, is the publicly subsidised 'short-time work' scheme that had already helped some European countries to weather the 2008 economic crisis relatively well, keeping far more people in employment than would otherwise have been the case. But the different institutions of a country are often complexly intertwined, so that one should be cautious of simple 'cut and paste' approaches.[5]

A crucial question, in all attempts at reform, is to what extent capital can be involved in carrying the costs of social insurance. The 'risk shift' that Hacker describes needs to be reversed – capital needs to pay its fair share in dealing with risks. One important aspect of this topic is the role of employers: which risks should they carry, which risks should they be allowed to shift to employees, which risks should be pooled between firms through state institutions, but with firms contributing financially? How are the risks and burdens distributed between different *kinds* of employers, such as companies of different sizes, and is this distribution reasonable? Of course, this issue raises larger questions about capital–labour relations, about globalisation and capital flight, about the power of large transnational corporations, and about tax harmonisation. The task may seem daunting. But the alternative of *not* starting to work on it seems even bleaker.

Social insurance systems can and should also experiment with new instruments that might help them to better achieve their goals. So far, when it comes to unemployment insurance, most systems have provided financial support, and the more developed ones also provide opportunities for training and skill development. But one can also imagine more ambitious programmes. One exciting proposal that might have some chance – if not for implementation, then at least for piloting and experimentation in the post-COVID phase of rebuilding the economy – is a job guarantee, in which the state acts as employer of last resort (Tcherneva 2020). This would also fit the logic of insurance: it would insure all members of society against the risk of *job* loss, in a way that goes beyond and complements the loss of *income*. State institutions at the local level could provide minimum-wage jobs in areas such as care work, environmental remediation or support for vulnerable groups. Accepting such jobs would be voluntary, and would, ideally, come with opportunities for further education or training. If successful, such a programme could take the sting out of the fear of unemployment, and thereby also put pressure on employers in the private sector to improve working conditions.

Conclusion

I have argued that the COVID-19 crisis has brought to light lingering problems of economic precarity and the lack of social insurance mechanisms for many individuals. Social insurance can be argued for on the basis of prudence, because pooling risks is a rational response to economic uncertainty. Such arguments can and should be combined with arguments about solidarity between citizens, which also finds expression in the institutions of the welfare state. In the COVID-19 crisis, some countries have done far better than others in protecting their citizens against the economic consequences of the crisis. But more can and should be done, not only in order to make sure that employers carry a fair share of economic risks, but also in order to develop the tools of social insurance further.

Albena Azmanova has recently claimed that the fight against economic precarity is a 'radical' policy that provides a way forward out of the 'precarity capitalism' that reigns in many countries (Azmanova 2020). She sees this as a precondition for turning the current dissatisfaction with capitalism and the political system, which all too often leads to right-wing populism, on to a more productive road. It is a sad commentary on the current situation that a strategy as basic as rebuilding social insurance can be described as 'radical'. But the COVID-19 crisis has brought the cracks in the current systems into open daylight. Many individuals and families will fall through them unless the process of reform gets started soon. Instead of trying to put small patches on the most obvious holes, a fundamental renovation is needed – and this action is neither unfeasible nor politically impossible. Maybe the experience of the pandemic can help build the political alliances that are needed to tackle this task.

Suggestions for further reading

- On structural justice: Iris Marion Young on 'structural injustice', see e.g. her *Responsibility for Justice* (Oxford: Oxford University Press, 2010), chapter 2.
- On the job guarantee as a proposal for reforming social insurance: Pavlina Tcherneva, *The Case For a Job Guarantee*. London: Polity, 2020.
- On a philosophical defence of the welfare state, from a Rawlsian perspective, see e.g. Jeppe von Platz, 'Democratic equality and the justification of welfare-state capitalism', *Ethics: An International Journal of Social, Political, and Legal Philosophy*, 131 (1): 4–33, October 2020.

Notes

1. Even Boris Johnson apparently realised, against Thatcher's famous line, that 'There really is such a thing as society', after having been admitted to hospital with COVID-19. See e.g. https://www.theguardian.com/politics/2020/mar/29/20000-nhs-staff-return-to-service-johnson-says-from-coronavirus-isolation (accessed 5 September 2020).

2. A powerful illustration of these mechanisms, in the UK context, can be found in Ken Loach's 2016 movie *I, Daniel Blake*. However, the UK is not alone as a system that uses draconic punishments for small failures on the part of individuals, such as showing up late for an appointment.

3. Such arguments resemble those made by Elizabeth Anderson (1999) in her criticism of luck egalitarianism. But it is not clear that she herself would see them as a reason for rejecting *all* forms of means-testing.

4. I cannot here discuss the problems that arise *between* countries with different social insurance systems. It is an old criticism that generous social insurance systems would be overrun by immigrants, but it is not clear that it is justified – many migrants bring more to economic systems than they take. For reasons of scope, I need to leave this discussion for another time.

5. For reasons of scope, I cannot discuss here other system-wide changes that would reduce economic precarity – for example support for worker-owned companies, which are often successful in preserving jobs in crises.

References

Anderson, E. (1999), 'What is the point of equality?', *Ethics*, 109 (2): 287–337.

Azmanova, A. (2020), *Capitalism on Edge: How Fighting Precarity Can Achieve Radical Change Without Crisis or Utopia*, New York: Columbia University Press.

Hacker, J.S. (2019), *The New Economic Insecurity and the Decline of the American Dream*, New York: Oxford University Press.

Hacker, J.S., P. Rehm and M. Schlesinger (2013), 'The insecure American: economic experiences, financial worries, and policy attitudes', *Perspectives on Politics*, 11 (1): 23–49.

Hall, P.A. and D. Soskice (2001), 'Introduction', in P.A. Hall and D. Soskice (eds), *Varieties of Capitalism: The Institutional Foundations of Comparative Advantage*, Oxford: Oxford University Press: 1–70.

Oreopoulos, P., T. von Wachter and A. Heisz (2012), 'The short- and long-term career effects of graduating in a recession: hysteresis and heterogeneity in the market for college graduates', *American Economic Journal: Applied Economics*, 4 (1): 1–29.

Piketty, T. (2013), *Capital in the Twenty-First Century*, Cambridge, MA.: Harvard University Press.

Pink, D. (2011), *Drive: The Surprising Truth About What Motivates Us*, New York: Riverhead Books.

Rosenbaum, S.M., S. Billinger and N. Stieglitz (2014), 'Let's be honest: a review of experimental evidence of honesty and truth-telling', *Journal of Economic Psychology*, 45: 181–96.

Standing, G. (2011), *The Precariat: The New Dangerous Class*, London and New York: Bloomsbury.

Standing, G. (2016), 'Meet the precariat, the new global class fuelling the rise of populism', *World Economic Forum*. Available online: https://www.weforum.org/agenda/2016/11/precariat-global-class-rise-of-populism (accessed 9 November 2020).

Tcherneva, P. (2020), *The Case For a Job Guarantee,* London: Polity.

Widmer, J. (2009), '*Kurzarbeit:* An alternative to lay-offs', International Law Office, 27 May. Available online: https://www.internationallawoffice.com/Newsletters/ Employment-Immigration/Austria/Graf-Pitkowitz-Rechtsanwlte-GmbH/ Kurzarbeit-An-Alternative-to-Lay-Offs (accessed Oct 8, 2020).

Young, I.M. (2010), *Responsibility for Justice*, Oxford: Oxford University Press.

CHAPTER 8
PANDEMIC SOLIDARITY AND UNIVERSAL BASIC INCOME
Diana Popescu

Introduction

In the wake of the COVID-19 pandemic, governments across developed nations have increased their spending on healthcare, unemployment benefits, job retention and housing programmes to levels unprecedented since the post-Second World War era. Then, as now, governments expanded the reach and breadth of the welfare state, in terms of both the number of beneficiaries and the size of their payments (Obinger and Schmitt 2017, Sandher and Kleider 2020). But the COVID-19 pandemic has also directed increased attention to proposals for a universal basic income (UBI), with calls for UBI made by the Scottish First Minister (Paton 2020), a cross-party Parliamentary and Local Government group in the UK (Partington 2020), The Liberal Party in Canada (Jamal 2020), and even the Pope (Clifford 2020). Whereas access to cash welfare benefits is typically conditional on satisfying eligibility criteria (or means-tested), UBI is an unconditional sum paid to every citizen 'without means test, regardless of personal desert, with no strings attached and, under most proposals, at a sufficiently high level to enable a life free from economic insecurity' (Bidadanure 2019: 482). But what is the most appropriate normative justification for this generosity? And does it support or frustrate the case for UBI?

In this chapter, I explore two moral motivations for expanding benefits during the COVID-19 pandemic, namely the *insurance model* and the *solidarity model*. The insurance model views enlightened self-interest as the main motivating force behind distributing benefits. This model's concern for restricting access so as to pre-empt free riders is in tension with the unconditional nature of UBI. Yet I argue that the most appropriate moral motivation for understanding the expansion of welfare provisions during the COVID-19 pandemic is solidaristic, which strengthens the case for introducing UBI, vindicating the recent interest in this 500-year-old idea whose time has come (Haigh 2016).

Which motivation? From insurance to solidarity

What is the moral motivation for the extensive redistribution needed for providing generous benefits to those affected by the COVID-19 pandemic, as distinct from both economic motivations (e.g. protecting purchasing power) and political justifications (e.g. appealing to the electorate)? One possible candidate is the received view regarding the motivational bases for the Second World War era welfare expansion, viewing it as a form of individual insurance against risks which could reasonably befall each citizen (Dryzek and Goodin 1986). In the face of a common threat, it is in the interest of individual citizens to pool risks by paying into a scheme which then distributes dividends to those unfortunate enough to incur loses. In a situation of profound uncertainty about who will be negatively impacted (and relative certainty that there will be an impact, and of its relative severity) 'partiality and impartiality are fused and institutions for promoting social justice serve self-interest as well' (ibid.: 9). Welfare policies thus function as 'a sort of insurance arrangement which selfish people accept to make sure they will not be mistreated and pay for it by providing assurance to others that they, too, will not be mistreated' (Baumol 1982: 640, cited in Dryzek and Goodin 1986). Hence, a collective system of redistribution appears to be in the enlightened self-interest of each, as it safeguards every participant against unmitigated, devastating loses.

The palpable uncertainty about which jobs will be lost and which will be in high demand created by the COVID-19 pandemic could indeed be said to mimic the common threat felt by people in South-East England during the Battle of Britain that inspired Dryzek and Goodin. Just as during the Battle of Britain 'no one could say for certain where the bombs would land' (Dryzek and Goodin 1986: 9), so during the pandemic it was unclear whose job was secure and whose wasn't. The pandemic called into question the very definition of a secure job, with delivery drivers and supermarket clerks elevated to the status of essential workers, while airline pilots or West End and Broadway producers faced unemployment. On this understanding, the moral motivation for redistributive policies such as the furlough scheme in the UK, holidays from rent and utility payments in France, or stimulus checks in the US is that, since anyone in society could have been in a position to lose their job, face homelessness, or suffer significant threats to their income, it is in the enlightened interest of all to pay for securing against this risk.

Nevertheless, the current situation does not quite match the pervasive uncertainty of the Second World War. Firstly, in contrast to the absolute unpredictability of whose house would be bombed, there is more certainty about whose jobs and whose health are at risk in the COVID-19 crisis. From early on in the pandemic, performers and those working in the hospitality industry were known to be at higher risk of losing their source of income than nurses and delivery drivers. Similarly, people over 65 were known to be at higher risk of losing their lives than the young. If people were purely self-interested, many would not be motivated to support the extensive redistributive policies benefiting others that were put in place during the COVID-19 crisis given that they know their place in the distribution of risk. We would have pockets of demand coming from the most affected categories, and pockets of resistance coming from the more comfortably situated health- and work-wise. This might result in a resistance to the plight of the unemployed reminiscent of the inertia in reacting to the endemic job loss of people in low-skilled professions prevalent since the 1970s (Bonica et al. 2013). Yet that is not what we are witnessing.[1]

So, if the insurance model is left aside, what moral motivation best captures the current expansion of welfare measures? Political discourse has emphasised solidarity in the face of a common threat over efficiency in pursuing individual rewards when motivating spending decisions. The motivational oomph of insisting that 'we are all in this together' (Guterres 2020), 'all in the same boat' or that various categories of workers 'have not been forgotten' (Sunak 2020) comes from solidarity and a sense of a shared fate – not from the pooling of insurance policies of individual rational agents. References to solidarity have been made specifically as a corrective to the two central tenets of the insurance model, namely *individual responsibility*, which takes prudent behaviour as a condition for receiving benefits, and *self-reliance*, which presents independence as the norm and dependency as deviant (Fraser and Gordon 1992; Anderson 2004).[2]

The individual responsibility tenet of the insurance model is motivated by discouraging free riders and guarding against exploitation. This is manifested as a primary concern for blocking undeserving recipients from accessing benefits. However, welfare benefits during the COVID-19 pandemic have not come with increased scrutiny of claimants but, on the contrary, with an increased scrutiny of whether anyone is unfairly excluded. As the former head of the United Nations Development Programme Kemal Dervis puts it, 'the hoary argument that support for the poor undermines work incentives, hardly convincing in normal times, loses all credibility during a pandemic' (Dervis 2020). Indeed, the expansion of benefits during the pandemic came with lowering, not increasing, conditionality.

Against the assumption of self-reliance, the COVID-19 crisis has emphasised our common vulnerability. This was most apparent in shifting approaches to public health. Arguments for mask-wearing emphasise not the individual dividends to the person wearing the mask, but the collective benefits of each altruistically wearing the mask to protect others. Not only is it the case that 'you cannot in an epidemic just take your own risk [as] you are taking a risk on behalf of everybody else', as Professor Chris Witty has argued (BBC News 2020). Collective vulnerability is also at the very heart of the policy of mask-wearing which 'shifts the focus from self-protection to altruism . . . and is a symbol of social solidarity' (Cheng et al. 2020: 2). The COVID-19 pandemic has shown people's individual vulnerabilities tie in with their work lives, creating a continuity between shared finitude and socio-economic interdependence. The physical security and productivity of workers in sectors deemed essential depended partially on the compliance with lockdown measures of workers who were laid off or were working from home. In the new COVID-19 narrative, self-reliance is a privilege, not a moral obligation.

Moreover, it is not clear that the best way to understand the moral motivation for the initial, Second World War era expansion of the welfare state was indeed self-interest in the face of common risk, rather than solidarity. For Iris M. Young, interdependence and a shared fate, not self-reliance and individual responsibility, lie at the foundation of the modern welfare state. As she puts it, welfare states of the mid-twentieth century 'were founded on a notion that people in a modern society are interdependent . . . and that people owe one another a certain measure of reciprocal care because of these interdependencies' (Young 2011: 9). What is more, Nancy Fraser and Linda Gordon criticise the individual insurance approach to welfare on the grounds that it drives a wedge between worthy recipients, who get what they put in, and recipients of charity, who get something for nothing (Fraser and Gordon 1992: 47). In contrast they propose a social solidarity model embedded in social citizenship, which points to 'solidarity and interdependence' (ibid.: 63). Therefore, even before the COVID-19 era welfare expansion there was reason to believe that social solidarity is a stronger predictor of support for welfare redistribution than (economic) self-interest.

Overall, the individual insurance model does the job of supporting extended welfare measures but remains rooted in individual responsibility and self-reliance. However, the COVID-19 crisis has exposed self-reliance for the privilege that it is, and political leaders around the world have emphasised collective fate rather than individual responsibility as a motivation for increasing welfare measures. In other words, solidarity has worked as a corrective to self-reliance and enlightened self-interest. The added motivational pull of COVID-19 is thus for *solidarity* not individual responsibility as the basis for extending welfare benefits.

Solidarity and UBI

The solidaristic underpinnings of approaches to COVID-19 outlined above strengthen the case for universal and unconditional measures such as UBI. On a solidaristic understanding, the entitlement to extended benefits comes from being recognised as a full member of a political community in which each is similarly situated to the rest. As Barbara Prainsack and Elena Buyx put it, solidarity is a set of 'enacted commitments to accept costs to assist others with whom a person or persons recognise similarity in a relevant respect' (2017: 43). The emphasis is thus on commonality prompting assistance, not individually ensuring against risk. Solidarity looks away from each person's individual situation towards the similarities they share with others which prompt institutionalised assistance. Once individuals come to understand themselves in terms of their similarity with others, individual variations lose their importance. For example, Hannah Arendt illustrates the notion of solidarity in *Eichmann in Jerusalem* through the story of the Danish king wearing the yellow star as a sign of solidarity with the Jewish population during the Nazi occupation. By publicly positioning himself in the same boat as those marked out for oppression and genocide, the king was successful in making the intended separation between Jews and non-Jews unenforceable (Arendt 1963: ch. 10).[3] The act is one of solidarity because of – not despite – the king not facing the same individual risk as the Jewish people.

A solidarity-based case for assistance during the COVID-19 crisis therefore points to universal benefits rather than conditional ones. The moral motivation for redistribution is no longer that individual bombs fall on some presently unknown houses; it is that those sharing a common fate rise or fall together. Conditionality cannot make sense of a solidaristic rationale as it creates an internal 'us and them' division among contributors and recipients, the worthy and the unworthy of support, the ones previously in stable employment and the ones struggling to find work even before the pandemic hit, etc. A focus on sharing an equal status is what is needed to account for the existence of, for example, the precariat as a class of similarly situated people, as opposed to pitting certain elements of the class against one another (Standing 2011). Conditional measures which require recipients to successfully prove they are not 'one of those' – that is, one of the deserving poor – are by contrast atomistic. The status of an equal is not just different from but conflicting with being made to demonstrate inability, which requires making 'shameful revelations' about the reasons why people are debilitated or genuinely undesirable in their search for employment (Wolff 1998). A solidaristic understanding therefore supports unconditional assistance as a policy for tackling the effects of the COVID-19 pandemic.

Indeed, a solidaristic understanding is a fruitful way to capture Philippe van Parijs's early motivation for a UBI grant from the employed to the unemployed. Van Parijs argues that having a job should be viewed as a resource and that those fortunate enough to find a job do so partially because the jobless do not take up their share of the job market for whatever reason (1991: 123ff.). This connection highlights the interdependence of the employed and unemployed in constituting the labour market, as opposed to a self-reliance model in which the employed are understood as able to secure jobs through their merit and talent alone, independently of the relative positions on the labour market occupied by others. Although van Parijs does not use the vocabulary of solidarity, his rejection of exercising personal responsibility as a criterion, and his reframing of the labour market as an interdependent space made up of the employed and unemployed competing for limited jobs (as opposed to simply the sum of self-reliant workers) is compatible with solidaristic arguments for benefit provision.

The solidaristic understanding helps strengthen the case for universal basic income against criticism that, as a universal measure, UBI is inefficient by not being targeted and means tested. Firstly, a solidarity-based rationale for COVID-19 era redistribution posits that the value of universality resides in something other than its efficiency alone. Much like the value of social citizenship as independent of redistributive advantages proposed by T.H. Marshall, the 'shared experience and common status' of accessing a universal benefit acts as a 'qualitative element' which 'enters into the benefit itself' (1950: 64). This is not to say that efficiency concerns are misguided or that the findings of economists and behavioural scientists working on the feasibility of UBI are beside the point. But it is to say that if a certain level of UBI is feasible, then there is a good reason to resist trading off the universality of the benefit against the efficiency of a more targeted provision.

What is more, during the COVID-19 pandemic specifically, the inefficiencies of means-tested welfare measures might prove to be more damaging than the alleged inefficiencies of UBI. Non-compliance with

COVID-19 era measures such as self-isolation after being in contact with an infected person or when exhibiting symptoms is often motivated by fear of resulting economic hardship. The fact that such hardship – from losing one's job or one's customers – would be mitigated by conditional measures seems unable to assuage anxieties of nevertheless falling through the cracks. An unconditional income would act as a stronger guarantee that, whatever happens, a basic provision is reliably forthcoming and would protect people who are not comfortable with the level of exposure to COVID-19 enforced by their bosses.

In the context of the current pandemic, opting for unconditional, universal measures is not only beneficial for the unemployed, but also for other categories. The working mothers who could employ nannies or personal tutors with extra income, the victims of intimate partner violence who would have more means of escaping abusive relationships, people with mental health issues for whom income security would alleviate anxiety and stigma, would all benefit from UBI beyond unemployment. Far from being a measure designed for the unemployed, a social solidarity motivation which is uniquely triggered by the current crisis could help re-establish a society of equals on the foundations of economic downturn.

Conclusion

This chapter has argued for taking solidarity rather than enlightened self-interest as the main normative justification for the expansion of benefits during the COVID-19 pandemic. In turn, solidarity strengthens the case for UBI as opposed to conditional welfare measures. However, the period of current solidarity might be short-lived. Just as fish who collect together on dry land to keep each other damp would forget one another in the rivers and lakes (Chuang Tzu 1996: 76), so our present interdependence might not endure.

This does not weaken the present case, as even though heightened levels of solidarity represent a unique opportunity for introducing UBI, once introduced UBI can generate independent motivations for remaining in place. This was T.H. Marshall's view about the effects of social citizenship, whose unconditional nature would in time 'enter into the benefit itself' (Marshall 1950: 64). This motivational dynamic can be extended to UBI once we regard it as a matter of recognition for commonality rather than distributing income to alleviate job loss.

A distinct opportunity is for countries affected by the COVID-19 pandemic to take the crisis and recovery effort as a founding moment for UBI and pledge a small percentage of the post-COVID GDP growth to be divided equally among citizens. This collective entitlement would reflect the necessarily collective nature of the recovery effort in which some contributed by remaining indoors, some by volunteering, and others through waged employment. As GDP would grow, so would the dividend, creating the possibility of an incremental implementation of a radical policy.

Suggestions for further reading

- Bidadanure, Juliana (2019), 'The political theory of universal basic income', *Annual Review of Political Science*, 22: 481–501.
- Standing, Guy (2011), *The Precariat*, London: Bloomsbury Academic.
- Van Parijs, Philippe (2000), 'A basic income for all: if you really care about freedom, give people an unconditional income', *Boston Review* October/November 2000.
- Young, Iris Marion (2011), *Responsibility for Justice*, New York: Oxford University Press.

Notes

1. Sandher and Kleider (2020) make the case that 'It has been low-paid workers in sectors such as tourism, hospitality, retail and transport who have been the most likely to lose their jobs. High-skilled workers may still demand higher social insurance payments either because they are concerned for their own incomes or feel an affinity with the worst affected, but this is not guaranteed. If it is only the low-skilled few who demand a more generous welfare state, then governments will feel little pressure to deliver it.'

2. This motivation could capture the spirit of the newly found interest in UBI as a response to unemployment benefits (as in the Spanish case) as well as the theoretical case for UBI as a response to the 'Fourth Industrial Revolution'. This dynamic furthermore matches the type of arguments advanced by the Fourth Industrial Revolution camp; just as the London bombings did not discriminate among the rich and poor (Titmuss 1950: 506–7, cited in Dryzek and Goodin 1986: 10) so automation could affect truckers and surgeons, architects and manufacturers, accountants or shop assistants. Hence, the introduction of UBI could be said to fall into a characteristic pattern of the welfare state whereby 'welfare states grow out of periods of deep and widespread uncertainty in which

the barriers to redistribution- through-insurance have largely collapsed' (Dryzek and Goodin 1986: 9).

3. The story, however, appears to be a myth – see Lund (1975).

References

Anderson, E. (2004), 'Welfare, work requirements, and dependant-care', *Journal of Applied Philosophy*, 21 (3): 243–56.

Arendt, H. (1963), *Eichmann in Jerusalem*, New York: Viking Press.

Baumol, W. (1982), 'Applied fairness theory and rationing policy', *American Economic Review*, 72: 639–51.

BBC News (2020), 'Prof Chris Whitty: "If I increase my risk, I increase everybody's risk"'. *BBC News*, 21 September. Available online: https://www.bbc.co.uk/news/av/health-54235024 (accessed 9 November 2020).

Bidadanure, J. (2019), 'The political theory of universal basic income', *Annual Review of Political Science* 22: 481–501.

Bonica, A., N. McCarty, K.T. Poole et al. (2013), 'Why hasn't democracy slowed rising inequality?' *Journal of Economic Perspectives*, 27 (3): 103–24.

Cheng, K.K, T.H. Lam and C.C. Leung (2020), 'Wearing face masks in the community during the Covid-19 pandemic: altruism and solidarity', *The Lancet*, 16 April. Available online: https://doi.org/10.1016/S0140-6736(20)30918-1 (accessed 9 November 2020).

Chuang Tzu (1996), *Basic Writings* (trans. Burton Watson), New York: Columbia University Press.

Clifford, C. (2020), 'Pope Francis: "This may be the time to consider a universal basic wage"', *CNBC*, 13 April. Available online: https://www.cnbc.com/2020/04/13/pope-francis-it-may-be-the-time-to-consider-a-universal-basic-wage.html (accessed 9 November 2020).

Dervis, K. (2020), 'The Covid-19 solidarity test', *Project Syndicate*. Available online: https://www.project-syndicate.org/commentary/covid19-pandemic-solidarity-test-by-kemal-dervis-2020-03 (accessed 9 November 2020).

Dryzek, J. and R. Goodin (1986), 'Risk-sharing and social justice: the motivational foundations of the post-war welfare state', *British Journal of Political Science*, 16 (1): 1–34.

Fraser, N. and L. Gordon (1992), 'Contract versus charity: why is there no social citizenship in the United States?', *Socialist Review*, 22 (3): 45–67.

Guterres, A. (2020), 'We are all in this together: human rights and COVID-19 response and recovery', United Nations, 23 April. Available online: https://www.un.org/en/un-coronavirus-communications-team/we-are-all-together-human-rights-and-covid-19-response-and (accessed 9 November 2020).

Haigh, G. (2016), ''Basic income for all: a 500-year-old idea whose time has come?' *The Guardian*, 10 November. Available online: https://www.theguardian.com/business/2016/nov/11/basic-income-for-all-a-500-year-old-idea-whose-time-has-come (accessed 9 November 2020).

Jamal, U. (2020), 'In pandemic downturn, Canada's drive for guaranteed basic income picks up speed', *NPR*, 14 October. Available online: https://www.npr.org/2020/10/13/921606901/in-pandemic-downturn-canadas-drive-for-guaranteed-basic-income-picks-up-speed (accessed 9 November 2020).

Lund, J. (1975), 'The legend of the king and the star', *Indiana Folklore*, 8: 1–2.

Marshall, T.H. (1950), 'Citizenship and social class', in T.H. Marshall, *Citizenship and Social Class and Other Essays*, Cambridge: Cambridge University Press.

Obinger, H. and C. Schmitt (2017), 'The impact of the Second World War on postwar social spending' *European Journal of Political Research*, 57 (2): 496–517.

Partington, R. (2020), 'Covid job losses lead MPs to call for trials of universal basic income', *The Guardian*, 31 October. Available online: https://www.theguardian.com/society/2020/oct/31/covid-job-losses-lead-mps-to-call-for-trials-of-universal-basic-income (accessed 9 November 2020).

Paton, C. (2020), '"Time has come" for universal basic income, says Sturgeon', *Independent*, 4 May. Available online: https://www.independent.co.uk/news/uk/home-news/universal-basic-income-ubi-scotland-uk-nicola-sturgeon-coronavirus-a9498076.html (accessed 9 November 2020).

Prainsack, B. and A. Buyx (2017), *Solidarity in Biomedicine and Beyond*, Cambridge: Cambridge University Press.

Sandher, J. and H. Kleider (2020), 'Coronavirus has brought the welfare state back, and it might be here to stay', *The Conversation*, 24 June. Available online: https://theconversation.com/coronavirus-has-brought-the-welfare-state-back-and-it-might-be-here-to-stay-138564 (accessed 9 November 2020).

Standing, G. (2011), *The Precariat*, London: Bloomsbury Academic.

Sunak, R. (2020), 'Speech: Chancellor's statement on coronavirus (COVID-19)', 26 March. Available online: https://www.gov.uk/government/speeches/chancellor-outlines-new-coronavirus-support-measures-for-the-self-employed (accessed 9 November 2020).

Titmuss, R.M. (1950), *Problems of Social Policy*, London: HMSO and Longman, Green.

Van Parijs, P. (1991), 'Why surfers should be fed: the liberal case for an unconditional basic income', *Philosophy and Public Affairs*, 20 (2): 101–31.

Wolff, J. (1998), 'Fairness, respect and the egalitarian ethos', *Philosophy and Public Affairs*, 27: 97–122.

Young, I.M. (2011), *Responsibility for Justice*, New York: Oxford University Press.

PART III
DEMOCRATIC RELATIONS

CHAPTER 9
LEGITIMATING PANDEMIC-RESPONSIVE POLICY: WHOSE VOICES COUNT WHEN?
Rowan Cruft

Introduction

During the lockdowns, many voices have argued for restrictions to be lifted early, despite the risks to public health. The reasons given typically concern the detrimental economic, educational, mental health and non-COVID health effects of lockdowns. There is much good work (including in this volume) that assesses the force of these arguments on their own terms. My chapter proposes that the force of these arguments also varies depending on who makes them, and on how the arguments treat the views of others. For example, are the arguments being made by people with little to lose either from lockdown or its alleviation? Or are they made by people with more at stake? Are they offered in a dialogic spirit, or do they make assumptions about others' behaviour without engaging with them?

In this chapter, I will argue that these considerations throw doubt on the legitimating force of the claims of some of those wishing to open up the economy and keep schools open at the expense of public health during a pandemic. Insofar as those arguing for a return to 'business as usual' are supporting a move that harms others while benefiting themselves, their claims for this policy often do little to confer legitimacy on it. This is most especially true of those who are already well off, or who benefited from the *injustices* of the pre-pandemic 'business as usual'.

Democratic legitimation: the importance of public support

In a democracy, people's support for a policy is a reason in its favour, other things being equal. This chapter looks at some cases where 'other things' are not 'equal': cases where the nature of the voices supporting a policy, or the way those in support treat the voices of others, undermine some of the legitimating power of their support. (A different type of case in which 'other things' are not 'equal' is when the content of a policy is grossly unjust. People's support for fascist or racist policies is no reason in favour of such policies.)

Before going further, in this section I say a little about why people's support for a policy is *normally* a reason in its favour: why democratic politicians are rightly attentive and responsive to public opinion, and policies with little public support should rarely be enacted. There are two deep reasons that justify political power's responsiveness to people's support. One reason concerns where knowledge lies. Another concerns the importance of consent or disagreement. Both factors – knowledge and consent – bear on the justification of the use of force or authority.

Many philosophers argue that, if it is not to be 'bare' force exercised arbitrarily and illegitimately, the imposition of a particular policy by those with political power must satisfy two conditions: (a) the policy must be justified by good enough reasons (and the imposers must believe this, as must those on whom the policies are imposed); and (b) its imposition must receive some sort of agreement from most of those on whom it is imposed (or at least, they must refrain from dissenting to it).[1] Sometimes there will not be time to secure such agreement, as in the case of an immediate quarantine. But here there can be higher-level agreement, to institutions that can where necessary impose quarantines without seeking consent.

How can policy responses to the pandemic fulfil condition (a), the 'good reasons' requirement? In the UK, the government claimed its policies were 'following the science', developed with input from a group of expert scientists.[2] Such involvement of expertise is clearly conducive to satisfaction of the 'good reasons' requirement. But the empirical facts that science discovers cannot constitute good reasons all on their own.[3] If science tells us that a policy of recommending hand-washing will result in so many thousand excess deaths with such-and-such a probability, while a policy of lockdown will result in so many fewer thousand excess deaths with some different probability, none of this yet tells us what to do until we add practical or 'evaluative' premises about the relative importance of avoiding excess deaths vis-à-vis the importance of the liberty lost and the other opportunity costs of the policies.

Where do we find these evaluative premises? Some might call on moral experts here, akin to the scientific experts.[4] But what we need are experts on the substance, as opposed to the theory, of moral and evaluative claims: experts on the importance of job security, on the horrors of death in hospital, on the nuances of everyday child-rearing, on the stresses of housing in cities (to name just four of the many relevant areas). It seems to me that while moral philosophers might have expertise on theorising these issues, expertise on how we should *practically* evaluate trade-offs between such goods depends on life experience in the broadest sense, and is therefore fairly evenly distributed across people throughout society. For this reason, the best way to discover the evaluative premises that, together with the non-evaluative facts, determine the policies for which we have good reason, is to pool everyone's knowledge through democratic deliberation, debate and voting.[5] This is one deep reason why people's support for a policy, other things being equal, counts in its favour: moral and other types of knowledge are dispersed among people. Formal expertise has its role to play, but when it comes to the complicated trade-offs demanding evaluative understanding that characterise political questions, the people are often the experts.

In addition, public support for a policy is an indication that it might satisfy condition (b), by commanding agreement or at least not causing widespread disagreement. There is debate among philosophers about how to interpret the consent requirement on legitimate authority. If taken in too demanding a way (e.g. as requiring the explicit agreement of a citizen before their ruler can be legitimate) it makes most political authority illegitimate.[6] But it seems to me that some sort of agreement, or at least non-dissent, among enough people, is necessary for the imposition of power to be morally acceptable. An otherwise excellent policy that is very widely dissented from should not be imposed on people (again, other things being equal). Underlying this is a general principle requiring respect for a person's will or choice even if they have not chosen wisely. This includes people's social choice to work with others on joint policies. When several of us freely agree to the imposition of a policy, my assenting part in the agreement can help confer legitimacy on its imposition both on me and on my fellows.

People's will or choice cannot legitimate a policy on its own: the 'good reasons' condition must also hold. Even if most people wanted to allow the army to torture people, this would not legitimate such torture. But if a policy is 'good enough', *then* its legitimacy depends on whether people support or assent to it. For example, I think there is a range of acceptable evaluative positions about the relative priority of education and defence spending: policies involving a nil spend on education are outside the acceptable range; but policies including high spending on both education and defence, and many alternative spends, will all be within the acceptable range. Within this range, a position that would otherwise be appropriate for a given society can be made inappropriate simply by that society's free democratic dissent from it.[7] And a society's support for a position within this range can sometimes make it appropriate to enforce this position even on dissenters.[8]

In this section, I have presented the two deep reasons why public support for a policy normally counts in that policy's favour: public support reflects where moral knowledge lies (namely, with the public), and public support constitutes agreement with a policy (agreement that potentially legitimates its enforcement). These points have practical implications for the legitimacy of pandemic-responsive policies. One obvious implication is that such policies, and the decision-making generating them, should be subject to open democratic debate, with avenues for everyone to make proposals, to protest against and support policies. Another is that those designing policy should be wary of value judgements likely to reflect their particular elite position, unreflected in the wider democratic populace. (One example might be a tendency to prioritise economic activity that maintains current power structures, at the expense of public health.)

In the remainder of this chapter, I focus on cases where, despite the points above, support for a policy by some part of the public does *not* contribute to its legitimacy. I focus in particular on cases in which the *attitude to others' choice* or the *attitude to others' suffering* demonstrated by a person's or group's support for a policy undermines the legitimating force of their support.[9] By 'legitimating force', I mean the weight that a democrat should attach to a potential policy simply because it has public support: weight that, as we have seen in the current section, could help justify the policy's imposition.

Policy proposals in dialogic spirit?

If someone proposes or supports a policy *while intending to benefit from violating it*, this normally undermines the legitimating force of their support. For example, if I enter into a contract with you while intending to violate it for my own benefit (perhaps I intend to defraud you), my support for the contract is no moral reason for the courts or the police to insist that you uphold your side of the bargain. They can insist that I uphold my side, but they should not use my insincere assent as a reason to enforce your side of the bargain.

In the context of the pandemic in the UK, we might here think of the widely reported behaviour of Scotland's former Chief Medical Officer (Catherine Calderwood), or of the Prime Minister's Chief Adviser (Dominic Cummings), both of whom violated lockdown policies that they advocated. Matters are not as straightforward in these two cases as in the principle outlined in the previous paragraph. It is not clear that either of these individuals *intended* to violate the policies at all the points when they advocated them. Their support for the policies was also in their *official* roles, rather than as ordinary citizens. I suspect the first of these factors points towards lesser blameworthiness, while the latter points towards more. I will not assess blameworthiness here. I mention the cases simply as examples similar to what I have in mind: support for a policy by someone who intends to violate it for their own good does not carry legitimating weight. Support from such a person cannot help the case for enforcing the policy on others. Such support should not be given the serious attention that democrats should would otherwise give it.

There is an interesting interplay between the principle just mentioned and a different one: the principle that supporting a policy *in a way that excludes others from debating it* confers less democratic legitimacy on that policy than support offered in an open, dialogic spirit. Suppose I argue that we should end the lockdown early on the basis that people will grow tired of it and will fail to respect it. If this prediction is based on open, democratic discussion, in which my fellow residents express their belief that they will be unable to maintain the lockdown, then my support for easing the lockdown is prima facie unproblematic, and my argument for lifting the lockdown on this basis can confer (some) legitimacy on such a lifting. Similarly, if I reflect on my own position and argue that *I* will not be able to cope with a long lockdown, then my point carries (some) legitimacy-conferring weight. By contrast, though, suppose I make my prediction about others without discussing this with those I expect to violate the lockdown. Suppose I just use sociological data to support an assumption that people of your type are unable to respect rules like this, even though I think I can respect the rules. This seems disrespectful of you.[10] I am treating you as someone who could not choose the lockdown policy and live up to it, without having discussed this with you. (It is almost as if I am treating you like Calderwood or Cummings: as someone whose support for lockdown would be unable to legitimate it, even if you claimed to support it, because you are (so I think) already doomed to violate it.) In this way, I fail to treat you as an equal chooser jointly involved in the policy decision.

This does not forbid the kind of reasoning just mentioned. Often we cannot avoid choosing policies partly on the basis of predictions – rather than interpersonal discussion – about how far the policies will be respected by others. But we should recognise that the more we let that factor influence our choice, the less 'we' are choosing jointly and democratically with the relevant others, and the less respectful we are being of them. I think that the more we argue for a policy in this predictive rather than dialogic spirit, the less our support can confer legitimacy on its imposition.

Proposals to benefit from harming others, and from unjust harms

Public support for a policy can also lose its legitimating power if the policy would benefit its supporters at the expense of someone else. The clearest cases of such loss of legitimating power occur when the policy is unjust, the supporters are already in a strong position, and they stand to benefit from the injustice. A policy of aggressive imperialism, for instance, gains no legitimacy from the support of those who would benefit from it. Similarly, the policy to delay the end of chattel slavery gained no legitimacy from the support of those who held enslaved peoples on the plantations. Of course the illegitimacy of the policies just mentioned is overdetermined. There can be no good reasons for grossly unjust policies like imperialism or slavery. But there can sometimes be good reasons for policies that are *moderately* unjust, such as awarding examination grades based solely on the predictions of a single teacher. Such policies can be legitimate – but, I contend, only with the support of relevant groups.[11] Support for such a policy from people who are already well placed, and who stand to benefit from its injustice (such as administrators and state agents for whom it is easy and cheap), looks very different to support from those on whom it risks unjust harm (such as students).

I suggest that the cases just mentioned reveal four factors relevant to the legitimacy-conferring power of support for a policy: (1) whether the policy harms anyone; (2) whether its supporters stand to benefit from the policy; (3) whether its supporters are already starting from a position of relative advantage or disadvantage; (4) how just the policy is. Support for an unjust and harmful policy voiced by someone who is already in a strong position, and who would receive new benefits, confers very little legitimacy on the policy. This means that their agreement or support does very little morally to justify using power to impose the policy – much less than would the support of other people.

Matters are different when some but not all of these four factors are present. Advocacy of a policy by someone who would benefit from the costs it imposes on others, but who would benefit because the policy helps alleviate an injustice, can do much to legitimate that policy – as, for example, in the NAACP's role in the US civil rights movement.

If this is correct, then in democratic debates about when and whether to lift a lockdown and reopen the economy, attention must be paid to the particular positions of those proposing different policies. People in high-risk groups arguing to open up the economy (and thereby to place themselves at greater risk of harm) can confer more legitimacy on the position for which they are arguing than those in low-risk groups – especially if the latter are already doing well even during lockdown, but will gain extra benefits from a return to 'business as usual'.

I think this point requires some reorientation of our thinking about democratic debates. It demonstrates the importance of policymakers attending carefully to who will be benefited and who will be harmed by a policy *in relation to who is propounding it and their current position*. Where a policy benefits some at the expense of others, policymakers and imposers should attend to the justice of the policy, and to where its harms and benefits fall, in assessing the forcefulness of those arguing in its support.

This point can be seen as one of many possible departures from the utilitarian view that a policy's serving well-being (or indeed choices) confers legitimacy on it wherever that well-being (or those choices) are located. Instead, whose well-being or choice is at stake matters enormously. Many have stressed that the well-being of those who are worse off overall should be given greater weight (see Rawls 1971; Parfit 1991). The four factors outlined are additional complicating factors, taking us further from the simple view that serving well-being (or choices) wherever it is to be found is sufficient for a policy's legitimacy. We should not mistake general support for a policy, led by those who stand to benefit from its injustices, for legitimacy-enhancing support.

Injustice-generated dangers of school closures

School closures are an interesting example to illustrate the principles set out above. Let us distinguish three harms caused by closing schools (see also Brando and Fragoso in this volume). One is the impact on education in a narrow sense: reading, writing, arithmetic, fostered by trained teachers. A second is the broader social impact on children: schools ensure that children are fed, cared for and socialised outside potentially harmful home environments. Many experts highlight the second as a primary danger of school closures: the way it leaves some children without help and support in 'dysfunctional' homes.[12] A third is the effect on parents, employers and the wider economy: schools provide parents with childcare, freeing them for work and other activities.

The second harm reflects a wider injustice. That is, the harm that some children suffer when confined to their homes is itself an injustice: it is clearly unjust that some children live in households where they lack enough to eat, suffer from cold and mould or miss out on social or educational experience. This remains an injustice even when schools are open and it is thereby partly alleviated. Now, if someone asks for schools to be reopened on purely educational grounds, while at the same time campaigning against the broader injustices that leave children in danger at home, then it does not seem to me that they are proposing a policy in which they themselves benefit from injustice. By contrast, people in privileged positions who ask for schools to be reopened primarily as a 'sticking plaster' for the wider social injustices, and who do *not* support, or who actively *oppose*, further measures to address these injustices, seem to me often to be proposing an unjust policy from which they benefit. Why is it unjust? Because it proposes a partial, and conceptually misdirected (because educational rather than social), solution to an injustice that should be faced head-on. Why do they benefit from it? Because alleviating the relevant wider social injustices requires major changes that will be (moderately) costly, at least in the short term, for those in privileged positions: both in terms of tax payments, and in terms of social changes that will make (e.g.) a private education less of an advantage. (Less privileged parents also benefit from having more time available, but unlike privileged groups, their support for reopening schools does not come from a position of strength.) When we add the facts about how reopening schools increases the risk of catching COVID-19, and that this disproportionately affects the kind of families for whom the schools are supposedly being reopened as a safety net, the proposed analysis is strengthened: it looks more like a case of privileged groups attempting to benefit from injustice.

Of course, there will be many people – including many in privileged positions – who argue for schools to be reopened for reasons of wide social justice who do not themselves benefit from this injustice. But the concern just mentioned points again towards giving extra weight to those who have most to lose from the relevant changes, not only because they know most about what is best for them, but also because their support does more to legitimate the relevant change than the support of those who will benefit from the resultant injustices.

Harm and relevant alternatives

The previous section centred around my claim that support for a policy does little to legitimate it if the policy is unjust and the supporter is already privileged and stands to benefit from that injustice. At least three aspects of this claim deserve further thought: what counts as an injustice, what it is to be privileged, and what it is to benefit or be harmed by it. I will not analyse injustice or privilege here. But I do need to say more about benefit and harm.

One account says that someone is benefited by an event if it causes them to be better off than they were before it happened. This is too crude. The lockdown benefited many by slowing the spread of COVID-19, even though it made many people worse off than they were before the lockdown happened. The reason we say the lockdown benefited people is because it caused them to be better off than *they would have been* if the disease had been allowed to spread without a lockdown. Here we seem to be comparing the lockdown to a counterfactual situation involving *COVID-19 plus 'business as usual'*.

But in the schools example above, I used a different point of comparison. I said that – even without COVID-19 – 'business as usual' harmed certain children. This cannot be in comparison to 'business as usual'! Instead, the harms suffered by the relevant children reflect the ways they are worse off when compared to a situation in which injustice is alleviated. This is a fairly common move.[13] But it seems to me that we cannot define harm in comparison to too utopian an alternative (such as one where everyone behaves as well as possible): that would make us find harm too frequently, all over the place. Instead, we should compare the relevant situation to one in which people do what they should, within some reasonable standard of what is achievable. Relative to this, the children discussed in the previous section are harmed by the injustices outlined, because there is a reasonably achievable normatively required alternative relative to which what we actually do makes the children worse off.

One thing this warns us to beware of is claims that 'there is no reasonable or achievable alternative'.[14] Sometimes that could be correct. But sometimes it will be a method for excluding alternatives, comparison with which would make a particular policy count as harmful (and its proponents' support thereby not fully count as legitimating it). We can see this at work in responses to the problems of injustice for children outlined earlier: if one argues that there is nothing that can be done about this except the reopening of schools, then one is thereby closing off my claim that 'business as usual' (through schools opening and nothing more) itself harms children by failing to alleviate the relevant injustices.

Conclusion: 'good' policies from 'bad' sources?

In the first section ('Democratic legitimation: the importance of public support'), I argued that, other things being equal, public support for a policy helps legitimate its imposition. That is, other things being equal, public support for a policy suggests that its imposition through the force of law would not be arbitrary, but would be morally justifiable. Given that moral expertise is dispersed among the public, the fact that a policy commands public support is a reason in favour of it; such support is also a mark of the kind of assent that is necessary for power to be legitimate.

The rest of the chapter focused on cases where 'other things' are not 'equal': cases in which the legitimating power of a person's support for a policy is undermined by their attitude or relative position. In the second section ('Policy proposals in dialogic spirit?'), we looked at cases where support for a policy is proposed in an insufficiently dialogic spirit. And in the third ('Proposals to benefit from harming others, and from unjust harms') and fourth ('Injustice-generated dangers of school closures') sections, we looked at cases where those supporting a policy would stand to benefit from the way it harms others, in a manner that undermines the legitimacy that the support might otherwise confer.

It is important to notice that these arguments in the later sections focus on how the legitimating power of public support for a policy can be diminished. This is distinct from the policy's own merits. An excellent policy could be proposed by someone whose position means that their support for it does not contribute to the legitimacy of its imposition. For example, a policy of lockdown might be proposed by someone who would benefit financially from the consequent increased use of videoconferencing. That policy might nonetheless be a good idea, and the benefiting proposer might even be motivated by the right reasons – for example, concerns about stopping the spread of COVID-19. In a slogan, a 'good' policy could come from a 'bad' proposer or supporter. My argument has simply shown that, in such a case, the bare fact of support from the 'bad' proposer does not count either as evidence that the proposal is a good one, nor as a form of legitimacy-conferring consent to the proposal. (By contrast, in the normal case – where 'other things' really are 'equal' – a good democrat should indeed recognise support for a proposal as (some) evidence that it is a good one, and as constituting (some) legitimating consent to it.)

Because a 'good' policy can be proposed by any source, my argument does not point towards silencing less-than-just proposals by those in privileged positions who would benefit from them. It simply entails that when assessing whether it would be legitimate to impose such policies, we need to look at who is supporting them. In public discussion of the pandemic, there has been much focus on the opportunity costs of different policies. But it matters just as much on whom such costs – opportunity and actual – fall. Are they victims of injustice, or simply harmed by just policies? And are the relevant policies being proposed primarily by those who stand to gain from them? Even at the expense of others? These questions are all relevant to the legitimating power of the public support given to different policies.[15]

Suggestions for further reading

- For more on how to think about consent's role in legitimating institutions, see Amanda Greene's 'Consent and Political Legitimacy', in *Oxford Studies in Political Philosophy* vol. 2, eds. D. Sobel, P. Vallentyne and S. Wall, Oxford: Oxford University Press, 2016): 71–97.

- For a wide-ranging introduction to different theories of democratic legitimacy, including their costs and benefits, see Fabienne Peter's *Democratic Legitimacy*, London: Routledge, 2009.

- For discussion of the question whether all those affected by the decisions of a government should have a democratic right to participate in it, see e.g. Robert Goodin, 'Enfranchising all affected interests, and its alternatives', *Philosophy and Public Affairs*, 35 (1) (2007): 40–68.

Notes

1. Much work focuses on the legitimacy of authoritative power, rather on the legitimacy of particular policies, but the two are clearly related. On the epistemic aspect of legitimacy – the requirement that power enact policies for which there are good reasons – see e.g. Estlund (2008), Peter (2009), Raz (1986). On the importance of consent or non-dissent, see Greene (2016), Locke (1960 [1689]), Simmons (2001).

2. See https://www.gov.uk/government/organisations/scientific-advisory-group-for-emergencies (accessed 9 March 2021).

3. For David Hume's famous objections to deriving an 'ought' from an 'is', see Cohon 2018, section 5.

4. Compare Plato's 'Philosopher Kings' in *Politeia*.

5. Compare Goodin and Spiekermann (2018), Ober (2017).

6. Compare Hume's concerns about consent theory: 'My intention here is not to exclude the consent of the people from being one just foundation of government where it has place. It is surely the best and most sacred of any. I only pretend that it has very seldom had place in any degree, and never almost in its full extent' (1994 [1741]: 182).

7. See Richardson (2002: 140–1), for the idea of a 'normatively fruitful context', one in which an option's having been chosen can make it right. One example might be the choice between an adversarial and an inquisitorial criminal justice system: both have merits, and each can be made appropriate or inappropriate for a society by their assent or dissent. For further epistemic approaches to democracy which take deliberation according to appropriate procedures as partly constituting the deliberation's outcome as the right one, see Misak (2001), and the pure epistemic proceduralism in Peter (2009).

8. As democrats, we have to be willing to live under rulers and policies from which we dissent, if the majority chose them (and chose them for 'good enough' reason).

9. My concerns might seem to be related to Rousseau's distinction between the 'general will' that 'considers only the common interest' and the 'will of all' that takes 'private interest into account'. My discussion is related to these issues, but I resist any sharp distinction between 'common' and 'private' concerns (Rousseau 1973 [1762]: 203).

10. Of course a lot here depends on the detail: is the relevant data gained from surveys of other groups, or from surveys that include you? What about surveys of groups like you, but not including you? Thanks to Aveek Bhattacharya and Fay Niker for comments.

11. Compare the 'all affected' principle which says that all those affected by a decision should have a say on it (e.g. Goodin 2007). I am adding that the voluntary 'say' of those at risk of unjust harm does more to legitimate a decision than the voluntary 'say' of those who would benefit – if the beneficiaries are already privileged. This is not an argument in favour of extra or fewer votes depending on one's position, but rather concerns the legitimating weight of the relevant voices arguing in favour of the policy.

12. Now I am sure there are many children in this position, but I also think we should be wary of a middle-class fear of 'the other' at work in diagnosing 'dysfunction' here.

13. We use a moralised baseline as our point of comparison when we think that someone who fails to help their elderly neighbour harms them, or that somebody who fails to feed their children harms them. The agent in these cases does not make the neighbour or the child worse off than they were beforehand. Instead in these cases the agent makes the neighbour and the child worse off than they would be if the agent had done what they should. For a famous – and in my view flawed – use of a moralised baseline in measuring whether a choice is voluntary, see Nozick (1974: 263–4).

14. See e.g. the critical discussion in Finlayson (2015), Chapter 1.
15. Many thanks to Aveek Bhattacharya, Fay Niker, Felix Pinkert and Alexandru Volacu for comments.

References

Cohon, Rachel (2018), 'Hume's Moral Philosophy', *The Stanford Encyclopedia of Philosophy* (Fall 2018 Edition), Edward N. Zalta (ed), URL = <https://plato.stanford.edu/archives/fall2018/entries/hume-moral/> (accessed 9 March 2021).

Estlund, D. (2008), *Democratic Authority: A Philosophical Framework*, Princeton: Princeton University Press.

Finlayson, L. (2015), *The Political is Political: Conformity and the Illusion of Dissent in Contemporary Political Philosophy*, London: Rowman & Littlefield.

Goodin, R. (2007), 'Enfranchising all affected interests, and its alternatives', *Philosophy and Public Affairs*, 35 (1): 40–68.

Goodin, R. and K. Spiekermann (2018), *An Epistemic Theory of Democracy*, Oxford: Oxford University Press.

Greene, A. (2016), 'Consent and political legitimacy', in D. Sobel, P. Vallentyne and S. Wall (eds), *Oxford Studies in Political Philosophy*, vol. 2, Oxford: Oxford University Press: 71–97.

Hume, D. (1994 [1741]), 'Of the original contract', in K. Haakonssen (ed), *Political Essays*, Cambridge: Cambridge University Press.

Locke, J. (1960 [1689]), *Second Treatise of Government*, ed. P. Laslett, Cambridge: Cambridge University Press.

Misak, C. (2001), *Truth, Politics, Morality*, London: Routledge.

Nozick, R. (1974), *Anarchy, State, and Utopia*, Oxford: Blackwell.

Ober, J. (2017), *Demopolis*, Cambridge: Cambridge University Press.

Parfit, D. (1991), *Equality or Priority?*, The Lindley Lecture, Lawrence: University of Kansas.

Peter, F. (2009), *Democratic Legitimacy*, London: Routledge.

Rawls, J. (1971), *A Theory of Justice*, Oxford: Blackwell.

Raz, J. (1986), *The Morality of Freedom*, Oxford: Clarendon.

Richardson, H. (2002), *Democratic Autonomy*, Oxford: Oxford University Press.

Rousseau, J-J. (1973 [1762]), *The Social Contract and Discourses*, trans. G.D.H. Cole, rev. J.H. Brumfitt and J.C. Hall, updated by P.D. Jimack, London: Everyman.

Simmons, A.J. (2001), *Justification and Legitimacy: Essays on Rights and Obligations*, Cambridge: Cambridge University Press.

CHAPTER 10
LIVING ALONE UNDER LOCKDOWN
Felix Pinkert

Introduction

Actions speak louder than words. It is easy for governments to spout 'modern', 'liberal' and 'tolerant' rhetoric. But the lockdown orders many have implemented to curb the spread of COVID-19 belie these stated values. The specific ways in which governments have re-regulated our social lives have revealed an astoundingly narrow and outdated picture of how people live, or ought to live, with respect to their personal relationships. The typical public health regulations required people to stay at home, to venture outside only for particular purposes (such as grocery shopping and physical exercise) and to do so alone or with members of their own household. People were asked to keep minimum distances from all others, with the assumption that these 'others' were simply strangers one happened to come across outdoors. Governments thus assumed that people live together with the people with whom they have their most important personal relationships. They assumed that a person's physical household is also the nucleus of their social world. Subsequently, many governments supplemented these lockdown rules with special permissions for 'intimate partners' who live in separate households to meet. They thereby assumed that for everyone sexual relationships have paramount importance in our relationship networks, in a way that, for instance, close friendships, ties between siblings, or relationships to one's religious co-believers do not.

In this chapter, I argue that on the basis of these assumptions, governments have acted in a way that is harmful, unjust, and discriminatory towards people who do not fit into governments' picture of our social lives: people whose closest interpersonal relationships do not coincide with their physical households and are not of a sexual nature. The aim of this chapter is to highlight these harms and injustices in order to sketch a better way forward for public health measures, one that respects the diversity of household models and core social relationships. Furthermore, by bringing to light governments' and societies' lingering biases, the pandemic also enables us to better recognise these biases in other policy areas and wider culture.

Interpersonal needs and social rights

Assuming the nuclear family model as the basis for lockdown regulations is highly problematic for people whose home does not overlap with their central social relationships. These are, first, people who physically live alone in a self-contained household without sharing any rooms with others. In high-income countries, where more people can afford this relatively expensive living arrangement, people who live alone account for some 10 per cent (in the US) to 24 per cent (Sweden) of the total population (United Nations Statistics Division 2020, Eurostat 2020). As the total population also contains children, their proportion of the adult population is even higher. While there are people who live extremely secluded lives – such as *hikikomori* in Japan – the vast majority of these people are not recluses. They simply live their social lives differently – with partners who live separately, families who live elsewhere, friends whom they meet outside or invite over. Most of my discussion will focus on this group, as the social harms and injustices are clearest here. Yet note that the separation of physical household and social home, and hence many of my arguments, apply also to people who live together with others *physically*, but not *socially*. Most notably, with rising housing costs, many students and young professionals share households, often with complete strangers. In the UK, it is common for people in their twenties to live in such flat-shares, and Germans even have a special word for this kind of household: a '*Zweck-WG*', or 'utilitarian houseshare'. Young adults who have to live in their parents' household for economic reasons – something that might become more common due to the economic hardships of COVID-19 – can be in a similar situation. While they don't live with strangers, the focus of their own, independent social world often lies firmly outside of their physical household. Similarly, single parents find themselves in a multi-person household, but not one that provides them with a close adult relationship.[1]

For people who live alone, most stay-at-home orders have meant going without meaningful face-to-face contact or human touch for many weeks in a row (unless one had to be physically present at one's socially interactive workplace *and* has meaningful relationships with one's co-workers). This is a sacrifice qualitatively different from those made by people mostly confined to their family homes. For people who live in such homes, the COVID-19 measures mean a loss of in-person interactions with specific persons, such as close friends or relatives living in different households. This is a significant cost, which consists in an unwelcome *restriction* and *concentration* of social contacts. It is, however, not a loss of supportive face-to-face personal contact and human touch *altogether* – which is the cost borne by people who live alone.

This cost is highly detrimental to people's well-being, and consequently a matter of the utmost ethical seriousness. We are deeply social creatures, and our general psychological well-being, as well as our sense of belonging, purpose and security, depend on our social interactions. So too do our physical and mental health (see e.g. Holt-Lundstad, Smith and Layton 2010). Social interaction of a particular kind and quality is an essential human need. Indeed, this need is so essential that it is acknowledged in many human rights documents. For example, the UK Human Rights Act asserts a right to respect for one's private and family life, which courts have interpreted as including friendships and other relationships (Equality and Human Rights Commission 2018). Most strikingly, the United Nations Standard Minimum Rules for the Treatment of Prisoners, also known as the Nelson Mandela Rules, interpret the Universal Declaration's prohibition of torture or 'cruel, inhuman or degrading treatment or punishment' to also cover prolonged solitary confinement (UNODC 2015). The underlying line of thought is that our need for social relationships and human contact is just as essential for our well-being as our need for food, clothing and housing, which are protected by human rights (United Nations 1948, Article 25) and consequently likewise warrants protection by inalienable human rights. Political philosopher Kimberley Brownlee hence argues that we should explicitly acknowledge a general human right to sociability (Brownlee 2020).

The essential needs, and human rights, of people who live alone were thus seriously compromised by the lockdown measures. Granted, we were fortunate that COVID-19 struck at a time of widespread access to video telephony, which helped people to stay connected and feel less lonely. Yet such online interactions lack the crucial element of affectionate touch, a lack of which studies have shown to be associated with 'depression, stress, loneliness, insecure attachment, alexithymia, and the number of diagnosed mood/anxiety disorders and secondary immune disorders' (Floyd and Hesse 2017).

The Austrian Corona Panel Project, a representative longitudinal study with 1,500 respondents in each wave, demonstrates this particularly high social cost borne by people who live alone, even with online connectivity (which all respondents had, as the study had to be conducted online) (Austrian Corona Panel Project 2020: section 3.1). The study found that under the full lockdown restrictions, 13 per cent of people who do *not* live alone reported feeling lonely daily or almost daily, while in the most affected (and arguably most internet-connected) group of people who live alone, over 40 per cent of men, and 54 per cent of women under the age of 35, reported such frequent feelings of loneliness (Bacher and Beham-Rabanser 2020).[2]

Proportionality and discrimination based on household model

But was the social cost experienced by people living alone not necessary for combating the spread of COVID-19, where everyone just had to do as much as possible? If it was, then we should ask why such a sacrifice was not asked of people in multi-person households. After all, the most effective way to contain COVID-19 would have been for everyone to meet absolutely no one. In multi-person households, this would have meant following the guidelines usually applied only to households with a suspected case of COVID-19: to always stay in individual rooms, to use communal areas only one person at a time, and to always disinfect and air them after each use. Yet such drastic measures were not required. While practical (and legal) considerations may have been a factor here, it is fair to assume that the enormous social cost of disrupting close-knit household bubbles was deemed disproportionate to the limited additional benefit of completely atomising society into individuals. It was politically accepted that people in multi-person households would likely infect each other if one household member got infected.

Yet for people who live alone, such an atomisation was mandated: they were required to not meet anyone face to face. This was done despite the possibility of allowing them a similar level of risk-taking as people in multi-person households, namely by allowing them (as very few governments did) to 'bubble' up into 'virtual households' with other people or isolated multi-person households (see below).

People who lived alone and strictly abided by the lockdown rules were thus among the unsung heroes of COVID-19 restrictions. They displayed ideal containment behaviour, at an exceptional personal cost. Yet given the severity of this cost, and that it was not required of others, their self-isolation behaviour should have been considered what philosophers call 'supererogatory': laudable behaviour, but beyond the call of moral, and legal, duty.

Governments indirectly mandated near total self-isolation of people who live alone, as a result of general lockdown regulations that took households to be the smallest social unit. This reflected neglectful or wilful ignorance of the easily obtainable statistic that some 10–24 per cent of people live in households with only one person (or a lack of imagination of what the lockdown rules would do to the social lives of people who live alone). This ignorance did not only impose extreme personal cost on those living alone. It also made them, and their sacrifice, invisible. For example, the Austrian Chancellor Sebastian Kurz urged people to spend Easter only with the people with whom one shares a household – implying that everyone lived with at least one other person (Bundeskanzleramt 2020). In the UK, it took the government almost twelve weeks from the start of the lockdown on 23 March 2020 (UK Government 2020) to acknowledge the situation of more than seven million people who live alone (Office for National Statistics 2019), who were then allowed to form 'support bubbles' with one other household from 13 June onward (Hill 2020).

As well as inflicting serious harms on people who live alone, governments' neglect of their social lives also unfairly discriminated against them for their way of organising their home and their social relationships. In the typical lockdown regime, members of multi-person households were permitted to take the infection risks of being close to each other, relating face to face, and physically expressing affection, at home as well as in public. They could, for example, hug or even kiss each other in public. By contrast, two friends (or even a couple) who both lived alone were at best permitted to stand two metres apart from one other, and even this was typically not explicitly permitted but only an implication of the rule to keep distance from people one happened to encounter outdoors. If they dared to defy the social distancing rules and form their own small support bubble, then they were criminalised and stigmatised as life-threateners for activities, and a degree of risk-taking, that was legal and deemed perfectly acceptable for people from multi-person households.

It is almost as if governments were saying, 'You could have lived together with housemates or a partner, so it is your fault for choosing a living arrangement that now lands you in this situation.' Yet 'this situation' – losing all face-to-face human contact – is not a necessary consequence of the need to contain a pandemic. It is a political choice. And it is a choice that reflects governments, out of conviction or ignorance, deeming some forms of intimate social life – the nuclear family – to be particularly valuable and protection-worthy, but others – the 'family' of close friends who live separately – as somehow less important, less worthy of protection, and more acceptable to be sacrificed for the greater good.

Intimate partners vs other relationships

While most governments remained oblivious to the social deprivation and discrimination their policies entailed for people who live alone, many did take notice of one particular subset of that group: couples who live in separate households. They then introduced a permission to meet and visit one's 'intimate' partner even if they live in another household, by clarifying that doing so fell into the category of activities necessary to fulfil one's basic needs.

This permission was appropriate – recall the picture of one couple kissing in the park, while the other had to stand two metres apart. But by introducing *only* this permission, governments committed yet another kind of discrimination: namely, against people whose most important relationships do not qualify as 'intimate' (i.e. sexual). Having sex, or just coffee, with one's intimate partner was deemed a basic need that people could not be required to leave unfulfilled for the sake of public health, while for a single person to have coffee with their closest friend was not deemed so important. Governments' actions basically said, 'If you're single, or asexual, your social needs don't matter that much, and you don't really have any relationships comparably worth protecting.'

By granting permission to meet only to intimate partners, governments have unjustly discriminated against other people who live alone. They have also acted in a highly illiberal manner, by buying into what philosopher Elizabeth Brake calls 'amatonormativity', a privileging of amorous love relationships as particularly valuable types of relationships, which one should aim at over and above other types of relationships (Brake 2012: ch. 4. iii). It is, however, not appropriate for governments to treat some forms of living – such as the nuclear family or the intimate couple – as more important or protection-worthy than others – for instance the close-knit non-sexual friendship or a close sibling relationship. To use an analogy provided by philosophers Stephanie Collins and Luara Ferracioli, governments' actions were akin to closing Muslim schools but keeping Catholic schools open – treating people differently without good pandemic-related grounds for doing so (Collins and Ferracioli 2020).[3]

Objections to my diagnosis, and replies

At this point, the reader may be tempted to defend governments, particularly those that imposed very stringent and successful lockdowns. After all, governments had to react quickly and strongly, there were many unknowns, and not every detail that appears in hindsight was clear then.

In response to this defence, let me point out that, for any government, the statistic of how many people live alone is not hard to come by, and with 10–24 per cent of the population, it is not a small group. While the welfare of these people may justifiably not have been at the forefront of governments' attention early on, it is not asking too much of governments to pay attention to essential interpersonal needs after a few weeks, especially since that is when social deprivation had started to become acute, and when it became clear that the lockdowns would persist for a matter of months. Moreover, some countries made special allowances for people who live alone very early on in the pandemic, most notably New Zealand with its 'social bubbles' (Long 2020) and Belgium, which permitted households to exercise outdoors with one additional friend (Galindo 2020; Office of Sophie Wilmès, Belgian PM 2020), and such policies were also discussed by some epidemiologists (Tiffany 2020). These policies show that even in the midst of an emergency situation, it was possible to be attuned to people's different social situations. And once some governments had taken such measures, other governments could have seen this and followed suit, even if the issue had not occurred to them initially.

Furthermore, responses to stress and uncertainty are not random. Often they clarify our priorities and deeply held convictions. Most governments did not act in a blind panic. It was, for example, immediately obvious to governments that jobs would be at risk and needed protection. It is therefore revealing that it was not as obvious to governments that people who live alone would face a situation awkwardly close to solitary confinement, or that people without intimate partners might still need to see other people.

A second line of defence is that the legally binding lockdown regulations were not as stringent as I have made them out to be. Some lockdown regulations, such as Austria's general 'stay at home' order, turned out to lack legal basis and were judicially overturned. And with some legal creativity and perhaps economy with the truth, one could meet friends. For example, one could just so happen to spend one's permitted time exercising outside at the same time as one's friend, running in parallel at a two-metre distance. Or one could just so happen to walk past one's friend's house and accidentally enter it, thereby 'unintentionally' leaving public space and entering a private space where the lockdown rules no longer applied. Or one could simply claim that one is about to have sex with the friend with whom one was just taking a stroll.

This defence, however, is woefully inadequate. For the harms and discrimination suffered by the lockdown measures, it does not matter what exactly the legal status of a given government requirement was, whether it was actually backed by the force of law, merely intended to be so backed or only intended as an urgent request.

This is because, first, all of these kinds of government communications were aimed at, and succeeded in, restricting people's social lives. Regulations which were later overturned in the courts nonetheless impacted people's lives while they were still in effect. Communications whose legal status was left ambiguous left citizens and police unable to readily distinguish legal requirements from mere recommended guidelines. So cautious or conscientious citizens as well as (perhaps overly) diligent police ended up treating many publicly announced requirements as legally binding, irrespective of their actual legal status. Lastly, even those communications that were framed as not legally binding requests still restricted people's actions, by way of shifting 'softer' social norms. For example, no one aims to legally enforce 'wash your hands' or coughing hygiene advice, yet constant reminders of this advice change social norms nonetheless. It is much less acceptable to be seen coughing into one's hand, or to be seen to only very briefly (or not at all) wash one's hands in a public bathroom. Likewise, any mere requests pertaining to our interpersonal relationships started to change social norms (e.g. by deliberately stigmatising certain behaviour as 'life-threatening' in the UK). Through people's own conscientiousness, and social control by others, these new norms restricted people's interpersonal contacts.

Because all kinds of government lockdown regulations – legally binding, legally ambiguous, as well as clearly not legally binding requests – were effective in restricting people's options, they must be subjected to the same standards: to not inflict serious harm to the fulfilment of essential needs, and to not discriminate against particular ways of living.

Finally, irrespective of the effectiveness of government regulations, being able to have face-to-face contact only in a legal grey area, with the Damocles' sword of punishment and social sanction hanging over one's head, while one's neighbours could happily hug in the park, is not to be treated with respect and as an equal. Neither is potentially getting questioned by police about whether one really does have sex with one's closest friend simply because you want to talk to them face to face. It is not unreasonable to demand that governments do better than that.

A better way forward: a flexible contact budget

So how could governments effectively contain the spread of a pandemic in ways that, first, permit all people to maintain a minimum of face-to-face contact, and, second, treat people with different modes of family and relationship life, and household organisation, equitably? One possibility is to start with stringent rules for typical multi-person households – the nuclear family – and then subsequently add special provisions for other groups. But such an arrangement would still take the nuclear family as the primary focus of policy, and treat it as a social default, with other lifestyles being a mere afterthought. Instead, it is preferable for governments not to take a stance on which relationship types and living arrangements are standard. Instead, people could be granted a 'contact budget', a sum total of face-to-face contacts, which they can freely 'spend' on whichever face-to-face interactions they deem most important.

The UK model of a 'support bubble', albeit developed far too late, captures this ideal of neutrality well: people who live alone were permitted to form 'support bubbles' with one other household, thereby being effectively treated as member of that household for the purposes of the lockdown restrictions. Notably, this permission did not specify the nature of the relationship to that other household one needed to have. One could form a support bubble with one's partner, a sibling, a close friend, but also with one's dance partner.

Most people in multi-person households would spend their limited contact budget on seeing their other household members, so for them this kind of arrangement works similarly to the typical 'stay at home' orders. But it automatically makes provision for people who live alone to be able to have some personal contact. Furthermore, in principle, one could also spend one's contact budget *outside* one's multi-person household. This is because the concept of a contact budget can do away with the assumed link between physical household and social bubble, by not only allowing people who live alone to *join other* households, but also allowing people in multi-person households to *disassociate* from the other members of their household. This would be helpful for people in multi-person households who prefer to socialise with people from another household. For example, people who live in more utilitarian house shares could see their closest friends or partners rather than their housemates, if they are willing to pay the price of setting up social distancing within their household. Likewise, young people who live with their parents might instead see their closest friends.

As legally enforceable rules, such a completely consistent application of the contact budget approach would likely be impractical and highly privacy-intrusive. But it can work as an ideal on which to measure policies, and if and when the pandemic is sufficiently under control to permit people leeway in their social interactions, the idea of a limited social budget can function as a social norm and personal ethic. By endorsing the norm of a limited contact budget, governments would clearly acknowledge that one's household need not coincide with one's social home – instead, our true home is the people we care most about, whoever they are.

Conclusion: beyond the pandemic

It is often said that the pandemic's disruption of our societies is also a chance for change. In their pandemic responses, many governments have inadvertently revealed that they hold very conservative, outdated and illiberal biases about what people's social lives are or ought to be, with unprecedented harmful and discriminatory consequences. Looking beyond the pandemic, this situation allows us to address these biases in other policy areas, as well as in other social norms and practices.

A few examples shall suffice here: governments regularly grant tax breaks, and some employers even offer salary subsidies, for married couples. Immigration regimes make special allowances for married people and intimate partners, but not, for example, for close friends. Landlords rent out some flats only to families, but not to house shares. At work, single people are sometimes treated as being generally more available, for instance for undesired weekend work, than people with family. Sports clubs routinely offer family or couple memberships, but only to people who live at the same address.

Just like the lockdown restrictions, these and other laws, policies and norms treat people who live alone, or without an intimate partnership as their central relationship, as a sort of exception or afterthought. Their living arrangements are not duly recognised as worthy of support and protection. We should emerge from the pandemic with a more acute awareness of such biases and their consequences, and move towards a more inclusive society that respects and supports the interpersonal relationships each of us values most, whatever form they take.

Suggestions for further reading

- Brake, Elizabeth (2012), *Minimizing Marriage: Marriage, Morality, and the Law*, New York: Oxford University Press.
- Brownlee, Kimberley (2020), *Being Sure of Each Other: An Essay on Social Rights and Freedoms*, New York: Oxford University Press.
- Cohen, Rhaina (2020), 'What if friendship, not marriage, was at the center of life?', *The Atlantic*, 20 October.
- Collins, Stephanie and Luara Ferracioli (2020), 'Sex under lockdown, but not friendship? The discriminations of intimacy', *ABC News*, 17 August.
- Taylor, Josh (2020), '"It gets into your bones": the unique loneliness of coronavirus lockdown when you live alone', *The Guardian*, 3 September.

Notes

1. Another much more seriously affected group are people, mostly women and children, whom lockdown orders have confined to a situation of domestic violence or emotional abuse. I do not focus on this harm, because it has received at least some media and political attention quite quickly, and has been discussed elsewhere (see e.g. Taub 2020; Bradbury-Jones and Isham 2020). And while the harms suffered there are *exacerbated* by lockdown measures, contrary to the harms I focus on here, they are not *created* by the measures in the first place.

2. These numbers decreased with increasing age of respondents, but still amounted to 36 per cent of men and 32 per cent of women in the age group 35 to 60 years, and 32 per cent and 17 per cent, respectively, for people over 61 years of age.

3. Collins and Ferracioli also point out that on a so-called 'perfectionist' liberal outlook, it *is* permissible for governments to favour and promote those forms of living that are objectively best. However, even on this outlook, favouring a romance-centred over a friendship-centred way of living is not permissible because, arguably, a social life that revolves around an intimate partner is but one of several good ways for humans to flourish.

References

Austrian Corona Panel Project (2020), 'Method Report'. Available online: https://viecer.univie.ac.at/coronapanel/austrian-corona-panel-data/method-report/ (accessed 27 October 2020).

Bacher, J. and M. Beham-Rabanser (2020), 'Allein Leben in Zeiten von Corona', Vienna Center for Electoral Research. Available online: https://viecer.univie. ac.at/corona-blog/corona-blog-beitraege/blog-23-allein-leben-in-zeiten-von-corona/ (accessed 27 October 2020).

Bradbury-Jones, C. and Isham, L. (2020), 'The pandemic paradox: the consequences of COVID-19 on domestic violence', *Journal of Clinical Nursing*, 29 (13–14): 2047–9.

Brake, E. (2012), *Minimizing Marriage: Marriage, Morality, and the Law*, New York: Oxford University Press.

Brownlee, K. (2020), *Being Sure of Each Other: An Essay on Social Rights and Freedoms*, New York: Oxford University Press.

Bundeskanzleramt (2020), 'Bundeskanzler Kurz: Stufenplan für schrittweise Öffnung von Geschäften nach Ostern, aber Maßnahmen weiter befolgen', 6 April. Available online: https://www.bundeskanzleramt.gv.at/ bundeskanzleramt/nachrichten-der-bundesregierung/2020/bundeskanzler-kurz-stufenplan-fuer-schrittweise-oeffnung-von-geschaeften-nach-ostern-aber-massnahmen-weiter-befolgen.html (accessed 27 October 2020).

Collins, S. and L. Ferracioli (2020), 'Sex under lockdown, but not friendship? The discriminations of intimacy', *ABC News*, 17 August. Available online: https:// www.abc.net.au/religion/sex-under-lockdown-but-not-friendship-victoria/12564864 (accessed 27 October 2020).

Equality and Human Rights Commission (2018), 'Article 8: Respect for your private and family life'. Available online: https://www.equalityhumanrights.com/en/ human-rights-act/article-8-respect-your-private-and-family-life (accessed 27 October 2020).

Eurostat (2020), 'Distribution of population by household type and income group'. Available online: https://ec.europa.eu/eurostat/web/products-datasets/-/ tesov190 (accessed 27 October 2020).

Floyd, K. and C. Hesse (2017), 'Affection deprivation is conceptually and empirically distinct from loneliness', *Western Journal of Communication*, 81 (4): 446–65.

Galindo, G. (2020), 'Coronavirus: only outings of people living together "tolerated" during lockdown', *The Brussels Times*, 19 March. Available online: https://www. brusselstimes.com/belgium/101495/coronavirus-only-outings-of-people-living-together-tolerated-during-lockdown-covid-friends-out (accessed 27 October 2020).

Hill, A. (2020), 'Support bubbles: what is new policy in England and how does it work?', *The Guardian*, 11 June. Available online: https://www.theguardian.com/ politics/2020/jun/11/support-bubbles-what-is-new-policy-in-england-and-how-does-it-work (accessed 27 October 2020).

Holt-Lunstad, J., T.B. Smith and J.B. Layton (2010), 'Social relationships and mortality risk: a meta-analytic review', *PLoS Medicine*, 7 (7): e1000316.

Long, N. (2020), 'New Zealand did "support bubbles" first: here's what England can learn from them', *The Guardian*, 12 June. Available online: https://www. theguardian.com/commentisfree/2020/jun/12/new-zealand-support-bubbles-england (accessed 27 October 2020).

Office for National Statistics (2019), 'The cost of living alone', 4 April. Available online: https://www.ons.gov.uk/peoplepopulationandcommunity/ birthsdeathsandmarriages/families/articles/thecostoflivingalone/2019-04-04 (accessed 27 October 2020).

Office of Sophie Wilmès, Belgian PM (2020), 'Coronavirus: mesures renforcées', 17 March. Archived copy available online: https://web.archive.org/web/ 20200331135442/https://www.premier.be/fr/Coronavirus-Mesures-renforcees (accessed 27 October 2020).

Taub, A. (2020), 'A new Covid-19 crisis: domestic abuse rises worldwide', *The New York Times*, 6 April. Available online: https://www.nytimes.com/2020/04/06/ world/coronavirus-domestic-violence.html (accessed 27 October 2020).

Tiffany, K. (2020), 'The dos and don'ts of "social distancing"', *The Atlantic*, 12 March. Available online: https://www.theatlantic.com/family/archive/2020/03/ coronavirus-what-does-social-distancing-mean/607927 (accessed 27 October 2020).

UK Government (2020), 'Staying at home and away from others (social distancing)', gov.uk, 23 March. Available online: https://www.gov.uk/government/ publications/full-guidance-on-staying-at-home-and-away-from-others (accessed 27 October 2020).

United Nations (1948), 'The Universal Declaration of Human Rights'. Available online: https://www.un.org/en/universal-declaration-human-rights/ (accessed 27 October 2020).

United Nations Statistics Division (2020), 'Population in households by type of household, age and sex'. Available online: http://data.un.org/Data. aspx?d=POP&f=tableCode:329 (accessed 27 October 2020).

UNODC (2015), *The United Nations Standard Minimum Rules for the Treatment of Prisoners*. Available online: https://www.unodc.org/documents/justice-and- prison-reform/Nelson_Mandela_Rules-E-ebook.pdf (accessed 27 October 2020).

CHAPTER 11
SHOULD WE HOLD ELECTIONS DURING A PANDEMIC?
Alexandru Volacu

Introduction

As this volume shows, the COVID-19 pandemic has left its mark on many aspects of our lives. Electoral politics is no exception. Though this may seem less of a pressing issue in the short term, compared to the impact of the virus on our health, economic circumstances or freedom of movement, the exercise of political power affects each of these, but also the public and private life of our communities. The process of authorising the exercise of political power, therefore, lies at the heart of any polity and – in a democratic polity – this is fundamentally embodied in the electoral process. In fact, it could be said that this authorisation process is even *more* important in the special circumstances raised by the pandemic, since governments are enabled to use their power in extraordinary ways, for example by imposing curfews, quarantining entire cities, banning public gatherings, and closing down schools, shops, restaurants and so forth.

Elections have been heavily affected by the pandemic. The Institute for Democracy and Electoral Assistance (IDEA) reports postponements of elections in at least seventy-three countries, with at least seventy-one countries either holding or projecting to hold elections as originally planned and at least thirty-five countries holding elections that were originally postponed, as of 11 October 2020.[1] In some places where elections have been held in the traditional fashion, they have faced heavy criticism (Seitz-Wald and Brewster 2020) and sometimes experienced severely depressed turnout (Chazan 2020).[2] All of this prompts the question of what the appropriate governmental response should be in respect of holding elections during pandemic times. Three broad categories of options are available. The first is to go on as usual and hold *in-person voting*, which is the standard way of organising elections in the overwhelming majority of democratic polities. The second is to still hold elections, but move from in-person voting to *convenience voting* mechanisms that do not require in-person attendance, such as postal or e-voting.[3] Finally, the third is to opt for *postponing elections*.

The chapter is structured as follows: in the next section I introduce what I call the *pandemic electoral trilemma*, which maintains that each of the three responses outlined fails to meet at least one fundamental principle of electoral justice. With this set up, I then explain how further institutional measures complementing each of the three responses can alleviate, but not extinguish, the concerns raised for electoral justice. Next, I argue that there are a variety of contextual circumstances which might make one response better than another, within the boundaries of a particular polity, and sketch out some of these circumstances.

The pandemic electoral trilemma

Any ethical inquiry into the design of electoral institutions should rely at its most fundamental level on a plausible and coherent set of values, which the electoral system should aim to meet. Dennis Thompson (2002) has provided what is perhaps the most influential account of such a set of values, which he labels as the principles of electoral justice:

1. *equal respect*, which states that 'the electoral process should provide citizens with equal opportunities to have their votes counted equally, unless respectful reasons can be given to justify unequal treatment';

2. *free choice*, which states that 'the process should give citizens adequate opportunities to put an acceptable set of alternatives on the ballot, acquire appropriate information about the candidates, and make their decisions without undue pressure'; and

3. *popular sovereignty*, which states that the majority of citizens 'should finally decide the rules that govern elections and the disputes they sometimes generate' (Thompson 2002: 9–11).

This framework aims to give a complete account of electoral justice, with the principles serving as guidelines to shape normative evaluations and debates on the design of electoral institutions. In spite of some objections to them (e.g. Cain 2005; Garrett 2005), the principles are sufficiently well specified and sufficiently appealing to help us in thinking about the ethical issues surrounding the holding of elections during a pandemic.

Let us return to the three broad categories of options outlined in the introductory section: (1) in-person voting; (2) convenience voting; and

(3) postponing elections. With Thompson's principles in hand, we can evaluate each of these options from the perspective of electoral justice. Engaging in such an assessment will, I believe, lead us to what I subsequently call the *pandemic electoral trilemma*:

> P1: Reasonably just elections should adequately satisfy the principles of equal respect, free choice, and popular sovereignty.

> P2: In-person voting during a pandemic fails to adequately satisfy the principle of equal respect.

> P3: Convenience voting during a pandemic fails to adequately satisfy the principle of free choice.

> P4: Postponing elections during a pandemic fails to adequately satisfy the principle of popular sovereignty.

> —

> C: No electoral policy during pandemic outbreaks can ensure that elections are reasonably just.

P1 is a normative premise, which is taken for granted if we accept Thompson's framework. P2, P3 and P4, however, require further explanation. I will begin with the first.

The obvious concern with in-person voting is that it would exacerbate the public health crisis, since many people would be in close proximity to one another and would have to touch some of the same objects (ballots, stamps, ID cards etc.) as part of the regular voting process. With months of restrictive measures taken in order to combat the outbreak, the social interaction required for holding elections would threaten to undo much of the progress obtained. Some tentative evidence for the damaging effect of holding in-person elections on the spread of COVID-19 has already been offered by Cotti et al. (2020), who estimate that 7.7 per cent of cases identified in Wisconsin in the five weeks following the Wisconsin primary elections in April 2020 are traceable to the election.[4] But the differential health impacts of COVID-19 raise concerns that are strongly tied to the principle of equal respect as well. While holding in-person elections puts everyone attending at a greater risk of getting the virus, the risks (and participation costs) are unevenly distributed amongst age groups and between medically vulnerable citizens and healthier citizens. Furthermore, those who frequently interact with more vulnerable persons, such as care workers or adults living with their aged parents, would also be disproportionately affected since their exposure would increase the chances of spreading the virus to them. Thus, if the equal respect principle is to embody a substantive component of fairness, the state must ensure equality of opportunity in voting, which it fails to do when it does not mitigate the unjust burdens of voting placed on some demographic groups and not others. In-person voting is therefore bound to violate the equal respect principle as it provides unequal opportunities to vote for senior citizens, medically vulnerable citizens and caretakers by comparison with other groups. Some preliminary evidence supporting this conjecture is offered by the two-round presidential election held in late June and early July of 2020 in Poland, where the overwhelming majority of citizens voted in person. In both rounds, citizens over the age of sixty had the lowest rate of turnout of any age group. This is in stark contrast with the 2018 local elections and the 2019 EP elections, where turnout among older voters was above average (Polish News 2020).

Some have argued that, under pandemic conditions, convenience voting mechanisms such as postal voting (Harwood 2020) and e-voting (Wolf 2020) should be considered, or expanded where they are already in place.[5] One concern with convenience voting is that it might increase the incidence of voter fraud. Indeed, as this chapter is being written there is an ongoing debate within the United States on this subject – partly driven by the fact-free tweets and comments of Donald Trump – though studies have systematically shown that voter fraud is very rare in the US (Brennan Center for Justice 2017). Of course, this is not to say that postal voting fraud would not be a genuine problem in the case of other polities, especially if it were to be introduced for the first time during the pandemic (Parvu and Stefan 2020), and widespread voter fraud would be inimical to any plausible account of electoral justice. However, even if we assume that electoral fraud is not genuinely concerning for a specific polity, there is also a second worry with convenience voting which is not particular to the pandemic, but which is at odds with one of the principles of electoral justice discussed earlier: free choice.

Since the privacy of the polling booth is no longer available in the case of convenience voting, ballot secrecy can no longer be ensured. This, in turn, makes individuals more vulnerable to the use of coercive practices against them. Convenience voting thereby clashes with the principle of free choice, which requires that electoral decisions are to be made without undue pressure. While I am not aware of any research comparing electoral coercion in convenience voting systems versus in-person voting, some empirical research offers credence to concerns over convenience voting. In a recent study in the US, Dowling et al. (2019) find that people voting by mail have less confidence in the secrecy of their ballot, being 15 per cent more likely to believe that elected officials could find out who they voted for than those who voted in person. Moreover, another US study shows that such perceptions may distort voting choices: Gerber et al. (2013) find that social pressure plays a larger part in the electoral choices of those who believe their ballot is not secret. According to them, 'it appears that beliefs about the formal secrecy of the ballot are particularly relevant when a voter fears formal sanctions from a third party – such as an employer or the leader of an organization' (Gerber et al. 2013: 98). Electoral choice has been found to be distorted for a non-trivial group of individuals by the perceived lack of ballot secrecy in a diverse range of other contexts as well, such as Argentina (Stokes 2005), Ghana (Ferree and Long 2016) and Singapore (Ostwald and Riambau 2017). Thus, if it is true that people are less likely to perceive that their ballot is secret under convenience voting schemes, and if a negative perception of the secrecy of the ballot makes it more likely for them to vote on the basis of external pressures, there is a serious reason to fear that violations of the free choice principle would be more common with the widespread use of convenience voting.[6] Of course, such violations are also possible under in-person voting, but fairly simple technical measures can be taken in order to protect ballot secrecy in that case. For convenience voting, however, it is the design of the electoral process itself that facilitates violations of the free choice principle by largely forsaking such protections.

Finally, many policymakers have opted for postponing elections rather than going forward with in-person or convenience voting. This alternative is not without its own concerns. The relatively fixed periodicity of elections is a hallmark feature of democratic systems. As Thompson writes, 'periodicity keeps open the possibility of change – specifically, change in the membership of the legislature and thereby in the nature of the people's representation. In this respect, periodicity is an expression of the democratic value of popular sovereignty' (Thompson 2004: 54). The principle of popular sovereignty is therefore undermined by postponing elections, since without them the voice of the *demos*/people cannot be heard at the appropriate time. Without this voice, holding power becomes democratically illegitimate, a problem which is particularly worrisome if no time frame is given for the length of the postponement.

The pandemic electoral trilemma therefore suggests a grim conclusion. It entails that during a pandemic such as COVID-19 all options available raise deep ethical concerns. In the most pessimistic interpretation, this would amount to claiming that any electoral alternative pursued is democratically illegitimate, since it does not meet the principles of electoral justice. I do not believe, however, that this interpretation necessarily follows. Even if the trilemma is genuine,[7] failing to ensure that all principles of electoral justice will be *perfectly* met should not lead us to reject all feasible alternatives. Rather, it should guide our thinking in designing electoral institutions which will meet, to a sufficient extent – though imperfectly – the overarching value of electoral justice during pandemics, and which will be consistent with other relevant values as well.

Defusing the trilemma: institutional reinforcements

A reasonable way of proceeding is, I suggest, to select one of the three broad categories of alternatives on offer (in-person voting; convenience voting; postponement) and reinforce them with additional institutional measures that would go sufficiently far in protecting the principle of electoral justice that the chosen option threatens. It is, however, unlikely that there is a unique solution for defusing the trilemma, since the best solution will also depend on contextual factors, which I discuss in the next section.

Take, first, in-person voting, where the main concern raised for electoral justice is that the differential risks associated with participation, if left unmitigated, lead to a violation of the equal respect principle. In practice, however, there are some institutional remedies which could alleviate this concern – even if only to a limited extent. These include: spacing out the physical flow of voters by distancing voting booths; organising outdoor polling stations; expanding the number of polling stations; providing polling workers with masks and ample cleaning resources to disinfect surfaces; accommodating social distancing in the polling queues (and moving them outdoors); expanding early voting and extending voting hours, maybe even across several days; and/or using preferential time slots for senior citizens and other vulnerable groups (e.g. Carnovale 2020; Parvu and Stefan 2020).

Second, democratic polities which use in-person voting normally have some provisions in place for the limited usage of convenience voting, but citizens must apply for them and provide a legitimate reason for their request (Gronke et al. 2008: 441). This could be expanded so that senior citizens would automatically be eligible to vote by mail, without providing any reason, and COVID-19-related reasons would be acceptable for voting by mail in the case of other vulnerable individuals and care workers. Such measures aim to reduce the prohibitive costs experienced by particular groups when voting in person during the pandemic. But they can only be partly effective, since – especially if in-person voting is required – voting may still be perceived as a high-risk activity even with safety measures in place. Furthermore, the measures themselves might raise some additional concerns. For instance, expanding the usage of mail-in voting will raise the same concerns regarding free choice that we discussed earlier in respect to convenience voting.[8] Also, as Thompson (2008) has argued, the use of convenience voting violates the principle of electoral simultaneity, which maintains that citizens should vote (as far as possible) at the same time. This violation is, in turn, detrimental to the value of equal respect, since citizens have unequal civic experiences when it comes to voting. Finally, the health risks associated with being a poll worker during the pandemic might also dissuade many people from accepting these positions,[9] reducing the number of available polling stations, and disproportionately reducing minority turnout (Cantoni 2020), on top of once again increasing the risks associated with attending for more vulnerable citizens.

Using convenience-voting mechanisms when holding elections during a pandemic is problematic, I have argued, because it endangers free choice. This is not only because some forms of electoral fraud simply lead to a misrepresentation of voter preferences, but also because it opens up the possibility that undue pressure will be exercised on voters, as ballots are no longer cast secretly. Unlike the previous case, the problem here does not spring from the particular circumstances of the pandemic, but these circumstances can exacerbate the problem in at least two ways. First, because convenience voting would fully replace in-person voting, it is expected that more opportunities for exercising undue pressure on voters will arise. Second, it is expected that election observation and monitoring will be made more difficult in the pandemic, due to both social distancing protocols and increased risk for observers. Still, there are ways of improving voter secrecy, even if imperfectly. For instance, in the case of postal voting, placing the ballot and identifying information in separate envelopes, and in the case of e-voting devising systems that permit fake credentials,[10] re-voting or are receipt-free (e.g. Juels, Catalano and Jakobsson 2010). But, on the one hand, even these mechanisms are unable to ensure anything close to the privacy of the voting booth. And on the other, the more secrecy is ensured in convenience voting the more it is likely that ensuring ballot integrity will be made more difficult, and – as mentioned – both fraud and coercion are damaging to electoral justice.

Finally, consider postponing the elections, a proposal which is fundamentally detrimental to the principle of popular sovereignty. In order to partially alleviate these concerns, I have suggested in another work the formation of national unity governments from the moment the election was initially scheduled until the new election date (Volacu 2020).[11] The logic behind such a move is that, absent the possibility of hearing the voice of the *demos* at the appropriate time, sharing power among a wide range of already elected political actors would go some way to ensuring that diverse interests are represented and that the preferences of a new majority are going to be reflected – among others – in the power-sharing structure.[12] Another proposal, suggested in a recent interview by Dennis Thompson,[13] is to replace unelected officials with randomly selected citizens' assemblies (e.g. Ferejohn 2008) as the main decision-making body, thereby safeguarding the principle of popular sovereignty to an extent, since such assemblies would be statistically representative of the underlying population. Of course, neither solution will ultimately be able to protect popular sovereignty in a representative democracy since political offices will not be occupied in accordance with the expressed preference of the electorate – and the longer the election is postponed the less legitimate any exercise of political power will be. But they might be able to temporarily lessen some of the main worries regarding this value.

Defusing the trilemma: contextual favourability

Ultimately, the most appropriate response to the electoral problems raised by the pandemic will depend not only on the ability and willingness to institutionally strengthen whichever option is deemed to be most acceptable, but also on a variety of contextual factors which themselves make these options more or less palatable.

Consider, first, the *electoral* context. Most democratic countries use in-person voting (with some justified exceptions) as the sole mechanism for voting. Others, however, have already used convenience-voting mechanisms widely (e.g. the US in the case of postal voting or Estonia in the case of e-voting). In these latter cases, where convenience voting has been proven to be relatively safe from fraud,[14] holding elections exclusively through convenience-voting mechanisms during a pandemic will be much more acceptable than in countries which would have to introduce such means for the first time. Indeed, recommendations on holding elections in this period have often stressed that where in-person voting is the standard norm, a move to postal voting should be avoided (Parvu and Stefan 2020) and that where postal voting has been widely used, a move to e-voting should be avoided (Ad Hoc Committee for 2020 Election Fairness and Legitimacy 2020). Other electoral features may also be relevant. For instance, postponing an election for lengthier mandates (e.g. six years, as in the case of US senators) may be more problematic from the perspective of popular sovereignty than postponing elections for shorter ones (e.g. three years, as in the case of New Zealand representatives), since the will of the majority has not been effectively exercised for a much longer period.[15]

Second, consider the *political* context. One of the main concerns regarding election postponement is that the governmental party can use such an opportunity for illegitimate power grabs. As Landman and Splendore (2020: 4) note:

> In elected authoritarian regimes . . . postponement can create a power vacuum, abuse of power, and the abuse of state of emergency measures, which further consolidate authoritarian rule, undermine the rule of law, and further threaten the protection of human rights (e.g. as has occurred in Hungary, where a slate of authoritarian measures have been passed under the premiership of Viktor Orban).

So postponing elections might be more acceptable in countries where there is a broad consensus at the level of mainstream political actors as to the liberal democratic foundations of the respective system. However, even this prescription is not as straightforward as it seems. First, if the political momentum favours the party in government (and 'rally round the flag' effects during crises often make this the case; see Jennings 2020), it might push to hold elections during the pandemic in order to consolidate its position. And second, the large-scale introduction of convenience voting mechanisms by illiberal governmental parties might raise serious concerns regarding voter fraud and further undermine the legitimacy of the elections. Arguably, both of these characterised the 2020 Polish presidential elections, even though the push towards full postal voting was ultimately unsuccessful (Vashchanka 2020).

Third, consider the *cultural* context. If the main problem with convenience voting is that it endangers free choice because of the unveiling of the vote, the extent to which it will be significantly concerning depends heavily on the cultural norms associated with voting. As Schaffer's (2014) overview of familial voting shows, patriarchal control over the electoral choices of women and younger members of the family is much stronger in certain regions and communities (such as Eastern Europe, Asia and Africa) than in others. Also, without engaging in comparative studies, several recent articles using list experiments[16] have uncovered ample evidence of electoral coercion, ranging from economic coercion exercised by employers in Russia (Frye, Reuter and Szakonyi 2014), to political coercion exercised by local officials in Romania (Mares, Muntean and Petrova 2017), and to familial coercion exercised mainly by the 'head of the household' in Turkey (Toros and Birch 2019). If the secrecy of the voting booth is eliminated it is likely that free choice would be severely damaged in such communities, to the point of rendering the process itself illegitimate. In others, however, where the capacity of third parties to control electoral choices is much weaker, convenience voting may raise few concerns for free choice and therefore be, on balance, preferable.

Fourth, consider the *demographic* context. The problem of equal concern outlined in the previous section is to a large extent related to the fact that, during the COVID-19 pandemic, senior citizens are more vulnerable to developing life-threatening symptoms if they get the virus. So holding in-person elections in ageing societies, such as Japan or Italy, where huge swathes of the electorate would be discouraged from voting – even with safety measures in place – in a way that potentially alters the electoral outcome is arguably more problematic than holding them in communities where the proportion of senior citizens is much lower. Postponing elections, if convenience voting cannot be safely relied upon, might be less detrimental to electoral justice and more acceptable in such communities, rather than in-person voting.

Finally, much will of course depend on the *epidemiological* context. Even advocates of temporary postponements of elections do not normally believe that the COVID-19 pandemic must be fully extinguished before elections are held. Rather, the current and projected state of the public health crisis is bound to be of fundamental importance in deciding whether in-person or even convenience voting can be held or whether elections should be postponed.[17] So, for instance, the South Korean 2020 legislative election was held on 15 April, when for the previous couple of weeks newly identified cases had remained below 100 per day at a national level. Holding the elections in late February or early March, when the numbers of cases would have likely surged, had rightly been considered unacceptable.

Of course, these are only some of the relevant contextual factors in deciding how to best proceed regarding elections in a particular community. The list is not intended to be exhaustive, but merely illustrative for the type of differential challenges which the pandemic might raise for the question of electoral management.

Conclusion

In this chapter I have mapped some of the major challenges posed by the COVID-19 pandemic for elections. I have argued that any alternative we choose to implement is bound to raise some concerns for electoral justice: no 'one-size-fits-all' approach should be endorsed, and thus institutional remedies and contextual factors need to be considered in selecting one alternative over others. Ultimately, although the ethical analysis of electoral design can provide valuable insights, it cannot determine what the best solution will be for a particular community in a legitimate way. It is incumbent upon the main political actors within the community to recognise the special challenges a pandemic like COVID-19 poses for their democratic system and to establish a broad consensus on how to proceed when it comes to the electoral process. As Tanja Hollstein (2020) aptly puts it, 'There's no "right" way to adapt elections to COVID-19 – but there is a right way to make those decisions.'

Beyond the immediate necessity of the analysis presented in this chapter in the COVID-19 pandemic context, it has more general implications, for several reasons. First, some of the value conflicts outlined in the chapter arise even in the absence of the extraordinary pandemic circumstances with which democracy has been confronted in 2020, and should be further explored. Second, parts of the analysis can also be extrapolated to other crisis situations, such as wars, even though some of the problems with in-person voting derive from the public health issues which are particular to a pandemic. Third, as numerous public outlets have reported throughout 2020 (e.g. Brulliard 2020; Tollefson 2020; Watts 2020), it is highly likely that pandemic outbreaks will be more frequent, and potentially worse than COVID-19, in the absence of significant individual and institutional changes in the proximate future. Consequently, the threats posed by pandemics for democracies and electoral justice are quite possibly here to stay.[18]

Suggestions for further reading

- Beerbohm, E. (2012), *In Our Name: The Ethics of Democracy*, Princeton: Princeton University Press.

- Birch, S. (2011), *Electoral Malpractice*, Oxford: Oxford University Press.

- Birch, S., F. Buril, N. Cheeseman, A. Clark, S. Darnolf, S. Dodsworth, L. Garber, R. Gutiérrez-Romero, T. Hollstein, T. James, V. Mohan and K. Sawyer (2020), *How to Hold Elections Safely and Democratically During the COVID-19 Pandemic*, London: The British Academy.

- Elster, J. (ed.) (2015), *Secrecy and Publicity in Votes and Debates*, Cambridge: Cambridge University Press.
- James, T. (2021), 'Running elections during a pandemic', *Public Money and Management*, 41 (1): 65–8.

Notes

1. See https://www.idea.int/news-media/multimedia-reports/global-overview-covid-19-impact-elections (accessed 11 October 2020).

2. This has not always been the case, however. To take just two examples, the South Korean legislative elections held in April 2020 saw the highest turnout since 1992 and both rounds of the Polish presidential elections, held in June and July 2020, saw the highest turnout since 1995.

3. We can define convenience voting as 'any mode of balloting other than precinct-place voting. Examples include casting a ballot early at a local elections office, at a satellite location or at a voting centre; filling out an absentee ballot and dropping it in the mail; phoning into a special system; or logging into a secure website and casting a ballot on the web' (Gronke et al. 2008: 438).

4. The evidence is not conclusive, however. Leung et al. (2020) maintain that no spike in the number of new SARS-CoV-2 cases in Wisconsin can be traced to the elections, though they study a shorter post-electoral time frame than Cotti et al. (2020).

5. Another option would be to opt for proxy voting, in which individuals can delegate their vote to someone else. But since it is possible for the proxy agent to vote in a way which contradicts the preferences of the principal agent (i.e. the one who delegates her vote), the problems with preserving the free choice principle are at least as bad as the former options.

6. Especially, as I discuss in the fourth section of this chapter, in certain cultural contexts.

7. Some, of course, might object to the existence of the trilemma to begin with. One way would be to argue that P1 does not adequately capture what just elections are. Another would be to show that there is a fourth category of policy options not yet explored which doesn't clash with any principles of electoral justice. Another still would be to show that one of premises P2 to P4 are in fact false. And another would be to lexically order the principles of electoral justice, so that the trilemma disappears in virtue of the fact that one of the principles is taken to be of paramount importance.

8. Albeit at a smaller scale, since convenience voting would still only take place in exceptional cases rather than being the default (so fewer people will actually vote through such a means).

9. Especially if, as in the United States, a core part of poll workers is usually made up of senior citizens (Levine 2020).

10. So that the voter can trick the actor attempting to coerce her into believing that she voted, when in fact the vote cast during the session where fake credentials were used is not registered.

11. A national unity government consists of a broad coalition of political parties, normally encompassing all (or almost all) the major parliamentary parties. Such coalitions are usually formed only in extraordinary circumstances, such as during wars or other crises.

12. A national unity government was widely favoured by the public in the United Kingdom in the early stages of the COVID-19 pandemic (Smith 2020), though it ultimately did not come to fruition. Such a government has, however, been formed in Israel during April 2020, albeit helped by the political instability generated after an inconclusive election one month earlier (BBC News 2020a).

13. http://www.redem-h2020.eu/insights.html#thompson (accessed 4 July 2020).

14. See BBC News (2020b) for the former and Postimees (2014) for the latter.

15. I thank the editors of the volume for this suggestion.

16. List experiments are usually used in order to elicit responses on very sensitive topics, where the data obtained would otherwise be seriously flawed by an expected response bias. For example, if respondents were asked to report whether they have been offered bribes by local officials to vote in a certain way in the last election, they would understandably be concerned that an outright positive response may lead to legal and social repercussions against them. List experiments address this problem by using (variations of) the following protocol: 'as originally conceived, the survey sample is split into two groups. Control group respondents receive a list of nonsensitive, yes/no items and are asked to tell the interviewer how many of the listed items they do/believe, and specifically not which items they are. Treatment group respondents, meanwhile, receive the same list as the control group, plus one more item that measures a sensitive topic, and receive the same instructions' (Corstange 2009: 48).

17. See IDEA (2020) for a more extended discussion on the question of electoral feasibility during a pandemic.

18. I thank Anca Gheaus, Andrei Poama, Annabelle Lever and Dennis Thompson for comments and discussions on a blog post where I originally outlined some of the ideas developed in this chapter, and Rowan Cruft, Adelin Dumitru, Felix Pinkert and Vlad Terteleac for comments on a first draft. I am especially grateful to Aveek Bhattacharya and Fay Niker for detailed feedback on the various stages of the chapter. This work has been carried out as part of the project "Reconstructing Democracy in Times of Crisis: A Voter-Centred Perspective" which has received funding from the European Union's Horizon 2020 research and innovation programme under grant agreement No 870996.

References

Ad Hoc Committee for 2020 Election Fairness and Legitimacy (2020), 'Fair Elections During a Crisis', *UCI Law*, April. Available online: https://www.law.uci.edu/faculty/full-time/hasen/2020ElectionReport.pdf (accessed 19 July 2020).

BBC News (2020a), 'Israel's Netanyahu and Gantz sign unity government deal', 20 April. Available online: https://www.bbc.com/news/world-middle-east-52358479 (accessed 21 July 2020)

BBC News (2020b), 'US election: do postal ballots lead to voting fraud?', 25 September. Available online: https://www.bbc.com/news/world-us-canada-53353404 (accessed 27 September 2020)

Brennan Center for Justice (2017), 'Debunking the voter fraud myth', 31 January. Available online: https://www.brennancenter.org/sites/default/files/analysis/Briefing_Memo_Debunking_Voter_Fraud_Myth.pdf (accessed 20 July 2020).

Brulliard, K. (2020), 'The next pandemic is already coming, unless humans change how we interact with wildlife, scientists say', *Washington Post*, 3 April. Available online: https://www.washingtonpost.com/science/2020/04/03/coronavirus-wildlife-environment/ (accessed 28 September 2020).

Cain, B. (2005), 'An ethical path to reform: just elections considered', *Election Law Journal*, 4 (2): 134–8.

Cantoni, E. (2020), 'A precinct too far: turnout and voting costs', *American Economic Journal: Applied Economics*, 12 (1): 61–85.

Carnovale, M. (2020), 'Conducting elections during the pandemic', *Duke University Science & Society*, 26 June. Available online: https://scipol.org/track/policy-brief/conducting-elections-during-pandemic (accessed 18 July 2020).

Chazan, D. (2020), 'Record low turnout for French local elections amid coronavirus lockdown', *The Telegraph*, 15 March. Available online: https://www.telegraph.co.uk/news/2020/03/15/record-low-turnout-french-local-elections-amid-coronavirus-lockdown/ (accessed 15 July 2020).

Corstange, D. (2009), 'Sensitive questions, truthful answers? Modeling the list experiment with LISTIT', *Political Analysis*, 17: 45–63.

Cotti, C., B. Engelhardt, J. Foster et al. (2020), *The Relationship Between In-person Voting and COVID-19: Evidence from the Wisconsin Primary*, Cambridge, MA: NBER Working Paper 27187.

Dowling, C., D. Doherty, S. Hill et al. (2019), 'The voting experience and beliefs about ballot secrecy', *PLoS ONE*, 14 (1): pp.e0209765.

Ferejohn, J. (2008), 'Conclusion: the citizens' assembly model', in M. Warren (ed.), *Designing Deliberative Democracy: The British Columbia Citizens' Assembly*, 192–213, Cambridge: Cambridge University Press.

Ferree, K. and J. Long (2016), 'Gifts, threats, and perceptions of ballot secrecy in African elections', *African Affairs*, 115 (461): 621–45.

Frye, T., O.J. Reuter and D. Szakonyi (2014), 'Political machines at work: voter mobilization and electoral subversion in the workplace', *World Politics*, 66 (2): 195–228.

Garrett, E. (2005), 'Who chooses the rules?', *Election Law Journal*, 4 (2): 139–46.

Gerber, A., G. Huber, D. Doherty et al. (2013), 'Is there a secret ballot? Ballot secrecy perceptions and their implications for voting behaviour', *British Journal of Political Science*, 43 (1): 77–102.

Gronke, P., E. Galanes-Rosenbaum, P. Miller et al. (2008), 'Convenience voting', *Annual Review of Political Science*, 11: 437–55.

Harwood, M. (2020), 'Why a vote-by-mail option is necessary', *Brennan Center for Justice*, 7 April. Available online: https://www.brennancenter.org/our-work/research-reports/why-vote-mail-option-necessary (accessed 20 July 2020).

Hollstein, T. (2020), 'There's no "right" way to adapt elections to COVID-19 – but there is a right way to make those decisions', *Westminster Foundation for Democracy*, 9 June. Available online: https://www.wfd.org/2020/06/09/theres-no-right-way-to-adapt-elections-to-covid19-but-there-is-a-right-way-to-make-those-decisions/ (accessed 24 July 2020).

IDEA (2020), 'Managing elections during the COVID-19 pandemic: considerations for decision-makers', *IDEA Policy Brief*, 14 July. Available online: https://www.idea.int/sites/default/files/publications/managing-elections-during-covid-19-pandemic.pdf (accessed 26 September 2020).

Jennings, W. (2020), 'COVID-19 and the "rally-round-the-flag" effect', *UK in a Changing Europe*, 30 March. Available online: https://ukandeu.ac.uk/covid-19-and-the-rally-round-the-flag-effect/ (accessed 24 September 2020).

Juels, A., D. Catalano and M. Jakobsson (2010), 'Coercion-resistant electronic elections', in D. Chaum et al. (eds), *Towards Trustworthy Elections: New Directions in Electronic Voting*, Berlin: Springer: 37–63.

Landman, T. and L. Splendore (2020), 'Pandemic democracy: elections and COVID-19', *Journal of Risk Research*, 23 (7–8): 1060–6.

Leung, K., J. Wu, K. Xu et al. (2020), 'No detectable surge in SARS-CoV-2 transmission attributable to the April 7, 2020 Wisconsin election', *American Journal of Public Health*, 110 (8): 1169–70.

Levine, S. (2020), 'Elderly workers run elections. But COVID-19 will keep many home', *The Center for Public Integrity*, 13 May. Available online: https://publicintegrity.org/politics/elections/democracy-2020/elderly-workers-run-elections-but-covid-19-will-keep-many-home/ (accessed 21 July 2020).

Mares, I., A. Muntean and T. Petrova (2017), 'Pressure, favours, and vote-buying: experimental evidence from Romania and Bulgaria', *Europe-Asia Studies*, 69 (6): 940–60.

Ostwald, K. and G. Riambau (2017), 'Voting behavior under doubts of ballot secrecy', unpublished manuscript. Available online: https://pdfs.semanticscholar.org/b42d/eda937e4a0598e2e6eaa156412df4d5ddec8.pdf (accessed 26 September 2020).

Parvu, S. and L. Stefan (2020), 'Elections in pandemic: scenarios', *EFOR Policy Brief* 86.

Polish News (2020), 'Presidential election 2020. Second round. Attendance in age groups', 12 July. Available online: https://www.polishnews.co.uk/presidential-election-2020-second-round-attendance-in-age-groups/ (accessed 18 July 2020).

Postimees (2014), 'Electoral committee: online voting is safe', 14 May. Available online: https://news.postimees.ee/2794276/electoral-committee-online-voting-is-safe (accessed 27 September 2020).

Schaffer, F.C. (2014), 'Not-so-individual voting: patriarchal control and familial hedging in political elections around the world', *Journal of Women, Politics & Policy*, 35 (4): 349–78. Assembly

Seitz-Wald, A. and S. Brewster (2020), 'Wisconsin, facing heavy criticism, plans Tuesday primary despite coronavirus', *NBC News*, 1 April. Available online: https://www.nbcnews.com/politics/2020-election/wisconsin-facing-heavy-criticism-plans-tuesday-primary-despite-coronavirus-n1173361 (accessed 15 July 2020).

Smith, M. (2020), 'Almost two thirds of Brits support a national unity government', *YouGov*, 9 April 2020. Available online: https://yougov.co.uk/topics/politics/articles-reports/2020/04/08/almost-two-thirds-brits-support-national-unity-gov (accessed 23 July 2020).

Stokes, S. (2005), 'Perverse accountability: a formal model of machine politics with evidence from Argentina', *American Political Science Review*, 99 (3): 315–25.

Thompson, D. (2002), *Just Elections: Creating a Fair Electoral Process in the United States*, Chicago: University of Chicago Press.

Thompson, D. (2004), 'Election time: normative implications of temporal properties of the electoral process in the United States', *American Political Science Review*, 98 (1): 51–64.

Thompson, D. (2008), 'Electoral simultaneity: expressing equal respect', *Journal of Social Issues*, 64 (3): 487–501.

Tollefson, J. (2020), 'Why deforestation and extinctions make pandemics more likely', *Nature*, 7 August. Available online: https://www.nature.com/articles/d41586-020-02341-1 (accessed 28 September 2020).

Toros, E. and S. Birch (2019), 'Who are the targets of familial electoral coercion? Evidence from Turkey', *Democratization*, 26 (8): 1342–61.

Vashchanka, V. (2020), *Political Manoeuvres and Legal Conundrums Amid the COVID-19 Pandemic: The 2020 Presidential Election in Poland*, Stockholm: International IDEA.

Volacu, A. (2020), 'Electoral justice in pandemic times', *Justice Everywhere*. Available online: http://justice-everywhere.org/general/electoral-justice-in-pandemic-times/ (accessed 1 July 2020)

Watts, J. (2020), '"Promiscuous treatment of nature" will lead to more pandemics', *The Guardian*, 7 May. Available online: https://www.theguardian.com/environment/2020/may/07/promiscuous-treatment-of-nature-will-lead-to-more-pandemics-scientists (accessed 28 September 2020).

Wolf, P. (2020), 'The COVID-19 crisis – a much needed new opportunity for online voting?', *IDEA*, 13 May. Available online: https://www.idea.int/news-media/news/covid-19-crisis-%E2%80%93-much-needed-new-opportunity-online-voting (accessed 20 July 2020).

CHAPTER 12
THE PANDEMIC AND OUR DEMOCRATIC WAY OF LIFE
Marc Stears

Introduction

COVID-19 has played havoc with democratic politics all over the world. Already chipped away by populism, democracy was vulnerable before the pandemic hit; but when it arrived, a whole host of previously unchallenged practices and conventions flew out of the window. From the delays in New Zealand's general election to the attacks on mail-in ballots in the United States, the extension of the Mayor of London's term of office to the widespread deployment of emergency powers and the postponement of legislative sittings, democratic norms turned out to be surprisingly fragile. Each of these issues was troubling and each worthy of detailed examination. But something even more profound also lay at the heart of COVID-19's democratic impact; something more mundane, less widely noticed but nonetheless crucially important. The *everyday practices of democratic life* were eroded. These practices – including the exchanges between strangers in public spaces, the workplace lunch where the issues of the day are discussed, the sharing of ideas over a drink in the evening, the community centre get-together where plans are hatched – were particularly vulnerable to the pandemic but went peculiarly unnoticed by most commentators. Yet if we lose them, we lose too the culture and habits that comprise the civic virtue and solidarity that are the essential elements of democratic life (Allen 2016; Coles 2005; Rogers 2018).

Right from the outset, this everyday democratic culture was challenged by both the fundamental biological features of the pandemic and the political choices that structured nations' responses to it. The highly transmissible nature of the virus meant that individuals around the world instinctively and vigilantly attempted to maintain distance from each other to stem its spread. To protect one's fellow citizens from infection, after all, one needs to stay away. High levels of social anxiety also led to further demands for decisive top-down action from the world's leaders, even in typically anti-authoritarian societies. This led to vigorous restrictions that were previously entirely unimaginable, such as the curfew preventing any social interaction after 8pm in Melbourne, Australia (Walker et al. 2020).

In some places, a counterbalance to these trends did emerge in the early months of 2020. Indeed, some scholars and activists even suggested that the pandemic invigorated forms of connection, political advocacy, and democratic engagement that had long been dormant (see survey in New Local Government Network 2020). The most celebrated example was the explosion in infrastructure for mutual aid across the globe, as online local and neighbourhood groups began facilitating daily assistance for the vulnerable and supporting lively discussion about community needs and rights. Some more established and larger civil society organisations, too, began to use peer-to-peer and digital tools to build diverse and vibrant communities, galvanising across political and other differences to tackle some of the deep inequalities surfaced by the pandemic.

These mutual aid groups and civil society organisations demonstrate that the democratic way of life is not over, not by a long way. In fact, in at least some places we have seen that people are hankering for the kind of connection that is at democracy's heart. But none of them provides the full answer to the challenge that is presented. They are still relatively weak reeds in the storm. What they might help us do, however, is to start our search for more detailed answers to two vital questions. *First*, how do we fully appreciate the pandemic's impact on democracy, looking beyond the straightforwardly formal elements of our governing system? And *second*, what will it take to respond to those threats?[1] I sketch answers to both of these questions in this chapter.

Democratic equality and the pandemic

All of our analysis of the impact of the pandemic on democracy should begin with the core principle at the heart of our commitment to democracy itself: *equality*. At its root, democracy is both a system of government and a way of life that recognises that each and every one of us counts for the same as another. No one has more intrinsic worth, no one has less (Allen 2008).

When we consider the impact of the pandemic on this core ideal, we should almost instantaneously recognise that it has been terrible. Almost nobody believes we are 'all in it together' any more, even if television commercials across the world have spent months insisting that we are. Both the pandemic itself and the political responses that have been taken to it have affected different parts of our society in vastly different ways. For a minority, especially those with stable employment that they are able to conduct from home and no immediate dependents, societal shutdown was a luxury they could afford to endure. But so many people have not had this privilege. In countries across the globe, millions of people have been thrown out of work, have experienced deep loss and dangerous illness, and have been separated from their loved ones at some of the most crucial and irreplaceable moments.

Yet those who have made these enormous sacrifices have also been the least likely to have their voices heard or have their interests taken into account as the decisions about how to manage the pandemic have been taken. Those most seriously impacted by the pandemic have not been invited into the scientific advisory meetings or the governing commissions. They haven't written the newspaper editorials or shaped the media agenda. They haven't been consulted by their bosses. This gulf between what has been asked of people and what has been given to them marks the largest democratic deficit of the modern age. There simply has been no similar period since the end of the Second World War when people's everyday lives have been so deeply disrupted at the same time as their opinions and interests have been so cut out of the political process.

This democratic deficit is, in part, a function of interruptions in the formal democratic process, including the delay of elections or the postponement of legislative sittings (as Alexandru Volacu's chapter in this volume discusses). But it is also a result of the way in which in jurisdictions across the world people's ability to gather socially was effectively put on hold from early on in the pandemic. Healthy democracies – ones which give living meaning to the principle of equality – depend on the ability of those at the sharpest end of political and social life to have some sway in their polity (Han 2009). At the very least, they must be able regularly to hold the most powerful to account. That in turn requires that people are able to exercise the advocacy and vigilance that ensures the accountability of the governing to the governed. For many, though, the pandemic consistently made that kind of vigilance harder than ever. Right from the outset, there were fewer opportunities to gather and to organise; fewer chances to identify common interests; fewer moments for the powerless to grab the attention of the powerful and turn their gaze towards them. In many cases, all there was was Zoom.

It is vital to note that this democratic culture has been threatened not only by the biological risk at the heart of the pandemic itself but also by the ameliorative actions taken in response to it. The closures of public spaces and the move to online interactions that have made democratic organising and mobilising so difficult are the result of conscious governing decisions, not simply the impact of the disease itself. Likewise, the closures of borders which inhibit the interaction of people from different nations and different backgrounds have come about because of the actions of governments, not the behaviours of the virus. That is not to say that each of these decisions is wrong in itself. Public health interventions of the kind described here have been crucial in the pandemic, although the specific merit of each individual one has proven hard to evaluate, even by epidemiologists. But it is to note that democracy has nonetheless been inhibited by the deliberate actions of human agents, many of them invested with power already, and not solely by the invisible forces of biology.

Democratic engagement between citizens has been further undermined by the pervasive anxiety that has set in in most countries, in part as a result of these government actions. Suspicion and mutual disregard are engendered psychologically by the sight of one's fellow citizens avoiding contact with us, by signs that remind us to stay apart, by the need to keep people away from our doors and, for some at least, by the sight of people's faces being obscured behind masks. The Italian philosopher Giorgio Agamben starkly warned his readers of the potential dangers of these developments near the outbreak of the pandemic:

> Other human beings, as in the plague described in Alessandro Manzoni's novel, are now seen solely as possible spreaders of the plague whom one must avoid at all costs and from whom one needs to keep oneself at a distance of at least a meter . . . Our neighbor has been cancelled and it is curious that churches remain silent on the subject. What do human relationships become in a country that habituates itself to live in this way for who knows how long? And what is a society that has no value other than survival?
>
> *Agamben 2020*

Agamben's pessimism was widely mocked at his time of writing, but his judgement has turned out to be largely vindicated by what has transpired ever since. Nonetheless, this idea is still almost nowhere openly acknowledged.

It is far more common still to see commentators talking about the ingenuity with which people have maintained social connections – 'staying together by staying apart', as the political slogan has it – than it is to see it acknowledged that social distancing has had a dangerous impact on social interaction and thus on democratic culture. The supposition continues to be either that digital interaction can somehow replace the social interaction of the past or that controversial political matters can effectively be postponed while either the 'experts' or our elected officials map a path forward for us. Neither of these are even remotely true. For while it is true that people can have digital conversations in ways that we couldn't even a few years ago, allowing families and friends to stay in touch, there is no evidence yet that we are able to pressurise our governing parties that way or collectively capture the attention of those who are making decisions through the power of digital forces alone (see Crawford 2016). Similarly, there is no reason to believe that the pandemic has rendered those who enjoy positions of power somehow more beneficent or trustworthy than they were previously. One only has to spend the briefest of time studying the practices of leaders across the world, and across different kinds of pandemic response, to disabuse oneself of that notion. The public reputation of a host of world leaders – including but not confined to Boris Johnson and Donald Trump – has not been enhanced through the pandemic period.

Social connections and democratic culture

Difficult though it might be to hear, in all of these ways the pandemic has made it clear what we need for democracy to be durable and effective. In short, it has shown that the culture of democracy depends on a particular kind of gathering (see Honig 2017). It has revealed as clearly as ever, that is, the fundamental connection between our everyday social lives and the functioning of our democracies. The shutdown of places where we stand shoulder to shoulder with other citizens, listen to them, learn from them, forge common cause with them and start to take action, threatens the shutdown of democracy itself.

Even if the vital importance of these kinds of connection have not been openly acknowledged in political theory or public commentary, there are signs that some kind of realisation about the importance of everyday democratic culture is somehow seeping through into everyday life itself. The attentiveness to relationships within neighbourhood communities, particularly at the very smallest level, described at the outset of this chapter is a sign that the civic virtues of care and concern for our fellow citizens matter to many. The rapid growth of socially networked mutual aid groups, some admittedly using digital tools, at the outset of the pandemic displayed a powerful urge for people to meet and care for others in their neighbourhood even in the most pressing circumstances, as did the explosion of volunteering. In some quarters, indeed, it has been suggested that a 'kindness pandemic' has taken hold just as vigorously as the viral one.[2] Neighbours who had never met have found cause to make introductions, and able-bodied and healthy community members have been delivering food to the elderly and those reliant on services. More broadly, people's relationships with 'essential workers', such as health workers, cleaners and teachers, have also been reshaped, as the undeniable social value of such work is more widely accepted than it was before the pandemic hit (for more on this, see the chapter by Adams and Niker in this volume).

These reinvigorated civic relationships do not go to the root of the pressing challenges the pandemic has highlighted, of course, and many rely on a pool of goodwill that may well be dwindling over time. Nonetheless, they do highlight the fundamental role that social connections play in healthy societies. It is surely unarguable now that social connection is an essential precondition for pandemic resilience. The public health rules and restrictions currently democratic nations around the world have relied upon are only effective as long as they are abided by (Costello et al. 2020). And they are only abided by as long as citizens decide to follow official advice. No number of fines or police actions can hide that fundamental fact. This is even more true of the contact-tracing phone apps developed in many countries. Such apps only work if significant numbers of people download them and are willing to go into isolation; and that will only happen if people feel a sense of connection, relationship, and trust with one another. For this reason, experts and decision-makers must attend closely to any potential corrosion of trust, even if they do not want to, ensuring transparent governance of apps, availability of open-source code, and strong privacy protections.

All of this leads to one conclusion when it comes to the question of what needs to be done. Social connections, especially those everyday social connections that usually follow from the mundane activities of ordinary life, demand our attention right now. If democracy is to be protected, and if we are to have any chance of making our way through these difficult months and years while paying heed to the fundamental principle of equality, then we need a plan for how social connections, especially social connections across difference, are to be protected, maintained and even enhanced throughout this pandemic moment and beyond. When governments and citizens evaluate each and every response to this pandemic and future threats of the same kind, they should do so with the everyday practices of democracy in mind.

Three ways forward

Enhancing social connections at a time like ours will no doubt be an extraordinarily difficult task. Social connections were, after all, already under threat before the pandemic hit. As Bonnie Honig has shown, they had been eaten away by the disappearance and privatisation of public space (Honig 2017). They had also been undermined by the advance of social media, which despite its name has had a tendency to polarise and individualise at least as much as it has to bring people together (Crawford 2016). The reaction to such a challenge, however, need not be a deepening sense of emptiness and loss. Instead, it is possible to map a different kind of future. Thinking through these issues throughout the pandemic, and discussing them with both theorists and democratic practitioners from across the world, I have become convinced that there are three clear areas that we need to address ourselves to if we are to have any chance of improving the situation in which we find ourselves.

First, and most straightforwardly, we should take a lead from Agamben himself and learn to more forcefully interrogate the demands for increased social distancing and the other restrictions on social interaction which flow from those demands. There was precious little of this kind of challenge in the initial months of the pandemic, in part because people have understandably focused instead on ensuring – or trying to ensure – that their governments developed resolute programmes of pandemic suppression. But as the pandemic has aged and some restrictions are eased while others remain (and indeed are reintroduced), it becomes increasingly vital that attention is given to which restrictions fall into which categories. Pressure should be placed on governments – in so far as that is possible at these moments – to ensure that maintaining possibilities for real social interaction is placed as high in the reckoning when such decisions are made as both economic vitality and immediate public health no doubt will be. We often hear of governments having to 'choose' between health and prosperity, and although that is far too simplistic a way of putting it, at the very least our insistence should be that everyday sociality and democracy must be under consideration too. There are, in other words, three core elements of a good life to consider and not just two. In practice that means if public spaces are closed down, we need to know what the alternatives are. If one set of opportunities to gather are infringed, we need to know for how long and how we are going to measure the consequences and address any democratic inequalities that subsequently emerge.

Second, there is an urgent need to invest and innovate in mechanisms of social organisation that are best suited to socially distanced times so as to ensure that pressure like this can be brought to bear. There have already been experiments, some funded by progressive philanthropic foundations, to bring civil society and campaigning groups together internationally to learn from each other and share ideas as to how it is possible effectively to make demands of government at this time. There have also been training courses and makeshift workshops run by trade unions and community organisers examining how campaigns previously run 'on the ground' can be transitioned to an alternative space as effectively as possible. The experiments of groups like RadicalxChange, who specialise in maintaining a real sense of social connection through digital environments were already vital before the pandemic and are increasingly so now (RadicalxChange 2020). Civil society groups with strong networks have also been making the most of the fact that governments are overstretched by the pandemic right across the world, and revelling in the fact that their expertise is in high demand. Strikingly, of course, Black Lives Matter also provides a powerful reminder that the older, more conventional methods are still occasionally available too, at least when the cause is strong and wide-ranging enough.

Far more creativity is still required in this space, however. Outside of the United States, Black Lives Matter has been effectively shut down by its critics, often deploying public health rules to prohibit public gatherings, and beyond that the obstacles to effective campaigning in the 'new normal' remain intense (Boston Review 2020). We have yet to discover any means, for example, of recreating the incidental and serendipitous connections that are traditionally the bedrock of successful campaigning relationships. Zoom breakout rooms have limitations that a walk in the park or a drink in the pub do not for many trying to craft solidarity and design a programme of action. The hope remains, however, that the scholars and practitioners of radical democratic politics are turning their attention to these questions at this very moment – as they have at key moments in the past – and that their prescriptions shall become clearer as the months progress.

Third, as we think about those serendipitous relationships – 'the bump', as my colleague Robyn Dowling calls them, after the idea of 'bumping into' someone in the street – we need also to deepen our commitment to the social infrastructure that enables social connection during both pandemic and non-pandemic times. Architects and designers should be thinking of how to reshape public space to enable more of this kind of interaction. Educators should be striving to make genuinely interactional educational opportunities open to all, even when there is no physical classroom. Progressive businesses should be thinking not only of how they enable their staff to work from home but also how they can continue to support social relationships between workers, including social relationships protected by a right to privacy. None of this is entirely new, of course. Scholars like Danielle Allen and Eric Klinenberg have been calling for this kind of innovation for years (Allen 2008; Klinenberg 2018). But now might indeed be the moment to take these ideas to their next level and begin to realise them. There will be high streets empty of shops and public squares devoid of visitors for many months to come. Imagining how those spaces can be reimagined as environments for real social interaction is, in my view, one of the most compelling social reform tasks of our time.

Conclusion

None of these three ways forward constitutes a concrete answer by itself, of course. They are better seen instead as areas of concern or categories of priority. Within each, there are the beginnings of ideas taking shape, but there is no clear pattern to discern yet and there are still to be any major breakthroughs. None of this should dismay us too much, though. Rather, it is to be expected. The pandemic has knocked us all off our feet and it has taken a while for most of us to begin to feel the solid ground beneath us again. We can hope now, though, that we have begun to regain some of the composure needed to think about the path ahead. And we are strengthened most of all, I believe, by the realisation about what matters most. Put most simply, we have come to see that our democracy is in peril because our social interactions are in peril. The task that falls to us now is to protect those social interactions that have survived, to invest them with more power and more energy when we can, and to do all we can to enrich the possibility of creating more. That is not a simple task. In fact, it is almost the dictionary definition of complexity. But the stakes are about as high as it is possible for them to be, so it is up to us to try.[3]

Suggestions for further reading

- Allen, D. (2008), *Talking to Strangers: Anxieties of Citizenship since Brown versus Board of Education*, Chicago: Chicago University Press.
- Costello, A., L. Gilbert, Jeon, Y.-H. Jeon, M. Stears and G. Wardle (2020), *Citizen Action to Tackle the Public Health Crisis*, Sydney Policy Lab COVID Policy Paper 2, Sydney: Sydney Policy Lab. Available at: https://www.sydney.edu.au/sydney-policy-lab/news-and-analysis/news-commentary/covid-19-the-sydney-policy-papers.html.
- Honig, B. (2017), *Public Things: Democracy in Disrepair*, New York: Fordham Press.
- Rogers, M. (2018), 'Democracy is a habit: practice it', *Boston Review*, July 2018. Available at: http://bostonreview.net/politics/melvin-rogers-democracy-habit-practice-it.
- Stears, M. (2021), *Out of the Ordinary: How Everyday Life Inspired a Nation and How It Can Again*, Cambridge, MA.: Harvard University Press.

Notes

1. These questions have provided the focus for much of my own work during the pandemic, as well as of the work of the Sydney Policy Lab that I direct.
2. See https://www.thekindnesspandemic.org.
3. I am grateful to conversations with Danielle Allen, Frances Flanagan, Bonnie Honig, Melvin Rogers, Amanda Tattersall, the Sydney Policy Lab team and the editors of this volume in developing the argument presented here.

References

Agamben, G. (2020), 'Clarifications on *The Inventions of an Epidemic* (trans. Adam Kotsko)'. Available online: https://itself.blog/2020/03/17/giorgio-agamben-clarifications (accessed 30 September 2020).

Allen, D. (2008), *Talking to Strangers: Anxieties of Citizenship since Brown versus Board of Education*, Chicago: Chicago University Press.

Allen, D. (2016), 'Toward a Connected Society', in E. Lewis and N. Cantor (eds), *Our Compelling Interests: The Value of Diversity for Democracy and a Prosperous Society*, Princeton: Princeton University Press: 71–105.

Boston Review (2020), *The New Politics of Care*, New York: Random House.

Coles, R. (2005), *Beyond Gated Politics: Reflections on the Possibility of Democracy*, Minneapolis: University of Minnesota Press.

Costello, A., L. Gilbert, Y.-H. Jeon, M. Stears and G. Wardle (2020), *Citizen Action to Tackle the Public Health Crisis,* Sydney Policy Lab COVID Policy Paper 2, Sydney: Sydney Policy Lab. Available online: https://www.sydney.edu.au/sydney-policy-lab/news-and-analysis/news-commentary/covid-19-the-sydney-policy-papers.html (accessed 30 September 2020).

Crawford, M. (2016), *The World Beyond Your Head: On Becoming an Individual in an Age of Distraction,* New York: Farrar, Straus and Giroux.

Han, H. (2009), *Moved to Action: Motivation, Participation, and Inequality in American Politics,* Stanford: Stanford University Press.

Honig, B. (2017), *Public Things: Democracy in Disrepair,* New York: Fordham Press.

Klinenberg, E. (2018), *Palaces for the People: How to Build a More Equal and United Society,* London: Penguin.

New Local Government Network (2020), *COVID Mutual Aid Project* 2020. Available online: http://www.nlgn.org.uk/public/2020/covid-mutual-aid-project/ (accessed 30 September 2020).

RadicalxChange (2020), 'Concepts'. Available online: https://www.radicalxchange.org/concepts/ (accessed 30 September 2020).

Rogers, M. (2018), 'Democracy is a habit: practice it', *Boston Review,* July 2018. Available online: http://bostonreview.net/politics/melvin-rogers-democracy-habit-practice-it (accessed 30 September 2020).

Walker, P.G.T., C. Whittaker, O. Watson et al. (2020), *The Global Impact of COVID-19 and Strategies for Mitigation and Suppression,* London: MRC Centre for Global Infectious Disease Analysis.

PART IV
SPEECH AND (MIS)INFORMATION

CHAPTER 13
CORONAVIRUS MISINFORMATION, SOCIAL MEDIA AND FREEDOM OF SPEECH
Jeffrey Howard

Introduction

Misinformation about the novel coronavirus SARS-CoV-2 and the disease it causes, COVID-19, is ubiquitous. Some of the misinformation concerns the origin of the virus, as with the conspiracy theory that the Chinese government manufactured it in a lab as a biological weapon. Other misinformation addresses the various measures that reduce transmission, with a wide array of sources falsely claiming that people shouldn't wear masks on the grounds that they cause greater harm. Still more misinformation concerns the appropriate treatment for COVID-19, with many prominent figures – including the US and Brazilian presidents – advancing the false claim that hydroxychloroquine (an anti-malarial drug) is a proven effective treatment. And a raft of conspiracy theories concern the long-awaited vaccine, with a prominent theory falsely avowing that Bill Gates seeks to use the vaccine to implant location-tracking microchips in all of humanity (see Sanders 2020; Goodman and Carmichael 2020; Wong 2020).

Misinformation about coronavirus is problematic for a number of reasons, but the most important reason is that it can lead to harm. It can lead people to harm themselves – making risky decisions that increase their exposure or involve harmful self-medication, and may have caused such harm already (Islam et al. 2020). But misinformation can also lead people to harm others. In some cases, it does so by assisting the virus's transmission. Failing to wear a mask when one may be infected increases the risk that one will infect others. Likewise, refusing available vaccination endangers others, too, such as those who cannot be vaccinated. In other cases, misinformation is dangerous because it can inspire violence. For example, conspiracy theories alleging that the virus is a scam created to control citizens have resulted in death threats against contact tracers (Thomas and Gatewood

2020). Similarly, the mistaken assumption that the Chinese are to be blamed for the virus seems at least partly responsible for the considerable spike in anti-Asian hate crime, which is up 21 per cent in the UK (Grierson 2020).

That *something* should be done to confront this misinformation seems undeniable. The controversy arises when we consider what, exactly, the appropriate solution is. One possibility is to reduce the circulation of misinformation by insisting that social media networks remove it from their platforms, or at least reduce its dissemination. Yet in the public debate, this suggestion continually inspires a chorus of opposition from those who think that such a move would run afoul of one of the most cherished values of liberal democracy: *freedom of speech*. On this view, even if speech risks causing harm, suppressing it is typically not an acceptable response. The headline of a recent article nicely articulates the underlying sentiment: 'Don't let free speech be a casualty of coronavirus' (Mudde 2020).

Here, my aim is to argue that efforts by social media companies to repress coronavirus misinformation are perfectly compatible with freedom of speech, properly understood. This is true especially when such efforts are voluntarily undertaken by the companies themselves, as many have started to do. But such efforts would be acceptable, in principle, even if they were legally mandated by the state. My reason is that the moral right to freedom of speech, like all our moral rights, is limited by a moral duty we have not to impose undue risks of harm on others. When users post harmful misinformation they violate this duty, even if unintentionally. Accordingly, those who endanger others by posting misinformation are not wronged when their posts are removed. That does not mean that removal is the right response in all cases; in some cases, posting links to fact-checkers, or otherwise merely slowing the spread of the misinformation, will be the most sensible approach. But which exact technique ought to be used is largely a question of effectiveness. As a matter of principle, there is nothing wrong with taking aggressive action against this category of dangerous speech.

Defining the debate

Two clarifications will help to set the terms of this discussion. First, the term *freedom of speech* can be used in different ways. The most obvious thing it can refer to is *the moral right to free speech*. This is a moral right (or, if you prefer, a human right) that all people have to express themselves and to communicate with others – a moral right that should be (though in many places isn't) codified as a *legal* right. As Article 19 of the Universal Declaration of Human Rights states: 'this right shall include freedom to seek, receive and impart information and ideas of all kinds, regardless of frontiers, either orally, in writing or in print, in the form of art, or through any other media of his choice.' This right is codified in the First Amendment to the US Constitution, and in Article 10 of the Human Rights Act in the UK.

Importantly, this is a right that we hold *against the state*, which paradigmatically forbids the state from restricting our speech on the grounds that it disapproves of the viewpoint we are expressing. Everyone agrees that there can be exceptions here, such as speech that encourages violence or incites hatred (though even these are controversial); a chief task in what follows is to examine whether restrictions on harmful misinformation count as such an exception. For now, the point I want to emphasise is that the right to free speech is a right we hold against our government, not against the various private companies on whose forums we might choose to post content. Accordingly, the idea that a social media company violates our *right* to free speech by removing content that violates its community guidelines is difficult to accept. (Note, however, that if we viewed these social networks as crucial public infrastructure, albeit privately owned, the idea that they could violate our moral right to free speech becomes more plausible.)

Yet social media firms nevertheless routinely express their support for 'free speech' – even invoking this value to explain decisions not to suppress users' speech (Zuckerberg 2019). What is going on here? This helps us to see that there is a second meaning to free speech, understood not as a *right* but as a kind of *culture*. As Robert Simpson aptly puts it, the idea of a free-speech culture is one 'in which all are encouraged to speak their minds and to work through their disagreements in debate and discussion, instead of trying to silence or ostracize opponents' (2020: 290). Thus, when social media companies claim to support free speech, what's happening is that they are voluntarily committing themselves to the creation and maintenance of this kind of culture. And so those who complain that companies undermine free speech aren't saying anything incoherent. They are simply best understood as talking about the culture of free speech, rather than the moral right.

The second definitional issue concerns the term *misinformation*. It has become commonplace in the public debate to distinguish between *disinformation*, understood as the deliberate dissemination of content one knows to be false, and *misinformation*, understood as the dissemination of false content that one honestly believes to be accurate (Strauss 2018). I will focus here on misinformation for three reasons. First, it is often unclear whether content is disinformation, since it depends on whether the person posting it knows it to be false – yet the relevant decision-makers will seldom be in a position to establish this (with the possible exception of concerted state-run disinformation campaigns). Second, what begins as disinformation can swiftly become misinformation, as content created nefariously gets passed along by people who've been duped. Finally, it seems easier to justify restrictions on disinformation; indeed, disinformation is simply *lying* by another name, and prominent philosophers have argued persuasively that lying falls outside the protection of the moral right to free speech (e.g. Shiffrin 2014). The more difficult case is that of misinformation, where falsehoods are disseminated by those who believe they are (or could be) true. Yet even in this case, I will argue, restrictions on speech can be justified.

A duty not to endanger others

My starting point is a simple principle: everyone has a moral duty not to endanger others, unless they have a good reason for doing so. Sometimes we have a good reason; we endanger one another by driving our cars, even when we drive conscientiously and within the rules, but we consent to these risks and in any case benefit significantly from the existence of a system of automotive transit. In contrast, speeding is wrong because it endangers others without any such justification. In other work, I have argued that this same principle applies to our speech. For example, the reason why it is wrong for a religious leader to encourage his followers to kill members of other faiths isn't that such speech is offensive (though it certainly is); it is that such speech *endangers* others for no good reason. Likewise, hateful speech that stirs up hostility toward vulnerable groups is similarly objectionable, on account of its dangerousness (Howard 2019b: 217ff.).

My suggestion is that this same argument can help explain why the dissemination of harmful misinformation about coronavirus is morally wrong: it violates the duty not to endanger others without a good reason. This is clearest in the case of malevolent disinformation campaigns, where those posting the false content know it to be false and intend to cause the harm that will likely eventuate. But it is true even in cases of misinformation. Consider someone who disseminates a fake article indicating that wearing masks is futile or counterproductive, unsure about whether it is true or false. This is a case of *recklessly* endangering others by increasing the likelihood that one's followers will stop wearing masks (thereby imperilling themselves and others). (What if someone inserts a caveat, indicating uncertainty as to whether it is true or false? Given that the post nevertheless amplifies harmful misinformation, and thus still carries a risk that others will come to believe it, my sense is that such caveats are not sufficient to immunise one from accountability; see Rini 2017.)

What if the person honestly believes that the misinformation one posts is true? In these cases, posting misinformation can sometimes still be wrongful. Even if someone doesn't know that their post on masks is untrue, it may still be reasonable to expect her to do some background research on the matter before disseminating it. Sometimes, even if someone doesn't know that something is false, she really ought to know, and it is reasonable to expect her to refrain from disseminating it until she undertakes some minimal due diligence. Thus peddling misinformation can be *negligent*. Of course, negligently endangering others isn't as *blameworthy* as intentionally doing so, just as stepping on a stranger's foot through one's carelessness is less blameworthy than doing so deliberately. We likely wouldn't want to subject those who negligently circulate falsehoods to *criminal punishment* (though having one's post demoted or removed on social media is a far cry from that, and so much easier to justify). But it is, I think, still presumptively wrongful.

An interest in expressing or receiving misinformation?

Suppose I'm right that we have a duty not to endanger others, unless we have a sufficient justification for doing so. Maybe, in the case of coronavirus misinformation, there *is* a sufficient justification. What might it be? Well, we might think that the very interests that justify free speech – both as a right against the state, and a culture to be promoted in civil society – could do the trick here. Specifically, once we examine the reasons why we care about free speech in the first place, perhaps we will see that these can explain why people must be free to spread misinformation. If so, then even if spreading misinformation is harmful, we should be free to do so. While initially tempting, this strategy comes up short.

Consider the interest that we all have as speakers in expressing our sincere beliefs to each other. Even if we are wrong about what we think, it is arguably still valuable that we are free to express these thoughts to others. C. Edwin Baker defends a version of this thought in the debate on hate speech, writing: 'Respect for personhood, for agency, or for autonomy requires that each person must be permitted to be herself and to present herself' (1977: 992).

On this view, even if expressing one's authentic white supremacist convictions inspires one's audience to engage in racist attacks, one must still be free to speak, to express one's authentic identity as a person.

But just as I think we should reject this position in the context of hate speech, I think we should reject it here, too. Indeed, some coronavirus misinformation takes the form of hate speech, as in spurious claims about the danger or blameworthiness of people with Chinese ancestry which have motivated violence against them. Likewise, just because someone genuinely believes that masks are ineffective – and just because someone thinks this passionately and with certainty – does not justify endangering others by publicly expressing such a view.

The reason why is that our moral rights are limited by the moral duties we owe to others. In this respect, the right to free speech is like other moral rights we have. So consider, for example, the right to religious freedom. Imagine someone was commanded by her religious doctrine to sacrifice a newborn infant. We would not think her right to religious freedom gives her a right to do so. Nor would we say that it gives her such a right, but that the right sadly must be infringed in this case since it is outweighed by the infant's right to life. The tidier way of thinking about what's happening here is simply to say that our moral rights are limited by our moral obligations not to endanger others (unless a compelling justification can be offered) (Howard 2019b: 233).

Now consider another interest that is thought to justify freedom of speech, which concerns *the quest for truth*. On this view, we need free speech to achieve a 'marketplace of ideas' through which citizens can discover – and develop their appreciation of – the truth. A crucial feature of this view is that even if a view is false, we secure important benefits by engaging with it. As J.S. Mill argued, engagement with erroneous views can help us to sharpen our apprehension of *why* we believe what we believe – 'produced by its collision with error' (1978 [1859]: 16).

I have two objections to this view. First, it is highly doubtful that a wholly unregulated marketplace of ideas leads to the successful identification of the truth. The claim that it does is among the most criticised views within the scholarship on free speech (see Brietzke 1997). While there is clearly a range of questions about COVID-19 on which there is ongoing scientific disagreement, some questions really are settled, and the wrong answers to those questions are plainly dangerous. It's not plausible that banning a selective set of indisputable falsehoods about COVID-19 – or simply tamping down their spread online – would have the effect of subverting humankind's quest for knowledge, even granting that this is an important component of a system of free expression.

But second, even if suppressing some misinformation came with an epistemic cost – since it's valuable to engage with false views – it is a cost worth paying. Consider the fact that we allow the state to limit false advertising. Is it worth losing the epistemic benefit – that is, whatever benefits we might enjoy when having to confront misinformation – for the sake of offering increased protection from misinformation? The answer seems to me to be plausibly 'yes'. However valuable it might be for consumers to 'decide for themselves' whether a product does what its sellers say it does, it is more important to prevent harm. So it seems to be here, too.

I have only considered two interests underlying free speech: our interest in expressing our sincere beliefs and our interest in discovering truth. There are other interests that underlie freedom of speech beyond the ones I have considered; an extended treatment of this topic would explore these other interests in detail (see Howard 2019a: 96–100; 2019b: 219–37). But what I've said is enough to illustrate my basic suggestion: even if we have some interests in expressing mistaken views, or in engaging the mistaken views of others, these are unlikely to be weighty enough to justify seriously endangering one another.

Conclusion: the regulatory challenge and the path forward

I have argued that we have moral duties not to endanger others by propagating harmful misinformation about COVID-19. It might be suggested that these duties should not be enforced by the state, since it is too risky for the state to be entrusted with decisions about truth and falsehood. I am sceptical of this claim, since we entrust the state to adjudicate on matters of truth and falsehood all the time (in defamation law, in consumer protection matters and more). But suppose it were true. Even so, it would not show that there is a *moral* right to endanger others through propagating misinformation as part of our freedom of speech. It would simply show that legislation in this area is, all things considered, misguided – whether in the form of criminal penalties for individual citizens, or civil regulation of social media companies themselves (Howard 2019b: 246).

If state action against misinformation is indeed misguided, this would leave open an extra-legal solution: social media companies themselves could combat misinformation on their own accord. And this is precisely what many have started to do. So we are left with the question: given that social media companies avow to be committed to a *culture* of free speech, what ought they to do? Social media companies that seek to protect a culture of free speech are, in essence, aiming to protect citizens' speech *as if* they were states. Therefore any suppression of citizens' speech that would be wrong for a state to do, on this view, would be wrong for a company to do. But conversely, if it is not wrong for a state to suppress certain speech, it is certainly not wrong for a private company to do so on its private networks.

But this does not yet determine what form these efforts should take. The most obvious way to counter misinformation is to remove it from online platforms, but this is only one possibility. There are several further options. The first is to challenge the speech by offering links to official fact-checkers, targeting those who have shared misinformation with additional information. This constitutes a valuable form of 'counter-speech' against the harmful misinformation. Yet it is an open question whether such methods of challenging misinformation are actually effective at slowing its spread and reducing harm. Alternatively, companies can simply reduce the 'virality' of the misinformation (forgiving the pun) – for example, by limiting the ability of others to re-post it without comment, preventing users from forwarding it without having actually read it, or requiring users to click through an interstitial warning label in order to see it. Or it can pursue some combination of these methods, such as banning extremely harmful content while also sending fact-checks to those who shared it.

While few want social media companies to have this kind of power over public discourse, the alternative – a world in which social media companies do nothing – is, I suspect, even worse. *Given* that social media companies have this enormous power, it is vital that we determine which of these techniques are most effective at countering misinformation about COVID-19 – both offline and online. This is largely an empirical question, requiring knowledge of psychology, behavioural social science, and (in the case of social media regulation) the relevant technology. As a philosophical matter, however, we should be sceptical of those who condemn concerted action in this area as anathema to free speech. Morally speaking, all options are on the table.[1]

Suggestions for further reading

- Howard, J.W. (2019), 'Dangerous speech', *Philosophy & Public Affairs*, 47 (2): 208–54.

- Mill, J.S. (1859), *On Liberty*, Chapter 2 (any edition).
- Rini, R. (2018), 'How to fix fake news', *The New York Times*, 15 October. Available online: https://www.nytimes.com/2018/10/15/opinion/facebook-fake-news-philosophy.html.
- Scanlon, T.M. (1972), 'A theory of freedom of expression', *Philosophy & Public Affairs*, 1 (2): 204–26.
- Shiffrin, S. (2014), *Speech Matters: Lying, Morality, and the Law*, Princeton: Princeton University Press.

Note

1. I am grateful to the Leverhulme Trust for research funding. I am also grateful to the editors of this volume, and to the other authors in Part IV, for helpful comments and discussion.

References

Baker, C.E. (1997), 'Harm, liberty, and free speech', *Southern California Law Review*, 70: 979–1020.

Brietzke, P.H. (1997), 'How and why the marketplace of ideas fails', *Valparaiso University Law Review*, 31: 951–69.

Goodman, J. and F. Carmichael (2020), 'Coronavirus: "deadly masks" claims debunked', *BBC News*, 24 July. Available online: https://www.bbc.co.uk/news/53108405 (accessed 9 November 2020).

Grierson, J. (2020), 'Anti-Asian hate crimes up 21% in UK during coronavirus crisis', *The Guardian*, 13 May. Available online: https://www.theguardian.com/world/2020/may/13/anti-asian-hate-crimes-up-21-in-uk-during-coronavirus-crisis (accessed 9 November 2020).

Howard, J.W. (2019a), 'Free speech and hate speech', *Annual Review of Political Science*, 22: 93–109.

Howard, J.W. (2019b), 'Dangerous speech', *Philosophy & Public Affairs*, 47 (2): 208–54.

Islam. M.S., T. Sarkar, S.H. Khan et al. (2020), 'COVID-19–related infodemic and its impact on public health: a global social media analysis', *The American Journal of Tropical Medicine and Hygiene*, 103 (4): 1621–9.

Mill, J.S. (1978 [1859]), *On Liberty*, Indianapolis: Hackett.

Mudde, C. (2020), 'Don't let free speech be a casualty of coronavirus. We need it more than ever', *The Guardian*, 6 April. Available online: https://www.theguardian.com/commentisfree/2020/apr/06/coronavirus-free-speech-hungary-fake-news (accessed 9 November 2020).

Rini, R. (2017), 'Fake news and partisan epistemology', *Kennedy Institute of Ethics Journal*, 27 (2): 43–64.

Sanders, L. (2020), 'The difference between what Republicans and Democrats believe to be true about COVID-19', *YouGov*, 26 May. Available online: https://today.yougov.com/topics/politics/articles-reports/2020/05/26/republicans-democrats-misinformation (accessed 9 November 2020).

Shiffrin, S. (2014), *Speech Matters: Lying, Morality, and the Law*, Princeton: Princeton University Press.

Simpson, R.M. (2020), 'The relation between academic freedom and free speech', *Ethics*, 130 (3): 287–319.

Strauss, V. (2018), 'Word of the year: misinformation. Here's why', *Washington Post*, 10 December. Available online: https://www.washingtonpost.com/education/2018/12/10/word-year-misinformation-heres-why/ (accessed 9 November 2020).

Thomas, E. and C. Gatewood (2020), 'COVID-19 disinformation briefing no. 4', *Institute for Strategic Dialogue*, 5 June. Available online: https://www.isdglobal.org/wp-content/uploads/2020/06/COVID-19-Briefing-5.pdf (accessed 9 November 2020).

Wong, J.C. (2020), 'Hydroxychloroquine: how an unproven drug became Trump's coronavirus "miracle cure"', *The Guardian*, 7 April. Available online: https://www.theguardian.com/world/2020/apr/06/hydroxychloroquine-trump-coronavirus-drug (accessed 9 November 2020).

Zuckerberg, M. (2019), 'Standing for voice and free expression', speech at Georgetown University, *Washington Post*, 17 October. Available online: https://www.washingtonpost.com/technology/2019/10/17/zuckerberg-standing-voice-free-expression/ (accessed 9 November 2020).

CHAPTER 14
WHAT IS THE DEMOCRATIC STATE'S OBLIGATION OF TRANSPARENCY IN TIMES OF CRISIS?

Rebecca Lowe

Introduction

Let's imagine we're in the midst of a respiratory pandemic. Millions of people are suffering from a horrible disease, many dying painful deaths. Little is known about this disease yet, but it's certain that coughs and sneezes transmit it. Then, suddenly, you hear an astonishing rumour, from an excellent source. Apparently, a while ago, the government gained reliable information to suggest it's the case that wearing a mask likely not only significantly reduces one's chances of passing on the horrible disease, but also one's chances of catching it. Yet this information wasn't passed on to the public – not a jot. You weren't told that the state had reliable new information about mask-wearing, and you weren't told what it was.

Now, maybe this story sounds more familiar than your typical thought experiment. Try to abstract away from any beliefs or knowledge you may have regarding the likely costs and benefits of wearing masks during the time of COVID-19 – and away from any government's particular communications about these things. Rather, what do you think about the imaginary government's behaviour? Probably, it angers you. Perhaps, however, before you come to a proper conclusion about how the imaginary government behaved, you'll want to know about its reasons. Why did the government's decision-makers choose to suppress the important information they had?[1] Presumably, if you were to learn that it was to try to bring about as many deaths as possible, in order to attempt to reduce the elderly population and enable a decrease in healthcare spending, then you'd be even more angry – to say the least.

But might there be anything, perhaps less extreme, you could learn about the government's reasoning that would convince you to conclude that what had happened was acceptable, after all? What if it were part of a wider attempt to quell public panic, by reducing the number of pandemic-related communications? Or to try to protect a limited supply of masks, to ensure there were enough for healthcare workers? Different people will give different answers here – both in terms of agreeing or disagreeing that any further information could suffice to justify the government's behaviour, and also regarding what that further information could be. But let's say, for the sake of argument, that there is something that suffices. Yes, you're convinced it was OK, after all. But wait a second! Isn't it problematic that this further information has also only been revealed to you now, by your source – even if it seems to justify the government's suppression of its newly acquired knowledge about mask-wearing? Aren't you concerned that its reasoning was kept from you, too, regardless of the quality of this reasoning? Sure, it might seem difficult to let someone know the reason they're not being informed about something without also letting them know that they aren't being informed about it. But informing someone that something has been kept from them is different from telling them about that thing, itself!

In other words, this imaginary scenario represents the state being non-transparent in several ways: it failed to pass on important knowledge to the public; it failed to inform them that some important knowledge had been attained and kept from them; and it failed to inform them about its reasoning for behaving in this way. Again, different people will have different views about what could suffice to justify these interlinked failures, but there must be some right and wrong answers here. In this chapter, therefore, my aim is to set out a framework for determining, generally, which kinds of instance of state non-transparency can be deemed justifiable, and then apply it to the mask-wearing scenario, above. Central to my approach will be the contention that the application of a general theory of state transparency – regarding state actions and reasoning – should suffice at all times. That is, that all instances of state non-transparency should be held to the same standards, regardless of whether they occur during 'times of crisis' or not.[2]

Why should the state be transparent?

Transparency is an archetypical modern buzzword. Since the 1980s, there's been a marked increase in its written use,[3] correlating with the introduction, in democratic states, of laws and frameworks enabling greater public access to up-to-date facts about the state (see e.g. Ball 2009). In the UK, this can be seen in the public gaining new ways to obtain information about state behaviour, exemplified by the Freedom of Information Act (UK Government 2000). It can be seen in the state's formal acknowledgement of relevant responsibilities, as per the inclusion of 'accountability', 'openness' and 'honesty' in the seven Nolan Principles for public office-holders (Committee on Standards in Public Life 1995). And it can be seen in the empowerment of members of the public in their own interactions with the state – for example, regarding the NHS's growing emphasis on informed patient choice (Department of Health and Social Care 2015).

Increased societal focus on transparency correlates with mid-to-late twentieth-century theoretical trends. Much has been written in response to John Rawls's discussion of public reason (Rawls 2005), and the argument that, within legitimate political society, important public rules must be justifiable to all reasonable societal members (Quong 2018). For these rules to count as 'public', a baseline entailment is that their content, and the reasons for their existence, must be sufficiently well clarified and 'publicised'. Similarly, within Lon L. Fuller's influential eight desiderata for the 'internal morality' of law is the claim that laws should be public and clear (Fuller 1964). Indeed, good public knowledge about the relevant corpus of law is generally taken as central to the existence of the rule of law within a state, regardless of debate about the rule of law's conceptual breadth, constitutively (Waldron 2020). Moreover, the quality of being known about, widely and accurately, is also typically seen as a necessary condition for a law's legitimacy (Peter 2017). Transparency is an important factor not only in morally acceptable law-making and enforcement, however, but also with regards to wider state behaviour. Onora O'Neill's related thoughts have formed a key part of her work on the value of trustworthiness. She has argued that a situation of transparency does not equate to a lack of deception: that 'if we want to increase trust we need to avoid deception rather than secrecy' (O'Neill 2002).

Although the term 'transparency' has become popular recently, the idea that those with political power should be open with those over whom they are permitted to exercise it – and, particularly, about how they are doing so – is as old as the idea of the liberal state itself.[4] Not all liberals see state legitimacy as grounded in its citizens' consent, as per the early, contractarian, modern state theorists (see e.g. Locke 1980); rival liberal theories, including those grounded in public reason have emerged (see e.g. Rawls 2005), and also reflect philosophical thinking going back to ancient times. But it is central to a traditional liberal approach to conceive of democratic government as premised on equal respect, stemming from human beings' shared natural equality of fundamental status, as equal participants in political society (see e.g. Locke 1980). The English Civil War that led to the death of Charles I, and the other contemporary revolutions that bore the rise of modern democracy, centred on the unjustness of unaccountable power. And it seems no overstatement to suggest that accusations of illegitimately secretive policymaking will have been levelled at all governments that have considered themselves democratic: suspicion about the Behavioural Insights Team is relatively new (see e.g. Cassidy 2011), but criticisms of manipulative Government House Utilitarianism are not (see e.g. Williams's classic criticism of Henry Sidgwick in Williams 1986). Arguably, a key difference today is that there is now, generally, an open state recognition of the need to be transparent, even if that transparency is sometimes used to mask secrecy.

Regarding the grounding of the requirement for state transparency, it seems reasonable to conclude that rights-based liberal democratic accounts of the state include, implicitly or explicitly, an individual right, held by citizens,[5] to be informed about the behaviour of the state. Indeed, without that right, the value of other standard rights held by members of political society, not least the right to political participation, would be severely diminished. This chapter, therefore, focuses on state transparency not because it brings about good results on measures such as GDP growth or welfare standards – although there is much to suggest that openness, and other hallmarks of the democratic regime, do (see e.g. Acemoglu et al. 2014) – but rather, as a precondition of democracy itself. On this view, the general obligation to state transparency correlates with a right held by the democratic state's citizens, and, as such, should not be compromised.

What about obvious tensions?

This is an obligation pertaining to general state behaviour, however. And it's typically accepted that there will be some particular times at which, and things about which, the state cannot or should not be fully transparent. Some of these 'cannot cases' won't be backed up by a 'should not case' – stemming instead, for instance, from the limitations of a state's communications systems. But it is the normative basis for intentional non-transparency that I'm interested in here. Therefore, I shall remain focused on the justifiability of 'should not cases', and assume that 'cannot cases', where they don't correlate with a justified 'should not case', are in need of redress.

While a proliferation of standard 'should not cases' may help to illustrate that justifiable instances of suppression don't necessarily detract from the case that the state has a general obligation of transparency, the existence of these instances does not suffice to justify them. They provide useful initial examples, nonetheless. The most obvious of these standard 'should not' cases depend, at their root, on concerns of harm or privacy. First, let's consider the case of an ongoing counterterrorism operation, which is kept secret from the public because it's believed that revealing information about it would seriously limit the state's ability to prevent disaster. The apparent justification for this kind of suppression hinges on the pressing need to prevent harm. It's not that there is good reason proffered to keep certain information about state behaviour from the public, in general – but rather, to keep it from them for a limited amount of time, in order to prevent seemingly avoidable serious harm. And it is, of course, a fundamental obligation of the state to protect its citizens. This obligation to protect does not override all other moral concerns, however, and as such cannot suffice, alone, to justify non-transparent state behaviour. Moreover, none of this is to suggest that delaying the release of required information is unproblematic in itself. But a delay does seem inherently less problematic than persistent suppression, as long as good enough reasons are given for such a delay. And, in certain instances, the prevention of harm does seem a good reason for the temporary suppression of required information.

Next, let's turn to the removal of personal details within public releases of information about state behaviour. This might include information such as the home address of a civil servant who was visited by a politician on official business, or the mobile number of a member of the public who gave evidence to a public inquiry, and spoke about it, over the phone, with a committee clerk beforehand. These are commonplace examples of instances in which we'd expect personal details to be excluded from the public record. First, let's consider why this exclusion takes place; then the extent to which it's problematic. Unsurprisingly, a tension is often noted between concerns of transparency and privacy (see e.g. Cohen 2008). And it's standardly deemed in cases like those above that to release such personal information would unjustifiably go against the interests of the particular individuals involved, whether they count as state actors or not. This moves us beyond considerations of harm – although a failure to respect someone's privacy can, of course, put them at risk of many kinds of harm. Rather, it hinges upon an individual's right to privacy, and the extent to which the state's correlative obligation to respect that right should take precedence over the state's general obligation to be transparent. The first consideration here seems to be one of relevance. It will often be claimed that the bits of personal information suppressed in such instances amount to unnecessary tangential details, rather than required information. In many instances, this kind of suppression doesn't seem truly problematic, particularly if it's the content of the seemingly irrelevant information that's kept secret – through anonymisation or redaction – as opposed to its existence. Again, however, none of this is to suggest that it's easy to balance concerns of privacy and transparency. There are many examples of personal details, within accounts of affairs of the state, that surely would count as 'relevant', to the extent that anonymising or redaction would not suffice, and then further justification would be required for their suppression. But this is to be expected. Obligations often bump up against each other, and a reason for thinking hard about these matters is to be able to respond to those bumps in justifiable ways.

Now, this 'relevance' argument could also be proffered regarding the release of information in our previous case – the ongoing counterterrorism operation. However, that argument would only be grounded by the concern of privacy when it pertained to any personal details involved. It's quite different to suggest that counterterrorism activity, per se, is not of relevance to the public. And this brings us to a wider issue of public interest and scope. The public's right to be informed about state behaviour encompasses everything the state does, no matter how mundane or esoteric, and no matter how seemingly important or unimportant. Of course, a breach of the correlative state obligation could be deemed worse depending on the relative importance, in some sense, of the information suppressed: failing to inform the public of reliable new information about mask-wearing is bad for many reasons that other instances of suppression won't necessarily be. But it is, at best, patronising to suggest that citizens have no interest in counterterrorism matters. There is, however, space to argue that resources should be allocated prudently in terms of the publicising of information about state behaviour. It seems unnecessary, for instance, to send copies to every household of transcripts of every meeting of every government committee; that details are easily available online seems reasonable, as long as good general awareness of such activity is also ensured. Finally, as ever, it is not the case that all moral matters are reducible to the concerns of the state. The general obligation of state transparency surely doesn't generally extend to its being required to inform me of details it has newly acquired about my neighbour's bank balance.

What are the ground rules for justifiable cases?

What can we take from our discussion so far to determine some ground rules for justifiable cases of state non-transparency? First, let's consider some conditions that must be fulfilled for the obligation of state transparency to have been met. What should it mean, in practice, for the public to be properly informed about state behaviour? What counts as the state being transparent about its actions and reasoning? It seems clear that simply avoiding the suppression of information is not enough. Rather, the idea of publicity, as above, seems crucial – in the sense of both the content of and the reasons for something being sufficiently well publicised. And, to return to O'Neill, the idea that the value of transparency is dependent on its relation to relevant truths – to what is not revealed, as well as to what is revealed, to whom, and why – also seems of fundamental importance (O'Neill 2002). Indeed, public accessibility and truthfulness (in detail, and in context) seem baked into the notion of transparency. The concept of state transparency loses some of its essential value if what are taken to be instances of such a thing do not meet reasonable thresholds related to truthfulness and accessibility.

So, what might justify a state failure to meet these important thresholds – either in being insufficiently transparent about its behaviour, or in being completely non-transparent? Here, I shall note the distinctions between the act of suppressing information, the act of misinformation and the act of disinformation; I'll contend for now that state disinformation is unjustifiable, but I'll come back to this later. To pin down some ground rules, however, it seems clear that any particular justified case of non-transparency should be grounded in justifiable general practice. On a rights-based liberal democratic account, there must be rigorous and open debate and reasoning about what determines justifiable general practice. Beyond any relevant considerations that are already preconditions for the liberal democratic state – such as respect for certain fundamental rights and the rule of law – these are matters for public deliberation, grounded by moral truths arising from the kind of philosophical thinking attempted in this chapter. There should be clear and well-publicised democratically deliberated general rules, in other words, about the kinds of instance that count as justifiable cases, and the extent to which information can be withheld, while it is justified to do so.

As per our opening discussion, key to this is recognising that being fully transparent about the fact that you aren't being fully transparent about something is different from revealing the full content of that thing. That some kind of information suppression is taking place, therefore, should ideally not only be publicised at the time of the suppression, in as much detail as possible, but this should also only occur during types of situation about which the public is already aware that full transparency may not always take place immediately. In some justifiable cases, therefore, existing public awareness about these matters will suffice, while the temporary suppression is taking place. In other cases, specific publicity, pertaining to a particular suppression, will also be required. Therefore, that a crisis is 'unprecedented' – caused by a new variety of pandemic, for instance – is not enough, in itself, to justify the suppression of important information. Neither will it suffice to claim that it's a 'time of crisis'. The obligations of the liberal democratic state do not dissolve in difficult times; rather, the continued fulfilment of these obligations helps to hold political society together, in a legitimate manner.

Now, ideally, there will be evidence of both of these approaches – 'ongoing' transparency and 'in the moment' transparency – in any justifiable case. However, while the existence of 'general awareness' will form a necessary condition of any justifiable case, this general awareness will, in certain instances, require supplementing with 'specific awareness' for a sufficient condition of justifiability to have been met. And, while 'specific awareness' is an ideal condition of any justifiable case, it is not a sufficient condition of justifiability, and, as above, is necessary in some but not all cases. It also seems essential to reiterate that, on this framework, justified cases are, by nature, temporary. Any suppressed information should be fully released, reflecting normal practice, as soon as suppression is no longer justified. Moreover, it should be clear that any temporary delay to the need for full transparency must never be instrumentalised – in order to attempt, for instance, to justify related rights violations, such as the use of torture during counterterrorism operations.

Beyond the removal (or, better, anonymisation or redaction) of justifiably 'irrelevant' personal details, it seems likely, therefore, that standard justifiable cases of non-transparency will involve necessary state action against a direct, immediate and (as far as possible) well-publicised threat to citizens, during a moment in which detailed public knowledge of such matters would (with as high a degree of certainty as possible) directly impede the state's reduction of that threat. But most importantly, justified cases depend on as much transparency as possible about the situation that has arisen that seemingly demands non-transparency, the action taken, and why.

Back to the mask-wearing scenario: an unjustifiable case?

Now, let's return to our thought experiment: could the imaginary government's non-transparent behaviour be justifiable? First, let's consider the wrong that's taken place. Again, it's not just that new information about mask-wearing was suppressed; the public was also uninformed about the acquisition and withholding of this information, and about the government's reasoning. Clearly, a reasonable threshold for truthfulness and accessibility was unmet regarding the state's obligation to be transparent. But could the case be justifiable nonetheless?

We can rule out the idea that this case might hinge on claimedly irrelevant personal details, removed on privacy grounds. Rather, we need to assess the state's actual reasoning. So, let's consider the three options set out above: to reduce healthcare spending; to quell panic; and to protect the mask supply. Now, you might think the answer is that the state's behaviour – in any of these three variants – could have been priorly determined, via democratic deliberation, to be the kind of thing about which the state could be temporarily non-transparent, when necessary. But this doesn't seem right. First, it was your source who informed you about what was going on, and shocked you by doing so! So it seems unlikely that the public, of which you're a part, is generally or was specifically aware of any part of this. Second, all three reasons proffered seem inherently problematic anyway.

Holding back information that could save people's lives, in an attempt to decrease state spending by letting elderly people die, is a form of state behaviour that clearly has no place in a liberal democracy. And while cutting down on pandemic-related communications to attempt to quell rising panic in the short term may, arguably, seem reasonable in certain limited situations, it seems, at best, ironic to cause direct harm to people's interests in the name of potentially protecting them. But what about the third reason proffered? What if the state were to fail to tell the public that mask-wearing was beneficial, when it had reliable information to suggest that it was, in order to try to prevent public consumption reducing the supply of masks available to healthcare workers? Such an approach could be well-intentioned. But it's clearly not justified on the framework set out above.

This is because – as with the other two variants of the case – it's not that the rights of citizens to state transparency have been overridden temporarily, and as minimally as possible, in order to protect them from a direct, publicised threat, according to pre-determined, democratically deliberated parameters. Rather, the government has acted secretively and manipulatively in order to bring about unrevealed aims. This implies not only the belief that the public is not to be trusted to act with the common good in mind, but also that deceptive behaviour can be justified to bring about certain societal ends. This is reminiscent of the kind of secretive 'nudge'-type policymaking which, deriving from Cass Sunstein and Richard Thaler's 'libertarian paternalism' (Sunstein and Thaler 2003), has provoked renewed discussion about the need for political actors to employ open reasoning (see e.g. discussion of the 'manipulation objection' in Hanna 2015). Nudge theory is often defended on consequentialist grounds, on which it's argued, for instance, that clandestinely shifting the public's eating habits – by changing the default sizes of plates in cafeterias, or the standard sizes of snacks – is the most efficient way of reducing aggregate obesity. Other standard examples of deceptive state behaviour employed on the grounds of bringing about certain societal consequences include the following two examples: epistocratic state actors seeking, deviously, to protect the public from legitimate electoral outcomes that have been deemed by those actors to be suboptimal; and the persistent non-disclosure of details about state contract processes, on the grounds that, in the long run, the economy will benefit more if secretive preferential relationships are developed with certain companies.

Now, regardless of whether policy decisions can generally be justified solely by the ends they (may) bring about – I would argue they cannot – it's clear that non-transparency is not justified in any of these cases, on my framework. Indeed, a natural extension to this chapter would be to consider what the appropriate public response should be to cases in which state non-transparency involves manipulation and disinformation. What if, for instance, it were not only that the imaginary state had failed to inform you about its newly acquired reliable information about the benefits of mask-wearing – but had also told you that wearing a mask would be detrimental to your health? What would be the appropriate public response to such behaviour?

Conclusion

I have set out a framework for determining which kinds of instance of state non-transparency can be deemed justifiable, on a rights-based liberal democratic account of the state. Central to my approach is the contention that the application of a general theory of state transparency should suffice at all times – regardless of whether instances of non-transparency occur during 'times of crisis' or not. My framework hinges upon the recognition that being fully transparent about the fact that you aren't being fully transparent about something is different from revealing the full content of that thing. Therefore, that some kind of information suppression is taking place should, ideally, not only be publicised at the time of the suppression, in as much detail as possible, but this should also only occur during types of situation about which the public is already aware that full transparency may not always take place immediately. Indeed, such situations should have been publicly determined via democratic deliberation. On this framework, justified cases are, by nature, temporary: any suppressed information should be fully released, reflecting normal practice, as soon as suppression is no longer justified. I then applied this framework to three variants of the mask-wearing scenario that I introduced at the start of the chapter, finding the state's non-transparency, on each variant, to be unjustified.

Suggestions for further reading

- Freeman, Samuel (2007), 'The burdens of public justification', *Politics, Philosophy, and Economics*, 6 (1): 5–43.
- Heald, David and Christopher Hood (eds) (2006), *Transparency: The Key to Better Governance?* Proceedings of the British Academy 135, Oxford: Oxford University Press.
- O'Neill, Onora (2002), *A Question of Trust: Reith Lectures 2002*, Cambridge: Cambridge University Press.
- Runciman, David (2009), 'Bouncebackability', *London Review of Books*, 31 (2).
- Simmons, A. John. (2002), *Justification and Legitimacy: Essays on Rights and Obligations*, Cambridge: Cambridge University Press.

Notes

1. I shall use the term 'suppression' throughout this chapter to refer to the intentional holding back of information. I understand this term often holds negative connotations beyond any assumed in relation simply to this 'holding back', but I don't necessarily imply them.

2. Some caveats to this kind of general theory might be expected regarding times of war, but that consideration lies outside the remit of this chapter.

3. You can chart this on Google Ngrams.

4. There's no room here to discuss fully what is typically meant in liberal theory by 'the state'. Sometimes, it will be synonymous with 'the government', but, for present purposes, should be taken to include all national political institutions, and actors running these institutions, etc.

5. There is, of course, much normative debate about the different rights and freedoms held by citizens, denizens, visitors to a state and so on. Owing to time constraints, I focus here on citizens as a key subset within the set referred to in discussion elsewhere in this chapter as 'members of the public'.

References

Acemoglu, D., S. Naidu, P. Restrepo et al. (2019), 'Democracy does cause growth', *Journal of Political Economy*, 127 (1): 47–100.

Ball, C. (2009), 'What is transparency?', *Public Integrity*, 11 (4): 293–308.

Cassidy, J. (2011), 'The Cabinet Office Behavioural Insights Team', *British Medical Journal*, 342: d1648.

Cohen, J. E. (2008), 'Privacy, visibility, transparency, and exposure', *University of Chicago Law Review*, 75 (1): 181–201.

Committee on Standards in Public Life (1995), 'The Seven Principles of Public Life'. Available online: https://www.gov.uk/government/publications/the-7-principles-of-public-life/the-7-principles-of-public-life--2 (accessed 9 November 2020).

Department of Health and Social Care (2015), *The NHS Constitution*. Available online: https://assets.publishing.service.gov.uk/government/uploads/system/uploads/attachment_data/file/480482/NHS_Constitution_WEB.pdf (accessed 9 November 2020).

Fuller, L.L. (1964), *The Morality of Law*, New Haven: Yale University Press.

Hanna, J. (2015), 'Libertarian paternalism, manipulation, and the shaping of preferences', *Social Theory and Practice*, 41 (4): 618–43.

Locke, J. (1980), *Second Treatise of Government*, ed. C.B. Macpherson, Indianapolis: Hackett Publishing.

O'Neill, O. (2002), 'Lecture 4: Trust and Transparency', *Reith Lectures 2002: A Question of Trust*. Available online: https://www.immagic.com/eLibrary/ARCHIVES/GENERAL/BBC_UK/B020000O.pdf (accessed 9 November 2020).

Peter, F. (2017), 'Political legitimacy', in E.N. Zalta (ed), *The Stanford Encyclopedia of Philosophy* (Summer 2017 Edition). Available online: https://plato.stanford.edu/archives/sum2017/entries/legitimacy (accessed 9 November 2020).

Quong, J. (2018), 'Public reason', in E.N. Zalta (ed), *The Stanford Encyclopedia of Philosophy* (Spring 2018 Edition), Available online: https://plato.stanford.edu/archives/spr2018/entries/public-reason/ (accessed 9 November 2020).

Rawls, J. (2005), *Political Liberalism*, New York: Columbia University Press.

Sunstein, C. and R. Thaler (2003), 'Libertarian paternalism is not an oxymoron', *The University of Chicago Law Review*, 70 (4): 1159–1202.

UK Government, *Freedom of Information Act* (2000): Available online: https://www.legislation.gov.uk/ukpga/2000/36/contents (accessed 9 November 2020).

Waldron, J. (2020), 'The rule of law', in E.N. Zalta (ed), *The Stanford Encyclopedia of Philosophy* (Summer 2020 Edition). Available online: https://plato.stanford.edu/archives/sum2020/entries/rule-of-law/ (accessed 9 November 2020).

Williams, B. (1986), *Ethics and the Limits of Philosophy*, Abingdon: Routledge.

CHAPTER 15
DEFERRING TO EXPERTISE IN PUBLIC HEALTH EMERGENCIES
Viktor Ivanković and Lovro Savić

Introduction

COVID-19 confronts the countries of the world with a threat that is altogether novel and grave. Science continues to expand our knowledge about the virus, but for a long time to come we are likely to have to proceed under great uncertainty, warranting an extremely cautious approach. Still, consulting with the best available evidence seems imperative in producing and communicating appropriate recommendations to the public. Unfortunately, the meddling of laypersons, scholars from unrelated fields, and politicians with no relevant medical and public health background has been a constant nuisance in these efforts. Among the more preposterous claims about COVID-19, still spreading on social networks as we write, are that it is transmitted by house flies and by 5G mobile networks. We have also heard bizarre claims about the preventative measures that people should take. Most famously, Donald Trump has stated that drinking bleach and other disinfectant products may kill the virus, and that ultraviolet lamps may be used to prevent contracting it (Reality Check Team 2020).[1] To add insult to injury, some dubious claims have been offered by highly respected academics. The most well-known example is that of Richard Epstein – law professor at New York University – whose erroneous projections about the expected mortality from COVID-19 were disproven only weeks after they were made (Chotiner 2020).

Imagine that it were in our power to hit the reset button on COVID-19, or that a similar deadly virus emerges next year. Imagine that, as with COVID-19, we know little about the virus itself and its potential to cause widespread harm. As ordinary citizens, to whom should we defer in such times of crisis? If there are such individuals, how should they guide us, and how should we respond? We argue in this chapter that laypersons (i.e. non-experts) and experts should practise restraint in exercising public speech and deliberation in high-stakes public health circumstances, such as a global pandemic.[2] We offer two possible forms such restraint may take.

The first is an obligation upon laypersons to defer to experts whenever possible and not to undermine them in matters that the laypersons know little or nothing about; the restraint laypersons should thereby exercise concerns not meddling in empirical matters.[3] Spreading incomplete or outright false information can be extremely costly during public health crises, so laypersons should refrain from divulging their non-expert opinions about the nature and effects of the virus in social media posts and other communicative channels. The purpose of this obligation is to inspire a mindful and responsible attitude, an awareness that by meddling in affairs beyond our understanding in times of crises, collectively we may cause or facilitate great harm.

The second is an obligation upon experts to stick to what they know about COVID-19; that is, to remain within their empirical role. For instance, they should be as explicit as possible about what goal drives the recommendation they are putting forward, and they should not allow their advice to be 'contaminated' by non-epistemic influences such as political or corporate interests.

Both these manifestations of restraint seem to provide not only valuable rules for how to avoid widespread harm, but they express an acceptable way of treating our social peers during trying and volatile times. Nonetheless, several reasonable questions arise when we consider these obligations in more detail. We may wonder whether there is expertise that is proper in circumstances in which very little is known about the virus. If there are such experts, laypersons may wonder how to distinguish them from charlatans, or to choose between the conflicting recommendations of experts with comparable credentials. Similarly, experts may wonder how they can practise restraint if they are frequently prompted to offer predictions and ready-made solutions. In what follows, we deal with these and similar complications.

Public health emergencies

As hinted, we treat the COVID-19 pandemic as a high-risk, high-stakes public health issue – a public health *emergency*. Following Herington, Dawson and Draper (2014) and Gostin et al. (2002), we take public health emergencies to denote imminent threats of illness, in this case caused by an infectious agent. A public health issue becomes an *emergency* once it is established that it carries a high probability of a significant death toll, long-term disabilities, or significant risk of future harm to a large number of people. It seems safe to say not only that COVID-19 fits this bill, but that our experiences with this virus will help to set the ethical standards for future public health emergencies.

Furthermore, the COVID-19 pandemic and other public health emergencies require speedy reactions from policymakers. This involves instituting and upholding health measures such as lockdowns and social distancing. Immediate action in such circumstances is necessary to 'mitigate the expected harm'. As Herington, Dawson and Draper write:

> Typically, this is understood as meaning that there is one, and only one, opportunity to eliminate or substantially reduce the expected harm before the *actual* harm to population health is decided by fortune alone. A highly pathogenic infectious disease meets this condition because it is supposed that, absent immediate intervention, the severity of the actual harm will be 'out of our hands' and instead decided by the natural dynamics of the disease's epidemiology.
>
> *2014: 28*

Public health emergencies will spark debates on whether we should regulate our communicative channels so as to suppress potentially harmful diffusion of misinformation, and, if so, how we might go about this permissibly; Jeffrey Howard's chapter in this volume makes great strides in this regard. Our assumption here, however, is that because a public health emergency normally catches us by surprise, such regulations take time to be discussed and implemented. Until then, the burden of mitigating harm will be shouldered by individual citizens. Our aim is to explain how individuals, in their capacity as either laypersons or experts, are to play their individual part in mitigating harm in a public health emergency, most particularly with regard to potentially harmful speech.[4]

The layperson's obligation

We claim that, in public health emergencies, laypersons have a particularly strong obligation to defer to experts in their communication and action, and particularly to refrain from using public speech for meddling in empirical matters. But are there in fact relevant experts about COVID-19? The notion of expertise is meant to separate those who possess epistemic authority over a subject from those who lack it. Having lived with the pandemic for many months now, many of us feel that we have a fairly good handle on how viruses are transmitted and which policy response in a pandemic is more or less appropriate. At the same time, recommendations from epidemiologists and immunologists are constantly being changed, sometimes giving us the impression that they are being made on the fly. In relative terms, then, there may be less epistemic separation between the alleged expert on COVID-19 and the layperson than in standard circumstances of expertise.

But we should not overstate this point. Being an expert about the virus is not limited simply to knowing a significant body of truths about it, but, as Goldman says, includes being able to deploy knowledge to offer answers to new questions that may be posed, and to perform 'appropriate operations' on this new information (2001: 91–2). Although epidemiologists and immunologists might get things wrong, these epistemic dispositions are certainly within their skillset when it comes to the emergence of new viral agents. Laypersons, on the other hand, are not significantly helped by their real-time experience in a pandemic to separate the wheat from the chaff.

The Richard Epstein example is also important to keep in mind. The pandemic has prompted scholars from all walks of the scientific world to weigh in. Many are undoubtedly motivated to aid our collective scientific efforts to overcome the current crisis. However, the crisis has also created an incentive for academics and scientific journals to publish as much and as quickly as possible about COVID-19. Agoramoorthy, Hsu and Shieh note that from numerous virus-related publications fast-tracked by journals in the last several months, many have been retracted, but not before they reached policymakers and the news (2020: 633). The scientific world has thus eroded its own system of filtering out pseudoscience and misinformation, making it even more difficult for laypersons to know whose recommendations to trust.

Some help in identifying good expertise is provided by philosophers such as Hume (2000 [1748]), Walton (1989), Goldman (2001) and Martini (2014), who have discussed possible cues for laypersons to adjudicate between differing expert opinion. One of the most reliable cues that Goldman and Martini mention is checking the prospective expert's track record of producing correct answers to the most closely related scientific questions in the past.[5] Another is the support an expert receives from other credible and independent experts. Finally, it sometimes helps in figuring out which experts are less trustworthy if some of them have non-epistemic interests in defending a particular claim. Note, however, that none of these strategies are foolproof – track records can be used for political purposes (Martini 2014: 13), whole scientific communities could be wrong (Holst and Molander 2017: 239), and those with vested interests might still be right (ibid.). Nonetheless, they do improve the likelihood for laypersons to follow the better recommendations.

Moreover, given the time pressures of a public health emergency, it may sometimes be necessary (at least temporarily) simply to defer to government-appointed experts, assuming that their recommendations make sense in the context of exercising precaution. Along these lines, many governments around the world gathered their own expert teams when the pandemic first broke out. The expectation for these expert teams was not only to derive recommendations from the findings of the global scientific community, but to put them forward in light of the specific epidemiological circumstances in their cities and states. As we learn more about the virus and as we move away from a state of emergency, laypersons will not have to be as trusting of these government-appointed experts, as they listen in on expert debates and assess (at least superficially) which experts seem more responsive to new evidence.

So, the layperson's obligation commits her to defer to the most trustworthy expert, and to refrain from second-guessing the expert on empirical matters in a public forum. Yet it might seem that the obligation not to talk about COVID-19 is very demanding on the layperson. The virus has shaped our lives in recent months so profoundly, and pushed so many other matters to the side, that it has become the main occupant of our collective attention. How do we not talk about it, not share our impressions with others? Our view, however, is not that laypersons should refrain from saying *anything at all* about the virus, only that they should not meddle in empirical matters in a way that might undermine the authority of experts, given that the stakes are so high.

There are a number of ways for the layperson to provide valuable epistemic contributions to experts, public health practitioners and policymakers. For instance, those who have recovered can share their experiences of the illness. Others could warn about a health measure not being observed in their community. Sometimes it will be important to share the recommendations of relevant experts, when they aren't reaching the wider public or when dangerous non-expert opinions are having too much influence.

Still, laypersons must engage in these activities responsibly and mindfully. The whole point of the layperson's obligation of restraint is not to undermine social trust in expertise, so as to avoid expected harm from occurring in public health emergencies. If they share information concerning COVID-19, laypersons have to be mindful about whether the information itself, or the way they present it, may deter others from abiding by some preventative measures. For instance, sharing on social media that people aren't wearing masks in supermarkets or in public transportation may cause some people to believe that, in effect, it makes little sense for themselves to abide by that measure.

But can we reasonably expect people to stop talking about the empirical features of the virus altogether? Perhaps not. Seeing that the virus is still the main news item, exchanges with friends and family will unavoidably ensue. But once again, there are mindful ways to participate in such exchanges. Even when an expert's point makes little sense to them, laypersons can at least refrain from resisting, or mobilising others to resist, policy recommendations backed by those experts, especially when these recommendations make sense within a precautionary strategy.

In some cases, ordinary citizens will have to do more. Some laypersons will not only remain distrustful of expert recommendations and dismiss the layperson's obligation, but will be very vocal about their views. If other laypersons stay silent, then these views may often appear more widespread and supported than they in fact are. This may leave the false impression that the views and recommendations of the 'scientific elite' are divorced from the experiences and sentiments predominating on the ground. In order to avoid this, it will sometimes be up to laypersons to disseminate expert recommendations and engage with radical anti-expert views. This will rarely convince radical anti-expert laypersons of the importance of the layperson's obligation, and may in fact entrench their commitment in their mistaken view, but it may succeed with other laypersons who might have otherwise been recruited to their cause.[6] In response to some particularly dangerous proposals coming from those distrustful of experts, other laypersons may even consider public shaming. But public shaming should not be used lightly, given that it often spirals out of control and may permanently stigmatise its targets, as Paul Billingham and Tom Parr's chapter in this volume warns.

Finally, we raise two objections against our view. The first states that the kind of restraint we are advocating would stifle a good deal of important criticism against experts, who often turn out to be wrong during public health emergencies. This helps us to qualify our view a bit further. Laypersons should be able to challenge the views of experts (or those they suspect not to be real experts), but only if they are guided in these activities by other experts. The Richard Epstein interview in the *New Yorker* is an example of good practice. Here, the journalist Isaac Chotiner is challenging Epstein's expertise, but only by fact-checking his claims with an immunologist and an infections specialist (Chotiner 2020). This, in fact, engages differing expert opinions during a public health emergency and helps laypersons recognise a more reliable source of expertise.

The second objection is that the category of experts on our view is underinclusive – our argument primarily points laypersons towards epidemiologists, immunologists and other medical experts. But scholars from other fields may offer important guidelines to laypersons and contributions to policymakers. We do not deny this. But as we explicate in the next section, the chief aim in a public health emergency is precaution; deferring to medical expertise is likeliest to produce the most grounded and informed recommendations at an early stage. As we move away from a state of emergency, the notion of expertise becomes laxer and more interdisciplinary, with other valuable contributors weighing in.

The expert's obligation

Any recommendation made by an expert is informed not only by the most recent evidence she possesses, but also by a set of explicit or implicit aims. When the COVID-19 pandemic first broke out, the *default aim*, shared by both experts and policymakers, was to safeguard public health. Seeing that the pandemic was also a public health emergency, and that there were (and still are) many uncertainties regarding the characteristics of the virus, the best way to realise the default aim was to adopt a set of precautionary measures.[7]

Later, the aim of safeguarding public health was challenged by other aims, such as keeping the economy afloat or protecting personal liberties. All expert recommendations are made with these and other aims in mind and are in this sense non-neutral (Christiano 2012; Prijić-Samaržija 2017), and may be distorted by particular interests and biases (Goldman 2001: 104–5; Holst and Molander 2017: 241). While they can provide the most valuable input, public health experts don't have the final say on just how weighty the aim of public health should be in a functioning democracy (Cerovac 2016: 80); it will be up to deliberative democracy to determine the weight of particular aims.

In this section, we claim that experts should abide by a list of standards in order to prevent widespread harm and the undermining of social relationships during a public health emergency. We mentioned earlier that experts should stay in their empirical roles. How is this achieved if their advice is bound to be non-neutral? We explicate several ways in which this is achieved.

First, experts must be as explicit as possible about the aims that drive their recommendations, and report changes in aims whenever they occur. If a change in recommendation is made by the expert without any change in aim, she needs to be able to point to some new empirical source or explain the change in reasoning (preferably backed by the scientific community) that prompted the revised recommendation. For any changes in aims and/or recommendations, experts also need to be able to show that their views are not compromised by external pressures or vested interests. As we mentioned earlier, non-epistemic interests give laypersons a strong reason to defer to other experts, so it is vital that COVID-19 experts maintain their distance from the political and economic spheres, lest the social trust in expertise be deteriorated.

Second, experts need to show epistemic humility in their communication of evidence to the public. Much is still, and will remain for some time, uncertain about how the global COVID-19 pandemic will unfold. Experts should, as Angner (2020) says, be open about their current limitations in knowledge and display a degree of confidence that fits the available evidence. Epistemic humility can also be expressed if experts show a sincere openness to new kinds of evidence coming from other scientific sources, as we move beyond the state of emergency. A closed-minded and dismissive attitude by the experts might not only undermine informed policymaking, but could strike the public as elitist and erode trust.

Third, experts in public health emergencies should cultivate an additional talent of conveying their messages to laypersons in an intelligible way. An overlapping understanding (Christiano 2012: 38–40) must be established so that people can make sense of the recommendations that are meant to guide their behaviour. As Christiano notes, in standard deliberative circumstances this task is carried out in part by journalists and politicians. However, seeing that stakes are high in a public health emergency, an 'interactional expertise' (Holst and Molander 2017: 238) must be fostered by experts so that falsehoods and misconceptions in communicative channels can be quickly and effectively refuted.

Fourth, some expert obligations of restraint will depend on whether the expert is appointed by the government, sometimes precisely to convey intelligible messages and issue guidelines for laypersons. These experts may particularly erode public trust in expertise and undermine democratic decision-making if they do their job non-transparently or underhandedly. This is because they might either choose not to disclose some item of information relevant to collective decision-making, or they may use their spotlight to subtly frame issues and debates in order to steer public opinion (Ivanković 2015).[8] While experts may act with the best of intentions in such cases, being caught in the act may be particularly damaging to public trust in scientific expertise.[9]

Fifth, we mentioned earlier that local experts might possess specific information pertaining, for example, to epidemiological circumstances on the ground, or local behavioural patterns. This may give them reasons to deviate in their recommendations from more general scientific guidelines. For instance, it was believed at the early stages of the pandemic that Sweden's relative lack of mandatory restrictions would not be appropriate to other countries that lack Sweden's high levels of social and institutional trust.[10] But locally specific expertise should not be assumed. Local experts need to be able to make a strong case for why local circumstances call for a different approach to dealing with a public health emergency. Otherwise, laypersons are completely justified in deferring to non-local expertise.

Finally, experts should follow their own advice. In fact, a case could be made that their obligation to abide by their recommendations should be more stringent than the layperson's. For instance, a government-appointed expert that pleads with laypersons to observe lockdown, but then violates it, may justifiably be called to resign. Such was the case of Professor Neil Ferguson, who was formerly employed by the Scientific Advisory Group for Emergencies, a body in the UK specifically entrusted with providing scientific advice to government during public emergencies. In his resignation, Ferguson himself acknowledged the capacity of his actions to dilute the recommendations for social distancing; this is because laypersons may sense that the recommendations don't apply to everyone equally (Stewart 2020). Other experts must try to remedy these faults and show that these violations don't nullify the rationale behind the recommendations themselves.

Conclusion

As a prime example of a public health emergency, the COVID-19 pandemic confronts us with a number of challenges. Among other things, mitigating the harmful consequences of the pandemic calls for a careful weighing of obligations relating to communicating and disseminating information. We have argued that, in public health emergencies, laypersons should defer to experts whenever possible and refrain from engaging in communicative acts that might undermine scientific recommendations. Experts, on the other hand, should strive towards formulating recommendations within their areas of competence and be wary of potential non-epistemic influences. While specifying and discharging these obligations of restraint is not straightforward, the division of labour in times of public health emergencies should be informed by epistemic humility, due weight of expert-scientific findings, and a mindful approach to communicating both the best available science and public health recommendations.[11]

Suggestions for further reading

- Brownson, Ross C., Elizabeth A. Baker, Terry L. Leet, Kathleen N. Gillespie and William R. True (eds) (2011), *Evidence-Based Public Health*, 2nd edn, New York: Oxford University Press.
- Crease, Robert P. and Evan Selinger (eds) (2006), *The Philosophy of Expertise*, New York: Columbia University Press.
- Oreskes, Naomi (2019), *Why Trust Science*, Oxford and Princeton: Princeton University Press.
- Wolfsenberger, Markus and Anthony Wrigley (2019), *Trust in Medicine: Its Nature, Justification, Significance, and Decline*, New York: Cambridge University Press.

Notes

1. Fortunately, all of these claims have been publicly debunked (World Health Organization 2020).
2. Our recommendations here may go beyond public health crises; deferring to expertise may be relevant in similar ways in natural disasters and wars. However, the relevant case here will be public health emergencies.
3. We count politicians among such laypersons if they dabble in matters of expertise. The obligation applies especially in their cases because they are in a prominent position to influence behaviour. As health policy expert Ben Sommers has stated about Trump: 'When the president is calling the guidance wrong and endorsing the view that these public health experts are lying, it makes it incredibly difficult for the public to know what to do' (Olorunnipa 2020).

4. In addition, it is important to understand and internalise individual obligations since regulation can only ever do so much in non-ideal circumstances.

5. A problem resurfaces here as to whether the relatedness of past questions is close *enough* to those regarding COVID-19, given its novelty and the uncertainties surrounding it. Cooke (1991) and Martini (2014) believe that, even for infrequent events, we can find related matters for which expertise has been established, although caution should be exercised. This line of argument seems plausible for COVID-19. Surely, experts on other coronaviruses are more likely to offer valuable input than most others.

6. We are inspired here by John Stuart Mill's claim in *On Liberty*: 'I acknowledge that the tendency of all opinions to become sectarian is not cured by the freest discussion, but is often heightened and exacerbated thereby; the truth which ought to have been, but was not, seen, being rejected all the more violently because proclaimed by persons regarded as opponents. But it is not on the impassioned partisan, it is on the calmer and more disinterested bystander, that this collision of opinions works its salutary effect' (Mill 2003: 117).

7. Compelling objections may be raised that these measures weren't precautionary enough. Macer (2020: 129) states that it took the WHO until April to recommend wearing face masks.

8. Alternatively, they may merely be complicit with the state using such methods.

9. While other experts should be expected to raise flags when in serious doubt that recommendations are communicated non-transparently or underhandedly, they should be wary about which battles to pick with their opponents. For instance, a heated and long-lasting public debate between two experts about whether adequate social distancing during the COVID-19 pandemic should be 2.1 or 2.2 metres might fuel public sentiment that experts all disagree with each other and that their advice should not be taken all that seriously.

10. It remains debatable, of course, whether the approach was fitting for Sweden either. See Trägårdh and Özkırımlı (2020).

11. Lovro Savić gratefully acknowledges financial support from the Wellcome Trust Doctoral Studentship in Humanities and Social Science; grant reference number: 212764/Z/18/Z. We thank Fay Niker, Aveek Bhattacharya, Jeff Howard, Paul Billingham, Tom Parr, Rebecca Lowe, Ivan Cerovac and Elvio Baccarini for their helpful and insightful comments and suggestions during the writing of this chapter.

References

Agoramoorthy, G., M.J. Hsu and P. Shieh (2020), 'Queries on the COVID-19 quick publishing ethics', *Bioethics*, 34 (6): 633–4.

Angner, E. (2020), 'Epistemic humility–knowing your limits in a pandemic', *Behavioral Scientist*, 13 April. Available online: https://behavioralscientist.org/

epistemic-humility-coronavirus-knowing-your-limits-in-a-pandemic/ (accessed 12 June 2020).

Cerovac, I. (2016), 'The role of experts in a democratic society', *Journal of Education Culture and Society*, 7 (2): 75–88.

Chotiner, I. (2020), 'The contrarian coronavirus theory that informed the Trump administration', *The New Yorker*, 30 March. Available online: https://www. newyorker.com/news/q-and-a/the-contrarian-coronavirus-theory-that-informed-the-trump-administration (accessed 25 June 2020).

Christiano, T. (2012), 'Rational deliberation among experts and citizens', in J. Parkinson and J. Mansbridge (eds), *Deliberative Systems: Deliberative Democracy at the Large Scale*, Cambridge: Cambridge University Press: 27–51.

Cooke, R.M. (1991), 'Experts in uncertainty: opinion and subjective probability in science', New York: Oxford University Press.

Goldman, A.I. (2001), 'Experts: which ones should you trust?', *Philosophy and Phenomenological Research*, 63 (1): 85–110.

Gostin, L.O., J.W. Sapsin, S.P. Teret et al. (2002), 'The model state emergency health powers act: planning for and response to bioterrorism and naturally occurring infectious diseases', *Journal of the American Medical Association*, 288 (5): 622–8.

Herington, J., A. Dawson and H. Draper (2014), 'Obesity, liberty, and public health emergencies', *Hastings Center Report*, 44 (6): 26–35.

Holst, C. and A. Molander (2017), 'Public deliberation and the fact of expertise: making experts accountable', *Social Epistemology*, 31 (3): 235–50.

Hume, D. (2000 [1748]), *An Enquiry Concerning Human Understanding*, ed. T. L. Beauchamp, Oxford: Clarendon Press.

Ivanković, V. (2015), 'Christiano's deliberative expertism and choice architecture', *Anali Hrvatskog politološkog društva*, 12 (1): 79–97.

Macer, D. (2020), 'Wearing masks in COVID-19 pandemic, the precautionary principle, and the relationships between individual responsibility and group solidarity', *Eubios Journal of Asian and International Bioethics*, 30 (4): 129–32.

Martini, C. (2014), 'Experts in science: a view from the trenches', *Synthese*, 191: 3–15.

Mill, J.S. (2003), *On Liberty*, ed. D. Bromwich and G. Kateb, New York: Yale University Press.

Olorunnipa, T. (2020), 'Trump cites game show host on pandemic while undercutting doctors and questioning their expertise', *The Washington Post*, 14 July. Available online: https://www.washingtonpost.com/politics/trump-cites-game-show-host-on-pandemic-while-undercutting-doctors-and-questioning-their-expertise/2020/07/13/a083ea5c-c51f-11ea-8ffe-372be8d82298_story.html (accessed 17 July 2020).

Prijić-Samaržija, S. (2017), 'The role of experts in a democratic decision-making process', *Etica & Politica*, 19 (2): 229–46.

Reality Check Team (2020), 'Coronavirus: Trump's disinfectant and sunlight claims fact-checked', *BBC News*, 24 April. Available online: https://www.bbc.co.uk/news/world-us-canada-52399464 (accessed 15 May 2020).

Stewart, H. (2020), 'Neil Ferguson: UK coronavirus adviser resigns after breaking lockdown rules', *The Guardian*, 5 May. Available online: https://www.theguardian.com/uk-news/2020/may/05/uk-coronavirus-adviser-prof-neil-ferguson-resigns-after-breaking-lockdown-rules (accessed 21 October 2020).

Trägårdh, L. and U. Özkırımlı (2020), 'Why might Sweden's Covid-19 policy work? Trust between citizens and state', *The Guardian*, 21 April. Available online: https://www.theguardian.com/world/commentisfree/2020/apr/21/sweden-covid-19-policy-trust-citizens-state (accessed 6 October 2020).

Walton, N.D. (1989), 'Reasoned use of expertise in argumentation', *Argumentation*, 3: 59–73.

World Health Organization (2020), 'Coronavirus disease (COVID-19) advice for the public: Mythbusters'. Available online: https://www.who.int/emergencies/diseases/novel-coronavirus-2019/advice-for-public/myth-busters (accessed 16 May 2020).

CHAPTER 16

SHOULD WE SHAME THOSE WHO IGNORE SOCIAL DISTANCING GUIDELINES?

Paul Billingham and Tom Parr

Introduction

A notable feature of contemporary society is the prevalence of public shaming, especially online. This practice involves calling out perceived wrongdoing and subjecting the perpetrators to public censure, for example by posting, sharing, and liking descriptions, photos, or videos of their actions. Both high-profile figures and ordinary individuals can find themselves the subject of a 'Twitterstorm' due to their alleged transgressions, whether perpetuated online or offline. This often has serious consequences for their public reputation, mental health, and sometimes even employment.[1]

The COVID-19 crisis has provided new opportunities for public shaming, with social media becoming flooded with posts excoriating those who are seen to breach the rules of 'social distancing'. For the purposes of this chapter, we understand this term somewhat loosely to refer to the full range of public health guidelines that are associated with the COVID pandemic. Accordingly, it encompasses not only the directive to remain physically distant from others, but also the requirement to wash one's hands regularly and thoroughly, to wear a face covering when appropriate, and to self-isolate if symptoms develop.[2]

All over the internet and from many corners of the world, images have been shared of individuals attending raves or parties, sunbathing at crowded beaches, or failing to wear a mask on public transport (including on aeroplanes), often using the hashtag #COVIDIOTS. Even the authorities got in on the action. For example, in the UK, Derbyshire Police released drone footage of hikers in the Peak District contravening the demands of lockdown (see BBC News 2020a), and the Commissioner of the Metropolitan Police Service in London claimed that shoppers should be shamed into complying with the requirement to wear a face covering in a store (BBC News 2020b).

The BBC even ran an article offering advice on 'how to go for a walk safely, without getting shamed' (Cheung 2020).

What is particularly striking is that the social norms concerning social distancing emerged almost overnight. As lockdowns were implemented, the majority of the population were suddenly expected to spend almost all of their time at home, venturing out for only a handful of reasons, and being careful to maintain appropriate distance from others when they did. Even as lockdowns ease, new norms emerge, such as the requirement to wear a face covering in various public spaces. The online public shaming of those deemed to breach the relevant rules started almost immediately, reflecting the way in which this practice has become one of the go-to responses to perceived wrongdoing in contemporary society.

We think there are sound reasons to be critical of, and indeed deeply troubled by, the increasing prevalence of online public shaming, including social distancing shaming. The practice of holding individuals up for public vilification and rebuke is not one that we should engage in lightly, especially using the unpredictable and uncontrollable media of the internet. The oft-used language of the 'Twitter mob' and 'pile-on' aptly captures the conduct of many participants, as well as the feelings of attack experienced by the targets. Furthermore, those who engage in public shaming are often more interested in bolstering their own moral credentials through virtue-signalling and grandstanding than in correcting bad behaviour, still less entering into genuine moral debate.[3] The shaming of those who violate social distancing rules provides a helpful illustration of many of these reasons for concern, or so we will argue in this chapter.

If we are right about the prevalence of unjustifiable public shaming, both in relation to social distancing and more generally, then this raises the question of what we ought to do in response. One possibility is that social media organisations have duties to enact policies that make it harder for the snowball effect of mass public shaming to occur, in a similar vein to the policies that Jeffrey Howard discusses in relation to misinformation in his chapter in this volume. We will not consider this here, but we hope to explore it in future work.

The appeal and constraints of public shaming

Though we have serious reservations about the justifiability of public shaming, this is not to say that the practice has nothing going for it. Most importantly, it can be an effective mechanism for enforcing and strengthening morally authoritative social norms, including those that are not or should not be legally enforced, for either principled or pragmatic reasons. In particular, we can identify the following three valuable functions that public shaming can serve.[4]

First, it can *communicate* our condemnation of norm-violating behaviour, to both the wrongdoer and the victim. In the best-case scenario, this will prompt the target of public shaming to recognise that she has acted wrongly and to respond to this fact appropriately, say by apologising. Even where this is not the case, public shaming might represent an attractive means by which to affirm the rights of victims of wrongdoing and to demonstrate our solidarity with those individuals.

Second, it can *deter* the future violation of morally authoritative social norms by both the target of public shaming and others who would otherwise be tempted to act similarly. It can thus increase levels of compliance with the norm. This is because individuals are less likely to contravene social norms if they believe they will be sanctioned by others for doing so. Though there are few studies of this effect, the available empirical evidence lends support to this hypothesis. For example, a recent study reveals how public shaming a firm with low health and safety standards can lead it and similar firms in the local vicinity to improve their practices, resulting in significantly fewer workplace injuries (Johnson 2020).

Third, it can provide a means through which to *express* our commitment to the norm that was violated, and to the values that it promotes or respects. This is instrumentally valuable in so far as these expressions strengthen our affirmation of the norm. There might also be cases when such expression is intrinsically valuable, since it can itself be a fitting response to serious moral wrongdoing.

With these three roles in mind, it is clear what is distinctively appealing about *public* shaming. Most obviously, though privately criticising someone might make it more likely that she comes to recognise the error of her ways, this method is much less likely to be an effective *deterrent* to future norm violations (either by the target or by others). This is both because private criticism tends to impose fewer burdens than public shaming and because others might not be aware of its existence, and so not deterred from violating similar norms. Additionally, if an individual is to *communicate* her condemnation of norm-violating behaviour to the wider community and/or to *express* her commitment to the value of the norm that was violated, then it is essential that her response is public rather than private. In other words, viewed in its best light, public shaming is part of a practice of public accountability, in which individuals openly hold one another responsible for norm violations in a way that serves these three morally valuable purposes.

Many of these attractions arise with respect to social distancing shaming. Certainly, social distancing norms are morally authoritative, in the sense that individuals have duties to comply with them. Furthermore, states cannot always legally enforce compliance with these duties, and perhaps they ought not to do so in some cases. Public shaming therefore emerges as a potentially attractive alternative means by which to strengthen these norms, in ways that serve the purposes that we have identified.

Nonetheless, for it to be justifiable there are several demanding constraints that public shaming must overcome (Billingham and Parr 2020b, 2020c). First, it must be *proportionate*, meaning that its negative consequences are not excessive in comparison with its positive consequences. As we noted above, the targets of public shaming often suffer significant reputational and psychological harms, including distress, humiliation, embarrassment, and shame, and sometimes also face material costs, such as losing their jobs. The negative consequences can be considerable, such that the positive consequences – in terms of serving the functions that we have identified – must also be sizeable if shaming is to be proportionate. Second, it must be *necessary*, meaning that there is no less harmful way to achieve its ends. Third, while drawing attention to the conduct of norm violators, public shaming must respect individuals' rights to *privacy*. Fourth, it must be *non-abusive*. Finally, it must not permanently stigmatise its target but must make *reintegration* possible.

If public shaming violates any of these constraints then it is unjustifiable, since it imposes unjustified harms and/or violates other rights of its target. These constraints are not easily met, especially online, where the conduct of shamers and the impact on the shamed is very difficult to control. It is on this basis that we conclude that a great proportion of online public shaming is unjustified.[5]

We analyse these constraints and make this argument regarding online shaming in detail elsewhere (Billingham and Parr 2020b). We will not rehearse that material here, and nor will we simply apply the constraints in a mechanical way to social distancing shaming. Instead, our aim in the rest of this chapter is to zero in on those features of the COVID-19 context that bear especially heavily on the justifiability of publicly shaming those who violate social distancing guidelines.

Indeterminacy and unverifiability

In order for it to be justifiable, normally those who engage in public shaming must be confident that their target acted wrongly, for example by culpably violating a relevant social norm. This is an aspect of proportionality: the burdens imposed on the targets of shaming are disproportionate if those individuals have not acted wrongly, since in that case they are not liable to bear any such burdens.[6] In this section, we focus on two problems that emerge for defenders of social distancing shaming in the light of this idea.

First, culpability requires at least that the individual was able to gain knowledge of the relevant norm and that her conduct breached it in a way that she could have reasonably foreseen. However, it is significant that the precise content of the social norms that regulate conduct during a pandemic is far from obvious, both shortly after its outbreak and even long past that point. Some things are clearly out of the question, such as a house party with friends, or indeed a 'COVID rave' (see BBC News 2020c). But what about resting on a bench or playing a game of football with your kids in the park during a period of strict lockdown? What about going to sit in your parents' front garden? What if it is your father's birthday (Forrest 2020)? Even well-meaning individuals sincerely and reasonably disagree about where to draw the line. Since government guidelines are never perfectly precise, there is likely to remain a range of activities whose permissibility is not clear-cut. Because of this, it is easy to end up shaming those who are complying with social distancing rules, as they reasonably understand them. We call this the *problem of indeterminacy*.

Second, even in cases where the content of the norms is clear and widely known, it can be tricky to know if others have violated their demands. This is because what we can know about others' lives via a momentary observation is highly limited. Those who pack themselves onto public transport when 'stay at home' orders are in place might be healthcare workers on their way to the hospital. A group of youngsters having fun in a park could be a household getting their daily exercise. And a woman not wearing a mask on public transport or in a shop could be a rape or sexual abuse survivor for whom covering her face could trigger debilitating flashbacks (Ferguson 2020). While we were writing this chapter, a teenager on a train was verbally abused for briefly removing her face covering – yet she was doing so to allow her deafblind sister to read her lips (PA Media 2020). The concern here is not that the content of the social norms is indeterminate. The issue is that it can be difficult to verify others' compliance with a norm, even when its content is not in doubt. For this reason, it is easy to end up shaming those who are in fact complying or who have a sound excuse for not complying. We call this the *problem of unverifiability*.

The problem of indeterminacy emerges because it may be unclear whether an individual has culpably violated a social norm, due to ambiguities within the norm itself. The problem of unverifiability emerges because we may be unable to tell whether an individual has culpably violated a social norm, even when that norm is clear. This pair of concerns arises not only in the case of social distancing shaming, but in many other cases as well. For instance, let us consider the case of Justine Sacco, who, on her way from New York to Cape Town to visit family, tweeted 'Going to Africa. Hope I don't get AIDS. Just kidding. I'm white!' (Ronson 2015: 63–77). Many observers judged Sacco's remarks as racist, leading to a barrage of online criticism and abuse. But she had intended her tweet as an ironic comment about the attitudes of middle-class white Americans towards AIDS, which was meant to amuse her small number of Twitter followers.[7] No doubt, Sacco's tweet was misjudged. But it is far from clear that this makes her culpable, and much less clear still that others could reliably know this to be the case.

Put in more general terms, there is reasonable disagreement concerning the precise demands of many social norms, and we should not be too quick to condemn others based on our specific understanding of the norms – especially when this involves publicly calling on others to join us in this condemnation. And even when norms themselves are clear, our perceptions of whether others have violated them, based on a single photo, tweet, or report, are far from fully reliable. Public shamers frequently misunderstand and misinterpret the actions of their targets.[8]

Wide proportionality and other constraints

Of course, in emergency situations, the moral costs of imposing burdens on those who are not liable might seem rather minor in comparison with the significant benefits that public shaming promises. Strengthening social distancing norms could arguably save thousands of lives. Perhaps, therefore, the risk of public shaming that misses the target is a price we should be willing to pay. We can express this thought more precisely by distinguishing two types of proportionality. While *narrow proportionality* focuses on the burdens imposed on the target of public shaming, *wide proportionality* takes into account the full range of positive and negative consequences. Public shaming that imposes on its target burdens beyond those that she is liable to bear – for example, because she has not in fact acted wrongly – is narrowly disproportionate. But such shaming can nonetheless be justifiable if it is widely proportionate: if its overall positive consequences vastly outweigh its negative consequences. The argument under consideration thus claims that social distancing shaming is widely proportionate even if it is narrowly disproportionate.

The success of this argument depends on empirical questions that are hard to answer. Presumably, the claimed positive consequences come in the form of higher levels of compliance with social distancing guidelines, such that the spread of the virus slows and fewer individuals contract it. It is certainly possible that shaming does have these consequences, but it is very difficult to know for sure, especially with respect to any individual instance. Consequently, there is a clear risk of imposing costs on individuals for which they are not liable, or that exceed those to which they are liable, in the name of a mistaken sense that this is promoting a wider public good. Twitter mobs often feel that they are righteously advancing a just cause by making an example of their targets, but it is usually far from clear that this is in fact the case.

It is worth noting the contrast here between the *ex ante* and *ex post* perspectives on an instance of public shaming. *Ex post*, we can judge the proportionality of an act in the light of lots of information about the negative and positive consequences that resulted. *Ex ante*, when individuals are considering whether to engage in acts of shaming, they must make their decisions based on expectations of the consequences, which typically involves a high level of uncertainty. They must certainly take into account the risk that things will get out of hand, and the higher the risk is, the more difficult it is to justify the shaming. Indeed, our ignorance as to whether any instance of social distancing shaming will in fact be narrowly or widely proportionate should make us cautious, such that we might have reservations about the conduct of those who engage in shaming even when it happens to work out well. This suggestion leads us into complicated questions about the ethics of acting in the face of risk, which we do not have space to address here. But one's views on those questions will influence one's view on when individuals were justified in engaging in acts of shaming, given the available evidence about the associated risks.

As we noted above, other moral constraints also apply to public shaming, the violation of which make it unjustifiable even when it is proportionate. It must respect rights to privacy, which means that it must not publicise either irrelevant or highly sensitive facts about the norm violator's life or past. It must be non-abusive, which means that it must not involve threats of violence, demeaning insults and mockery, or attacks on the norm violator on the basis of socially salient characteristics, such as their race or sex. And it must aim at, and make possible, the violator's reintegration into the community, rather than permanently stigmatising them or marking them with an inferior status.[9]

These requirements raise particular concerns when shaming is carried out online, and thus potentially seen by an audience of many thousands. Even if the initial shamer respects these constraints, she may be unable to control the comments or actions of others who participate in or respond to the shaming. This fact raises additional concerns about proportionality, with respect to the magnitude of the costs imposed on the target.[10] But, as numerous examples show, it also often leads to the violation of other constraints. Such violations are wearily familiar, with targets subjected to extensive abuse and having personal information publicised. In the worst cases, an individual may reasonably experience a sense of exclusion from the moral community, such that she feels that she is a social pariah who is permanently tainted in others' eyes and thus unable to be seen as a member of the public in good standing. These things can render public shaming unjustifiable even setting aside concerns relating to culpability and proportionality. Individuals must also factor the likelihood of these occurrences into their *ex ante* judgements about whether to engage in acts of shaming.

Public shaming is more likely to avoid these outcomes when it is not targeted at identifiable individuals, but instead involves images of groups of unidentifiable norm violators. The Derbyshire police force faced well-justified criticism for their video footage, to which several of the concerns that we have raised apply. But they did at least maintain their targets' anonymity by blurring faces where necessary. This better respects privacy, protects individuals from targeted abuse, and is less stigmatising. Such shaming can alert viewers to the norm and might deter further violations, without directly shaming specific individuals. Still, this certainly does not mean that it is necessarily justifiable overall, since concerns about both proportionality and necessity still apply.

Conclusion: is shaming just a distraction?

Rather than rehearse our main findings, we conclude by commenting on a broader concern about the practice of public shaming in the current political context, namely that it may be a distraction from the work of holding our governments to account by scrutinising their decisions and conduct throughout a crisis.

To illustrate, let us take an extreme and perhaps surprising example. In May 2020, Dominic Cummings, Prime Minister Boris Johnson's chief advisor, was attacked online for travelling to Durham at the height of lockdown and for some of his activities while there, such as his infamous trip to Barnard Castle (see Reality Check Team 2020). Given Cummings's prominent role and his questionable conduct, plausibly this is a case where public shaming meets all of the relevant moral constraints and so was justifiable, even though it was individualised and non-anonymous.

Nonetheless, we worry that the extensive media attention given to incidents such as these risks distracting the general public from arguably more important issues, such as the government's handling of a pandemic. Given the limited nature of our time and attention, and indeed the scarce space on newspaper front pages, there is always an opportunity cost to focusing on whether specific individuals are complying with the rules. Our point is not that we feel a great deal of sympathy for Cummings or that we regard him a victim of serious mistreatment. Rather, our concern is that it can be a mistake to focus on instances of individual misconduct at the expense of putting pressure on governments to enact appropriate policies.

Stephen Reicher, an advisor to the UK and Scottish governments, neatly and even-handedly summarises this worry with public shaming as follows:

> All in all, while it is certainly true that individuals need to act responsibly and be held accountable for their actions, it is equally true that covidiots on a plane are a dangerous distraction. The problems in this pandemic are less to do with the inadequacies of individual psychology than systemic failures in the government response. And while it might suit some to focus our attention on the former, it will only make it harder for us to get out of the mess we are in.
>
> *Reicher 2020*

Critics might push back, insisting that there can be cases in which public shaming is not a mere distraction. Perhaps this is true of the shaming of Cummings. After all, the episode shone a spotlight on the attitudes and conduct of a high-profile figure within government who pioneered some of its headline policies. For what it's worth, we are sceptical of this defence of the public shaming of Cummings, or at least that it can justify the prolonged coverage that the story received, with newspaper front pages devoted to it for several days running. But little hangs on this for our purposes. Even if *this* instance of public shaming were appropriate, surely there are many others whose wisdom cannot be salvaged in this way.

Once again, this point generalises to cases beyond COVID-19. Even when it comes to crucial moral endeavours, such as the fight against racism, focusing on individual wrongdoing can take attention away from the structural nature of some injustices, failures in government policy, and inadequate responses by businesses and other large organisations. This is not to say that public shaming is never an appropriate response, but only to highlight that it can have considerable opportunity costs. This is true even in cases where the other concerns we have raised – concerning culpability, proportionality, abuse, privacy, and stigmatisation – have been adequately defused.[11]

Suggestions for further reading

- Billingham, Paul and Tom Parr (2020), 'Enforcing social norms: the morality of public shaming', *European Journal of Philosophy*, 28 (4): 997–1016. This article offers an elaboration and defence of the normative framework used within this chapter.

- Jacquet, Jennifer (2016), *Is Shame Necessary? New Uses for an Old Tool*, London: Penguin. This is an accessible discussion of shaming as a tool to bring about social change, jam-packed with examples and illustrations.

- Ronson, Jon (2015), *So You've Been Publicly Shamed*, London: Picador, 2015. This book tells the stories of many individuals who suffered from public shaming and reflects upon the lessons to be learned from their experiences.

Notes

1. We discuss some of the complications surrounding public shaming and firing employees in Billingham and Parr (2020a).

2. While our conception of social distancing shaming is broad, it does not encompass all COVID-related shaming activities. For example, individuals might be publicly shamed for spreading misinformation, the topic of Jeffrey Howard's chapter in this volume, or for violating the duties of restraint defended in Viktor Ivanković and Lovro Savić's chapter. We do not consider those possibilities here, but we can apply the same normative framework to them.

3. For a philosophical analysis of grandstanding, see Tosi and Warmke (2020).

4. In what follows, we draw on ideas presented in Billingham and Parr (2020b). For a defence of at least certain forms of public shaming, see Jacquet (2016).

5. For other recent critiques of online shaming, see Adkins (2019); Aitchison and Meckled-Garcia (2021); Klonick (2016); and Norlock (2017).

6. More precisely, the burdens are *narrowly* disproportionate. See our discussion below ('Wide proportionality and other constraints').

7. For Sacco's explanation, see Ronson (2015: 69).

8. This is true with respect to many of the stories told in Ronson (2015).

9. Critics might attempt to resist these claims by contending that we can satisfactorily account for the moral significance of some or all of these considerations merely as factors that bear on proportionality, rather than by treating them as independent constraints. We argue against this view in Billingham and Parr (2020b).

10. Importantly, these concerns apply even if the individual is culpable, and thus liable to bear some burdens as a result of their actions.

11. For helpful comments on earlier versions of this chapter, we owe thanks to Aveek Bhattacharya, Jeff Howard, Fay Niker, Tony Taylor, and the participants in a workshop on 'Speech and (Mis)information' in August 2020.

References

Adkins, K. (2019), 'When shaming is shameful: double standards in online shame backlashes', *Hypatia*, 34 (1): 76–97.

Aitchison, G. and S. Meckled-Garcia (2021), 'Against online public shaming: ethical problems with mass social media', *Social Theory and Practice*, 47 (1): 1–31.

BBC News (2020a), 'Coronavirus: Peak District drone police criticised for "'lockdown shaming"', 27 March. Available online: https://www.bbc.co.uk/news/uk-england-derbyshire-52055201 (accessed 24 September 2020).

BBC News (2020b), 'London police to enforce face masks as "last resort"', 22 July. Available online: https://www.bbc.co.uk/news/uk-england-london-53498100 (accessed 24 September 2020).

BBC News (2020c), 'Coronavirus: Inside the secret Covid rave scene', 3 July. Available online: https://www.bbc.co.uk/news/av/uk-53283351 (accessed 24 September 2020).

Billingham, P. and T. Parr (2020a), 'A sackable offence? Employers' responses to public shaming', *Ethical War Blog*, 9 July. Available online: http://stockholmcentre.org/a-sackable-offence-employers-responses-to-public-shaming/ (accessed 24 September 2020).

Billingham, P. and T. Parr (2020b), 'Enforcing social norms: the morality of public shaming', *European Journal of Philosophy*, 28 (4): 997–1016.

Billingham, P. and T. Parr (2020c), 'Online public shaming: virtues and vices', *Journal of Social Philosophy*, 51 (3): 371–90.

Cheung, H. (2020), 'Coronavirus: how to go for a walk safely, without getting shamed', *BBC News*, 25 March. Available online: https://www.bbc.co.uk/news/world-us-canada-52022743 (accessed 24 September 2020).

Ferguson, D. (2020), 'Rape survivors say they are being stigmatised for not wearing masks', *The Guardian*, 10 August. Available online: https://www.theguardian.com/society/2020/aug/10/survivors-say-they-are-being-stigmatised-for-not-wearing-masks (accessed 24 September 2020).

Forrest, A. (2020), 'Coronavirus: Stephen Kinnock issued warning by police after MP pays father Neil birthday visit', *The Independent*, 30 March. Available online: https://www.independent.co.uk/news/uk/politics/coronavirus-stephen-kinnock-labour-neil-birthday-visit-police-warning-twitter-a9433281.html (accessed 24 September 2020).

Jacquet, J. (2016), *Is Shame Necessary? New Uses for an Old Tool*, London: Penguin.

Johnson, M. (2020), 'Regulation by shaming: deterrence effects of publicizing violations of workplace safety and health laws', *American Economic Review*, 110 (6): 1866–1904.

Klonick, K. (2016), 'Re-shaming the debate: social norms, shame, and regulation in an internet age', *Maryland Law Review*, 75 (4): 1029–65.

Norlock, K. (2017), 'Online shaming', *Social Philosophy Today*, 33: 187–97.

PA Media (2020), 'Deafblind woman and sister verbally abused for lifting mask on train', *The Guardian*, 25 July. Available at: https://www.theguardian.com/society/2020/jul/24/deafblind-woman-and-sister-verbally-abused-for-lifting-mask-on-train (accessed 24 September 2020).

Reality Check Team (2020), 'Dominic Cummings: fact-checking the row', *BBC News*, 30 May. Available online: https://www.bbc.co.uk/news/52828076 (accessed 24 September 2020).

Reicher, S. (2020), 'Don't blame "selfish covidiots". Blame the British government', *The Guardian*, 2 September. Available online: https://www.theguardian.com/commentisfree/2020/sep/02/selfish-covidiots-blame-british-government-greek (accessed 24 September 2020).

Ronson, J. (2015), *So You've Been Publicly Shamed*, London: Picador.

Tosi, J. and B. Warmke (2020), *Grandstanding: The Use and Abuse of Moral Talk*, Oxford: Oxford University Press.

PART V
CRISIS AND JUSTICE

CHAPTER 17
HARNESSING THE EPISTEMIC VALUE OF CRISES FOR JUST ENDS
Matthew Adams and Fay Niker

Introduction

The negative effects of the pandemic upon individuals and societies across the world have been vast and wide-ranging. Most obviously, at the time of writing, over a million people have lost their lives due to the virus and millions of others have lost their jobs.[1] Tragically, these figures are set to continue rising. At the same time, one interesting aspect of the public debate over the COVID-19 crisis is the extent to which it has been infused with a sense of hope and renewal, in spite of these terrible events. There is a tangible sense that this deep rupture to 'business as usual' brings with it opportunities to forge a new and better social world.

Looking back over history, the author and political activist Arundhati Roy notes that pandemics tend to force humans 'to break with the past and imagine their world anew' (Roy 2020: 214). The COVID-19 pandemic, she claims, is no different: 'It is a portal, a gateway between one world and the next' (ibid.). Roy's metaphor of a portal is evocative. But it raises a number of questions. How exactly do crises provide an opportunity for such change? And how should we take advantage of such opportunities? In this chapter we try to sketch some answers to these important questions. In particular, our aim is twofold: first, to give a partial philosophical explanation of why crises can induce rational optimism; and second, on the basis of this, to examine how individuals might permissibly act to persuade others of the merits of understanding the lessons of and necessary policy responses to the crisis in a particular way. We begin by locating more precisely the grounds for this hope in renewal, arguing that it rests primarily in the fact that crises perform the epistemic function of transforming at least some people's social and political worldview. Drawing on interdisciplinary literature on salience and nudging, we go on to explore how this epistemic function might be enhanced using direct and indirect means, and discuss some psychological and ethical concerns, respectively, that may lie therein.

A couple of clarifications are in order before we get started. First, we do not presuppose that crises only provide opportunities for social progress; social and democratic backsliding are also, lamentably, a possible and actual historical outcome. This fact partly motivates our discussion about harnessing the epistemic value of crises. Second, although we focus on the epistemic function that crises perform, we do not think this is the only means of political change that they make available. Indeed, we remain neutral about whether crises facilitate far more radical opportunities, such as suspending standard judicial and democratic procedures, in order to realise a more just world.[2] We put these possibilities to one side in this chapter because they raise very general questions about issues such as democratic legitimacy. Furthermore, even if more radical and morally troubling options may be deemed permissible in an all-things-considered sense, they surely are far from optimal.

Locating the grounds for hope

What grounds the hope in renewal that has, to some extent, marked the debate over the COVID-19 crisis? We think there are two main sources.

The first source is the simple fact that the 'disruptions to societal routines and expectations' wrought by crises 'open up political space for actors inside and outside government to redefine issues, propose policy innovations and organisational reforms, gain popularity and strike at opponents' (Boin, 't Hart and McConnell 2009: 82). Such ruptures and dislocations to the *status quo* can, but do not necessarily, translate into significant political and policy change. Of course, this raises complex empirical questions, such as the degree to which and the causal reasons for which crises provide opportunities for social progress.[3] Given our present purposes, we simply note the socially and politically transformative potential of crises – a potential to which the origin of the word 'crisis' itself testifies: the English word, deriving from the Latin *krisis* ('decision'), has been used to mean 'decisive point' or 'turning point' since the early seventeenth century.

The second source is the transformative effect that such societal-level disruptions can have on how individual citizens understand their social world. The lived experience of the COVID-19 crisis – including the sense of threat and uncertainty it has induced and the enforced changes to all our lives it has caused – can have a profound impact on a person's understanding of the world around them and her place within it. In her reflections on this revelatory potential of the pandemic, the writer Zadie Smith draws on an analogy with post-Second World War Britain when she observes that a crisis, such as a world war or a global pandemic:

> transforms its participants. What was once necessary appears inessential; what was taken for granted, unappreciated and abused now reveals itself to be central to our existence.
>
> *Smith 2020: 14–15*

The idea of something that previously appeared inessential somehow revealing its hitherto concealed value (or vice versa) is suggestive. But how exactly does such a transformation occur, and how does it apply to a crisis like COVID-19 *per se*? Thankfully, we can draw on philosophical theory in order to build up a clearer understanding of both of these questions. As a first point of call, consider what L.A. Paul describes as *transformative experience*:

> When a person has a new and different kind of experience, a kind of experience that teaches her something she could not have learned without having that kind of experience, she has an *epistemic transformation*. Her knowledge of what something is like, and thus her subjective point of view, changes. With this new experience, she gains new abilities to cognitively entertain certain contents, she learns to understand things in a new way, and she may even gain new information.
>
> *Paul 2014: 10–11*

Paul's essential claim is that certain experiences can perform the epistemic function of transforming people's understanding of the world in significant, even if in specific rather than complete, ways.

The experiences forced on us by the COVID-19 crisis have engendered, or at least provided opportunities for, such epistemic transformations. For example, the governmental classification of 'essential' or 'key' workers during lockdown periods has revealed the gap between many of those we consider to be essential to the functioning of society, on the one hand, and how we value – in terms of recognition and recompense – these people's work, on the other. This revelation has changed some people's viewpoint, as Zadie Smith observes: 'People thank God for "essential" workers they once considered lowly, who not so long ago they despised for wanting fifteen bucks an hour' (Smith 2020: 15).

To see how such a process could work from a particular person's perspective, imagine a relatively privileged person called Zoe. Prior to the crisis, Zoe invests little effort in contemplating the predicament of certain workers. Insofar as she thinks about them at all, she thinks about them in relation to the economic function they perform for her; consequently, she resents their desire to receive more compensation for performing such a function. But during the crisis she comes to appreciate her own vulnerability and indeed her own dependence on certain workers – particularly when this is highlighted by the fact that the government classifies such workers as 'essential'. This vulnerability makes her more attentive to these workers and their interests as people. This generates a fundamental epistemic shift in her perspective: she doesn't merely recognise her own vulnerability and dependence. Rather, she becomes aware of and sympathetic to *their* interests, including the risks they are incurring in performing their essential role during this time. Essentially, the transformation starts from seeing them as serving a function, then recognising her dependence on them, and then – because of such recognition – appreciating their value independent of her own interests. This warms her up to policies that could improve their predicament, not merely facilitate the economic function that they perform for her with greater ease and efficiency.

This example highlights that the relevant epistemic transformation takes place relative to the beliefs and knowledge of *particular* individuals. To be sure, the fact that certain workers are fundamental to the smooth and productive functioning of our society may already be known in a theoretical sense, having been demonstrated by researchers, for example. But an epistemic transformation – or at least an epistemic shift – still occurs when such knowledge becomes integrated into a particular individual's worldview.[4]

There are numerous other examples, in which essentially the same phenomena as the case of Zoe occur. Consider, for instance, the action that governments have taken to house rough sleepers in empty apartment blocks and hotels in order to prevent the spread of the virus. This action has starkly exposed the lack of political will to house the homeless in normal times. Seeing this reality has changed some people's view on whether we can simply go back to not providing for this group of vulnerable people after the pandemic – especially as more people will become homeless as the full economic effects of this crisis come to be felt. Similarly, the experience of living through lockdown has led some to better appreciate the value and difficulty of caring for children or elderly relatives all day. This experience has caused a change in their beliefs concerning how household and care-based tasks ought to be distributed (see Gheaus, this volume). Both of these examples involve a fundamental epistemic shift in perspective at the level of individual citizens, with the potential for bringing about social and political change if it occurs across a wide enough portion of the population.

Readers may resonate with one or more of these examples or have examples of their own. What we are interested in here is the more general idea that crises perform an important *epistemic function*, revealing to people that (some aspect of) the current system is untenable and needs reform. In virtue of this, crises like the COVID-19 pandemic can make socially just policies – that otherwise could not have been implemented – feasible. The reason for distinguishing the two sources of optimism in this section, then, is because the question we wish to take up concerns the relations between them: how might the epistemic value of a crisis (i.e. the second source) be enhanced or amplified so as to make the most of the opportunities for significant political and policy change that it has opened up (i.e. the first source) for the purpose of bringing about a more just society?

Direct salience-raising measures

One way into considering how this value might be harnessed is, somewhat ironically, to reflect on its limitations. Only a subset of any actual population will have their social outlook appropriately changed in the light of the pandemic and the injustices exposed by their society's response to it. There is another subset whose worldview will remain fixed and resolute in the wake of it – or worse, will be transformed into support for more radically unjust policies like unwarranted military intervention or xenophobic policies. The fact that it is unrealistic to expect any crisis to transform everyone's outlook in the appropriate sense raises the question as to what actions we can and should undertake in an attempt to expand the reach of its epistemically transformative potential.

The case of Zoe shows that, whether the government intended or even might have wanted this to be the case, its designation of certain workers as 'essential' caused particular features of our social structure to become salient. As a psychological matter, something is salient if it is prominent or otherwise noticeable as compared with its surroundings. In this case, social facts about who Zoe is dependent on (not just during the pandemic, but in normal times too) were given prominence in a way that captured her attention and, via a process something like the one described above, brought about an epistemic shift in Zoe. Individuals who support socially just policies might seek to perform a function that is somewhat analogous to the state's designation of key workers – by making certain social facts and injustices salient to other people in order to instigate or influence these people's personal reflection on the crisis. Of course, attending to some relevant social fact does not necessarily mean that an epistemic transformation will occur. Indeed, this insight will have important implications for our analysis below. But we assume that at least some kinds of salience-raising measures make such transformations more likely.

The most natural suggestion is that such individuals should engage in efforts to make certain facts *directly* salient to others in the target group; for instance, by writing op-eds and blog posts, or using social media to amplify certain perspectives and findings, such as the racial disparities in the negative effects of COVID-19 (see Wolff and de-Shalit, this volume). Relatedly, perhaps, people should become involved in political action of various kinds. For instance, individuals can take part in large-scale coordinated actions like civil disobedience that perform the communicative function of making the questions and concerns raised by the crisis as clear and hard to avoid as possible within society. There are good justifications for such action (e.g. Brownlee 2012); though in the specific case of COVID-19, some of the standard forms of protest – namely those comprised of large gatherings – are ruled out, or at least are much more controversial, on public health grounds. Nonetheless, there are safe ways of engaging in coordinated action: Build Back Better, for example, is coordinating local organising, virtual rallies and the production of persuasive resources that can be shared with others.[5]

Such direct expressions of particular convictions, on either an individual or a political level, are central to democratic life and are uncontroversial actions that individuals may undertake. But there are reasons to doubt that such actions will achieve their desired effect among those in the target group. One reason for this relates to the property of salience itself. The philosopher Bernard Williams captures the key insight in this way: 'features of [a person's] environment display salience, relevance, and so on, particularly in light of what [one] sees as valuable' (Williams 2010: 82). Williams's essential point is that the core values that people hold act almost as a kind of perceptual filter. Consequently, we must consider how the subset of people whose outlook is not directly affected by the crisis are likely to view such direct expressions by other individuals. Bluntly put: if the values that they hold prevent them from seeing what has been revealed or further exposed by the crisis, then they (or at least most of them) are unlikely to change their minds in response to other citizens directly expressing their different reaction to the crisis.

Indeed, recent work in psychology has shown not only that attempts to persuade people in this direct sense are much less effective than expected, but that they may in fact prove counterproductive. The problem with these forms of salience-raising efforts, according to this research, is that they are the most susceptible to 'backfire effects'. A significant body of evidence shows not only that giving people strong arguments often fails to change their minds if people are motivated to reject the evidence (e.g. if it challenges some element of their existing worldview), but that such arguments can cause these people's views to become *more entrenched* than they previously were (e.g. Nyhan and Reifler 2010, 2015; Peter and Koch 2016).

These findings do not necessarily rule out the value of direct salience-raising measures. But they do highlight that such actions are likely to affect, in the sense of facilitating some kind of epistemic shift, only those people who are already somewhat predisposed to accept a particular view on account of their existing worldview. In her characterisation, L.A. Paul is clear to state that, 'For any epistemic transformation, the degree of epistemic change depends on how much the person already knows, and on the type of experience that is involved' (Paul 2014: 11). So, a person could come to know or appreciate something more deeply, to gain additional information or insight, as a result of reading an op-ed or listening to another person's experiences. The degree of epistemic change may be less in these cases, but we should not underestimate the potential ripple effects, politically speaking, of such changes. Yet, if we are to take the findings relating to backfire effects seriously, we need to acknowledge the limits – and perhaps even the negative consequences – of addressing these direct measures to some members of our target group.

Indirect salience-raising measures

This leads us to consider more *indirect* ways of trying to get people to notice and take account of what the COVID-19 crisis, and our response to it, has revealed about unjust features of our societies – or to put it another way, to make people more responsive to the evidence, as it were, that has been offered in favour of more socially progressive policies. One option is provided by a set of persuasive techniques that can be categorised as *epistemic nudges*. Epistemic nudging is defined as 'the act of intentionally making use of one's understanding of the cognitive processes and psychology of others in order to encourage them to form, retain and/or give up certain beliefs [or] epistemic dispositions', while not precluding them from retaining or forming non-preferred beliefs or dispositions (Smith 2021: 151).[6] So epistemic nudges steer people towards seeing things in a particular way, rather than directly confronting them with ideological convictions or challenges. Can this kind of influence be used in attempts to facilitate an epistemic shift in others?

Arguably the most obvious way that epistemic nudging might alter how a person sees a situation is by adjusting salience; for instance, 'by providing relevant information via a means that can be more easily noticed, absorbed, and interpreted' by those one wishes to influence (Niker 2018: 159; see also Noggle 2018). Epistemic nudges take into account the fact that people's background ideological beliefs influence how they process information. Using findings from the cognitive sciences, they provide a means of presenting evidence in favour of just policies in ways that can make people more responsive to it. How an argument is *framed*, for example, is a factor that can significantly affect how people receive and respond to it. Accordingly, Matthew Feinberg and Robb Willer have recently offered 'moral reframing' as a potential technique for effective and persuasive communication across the political divide.[7] This works by framing a position that a person would normally not support in a way that is consistent with her existing beliefs and values (Feinberg and Willer 2019). The aim is that, by making the reasons provided in the argument more salient to her, this reframing will positively affect the credence she gives to them.

In the context of COVID-19, consider people who resist initiatives such as Build Back Better and in general any type of policy that tries to improve the existing social net. One way of trying to reframe such policies is to present them not as demands of justice that people must accept but as certain demands that they should accept given their own commitments to, for instance, economic stability and prosperity. So, for example, perhaps they can be convinced that policies like universal basic income and improved healthcare should be introduced in order to reduce the likelihood of massive social unrest – even a political breakdown – which would jeopardise their economic interests. The potential change that this type of epistemic nudge can induce is different from the deeper epistemic shift experienced by people like Zoe. Such moral reframing, if successful, does not make people come to appreciate the value of other people in independence of their own interests and values. But a significant shift still occurs in their political outlook. By reframing the situation in this way, it can make certain people come to see the value of, and thus be more open to, political changes that will in fact address some of the injustices and inequalities within their society.

Similarly, a person's response to information – whether she welcomes or rejects it as part of her deliberations – can be affected by *who delivers it*. We give some agents preferential access to influencing our belief-forming and decision-making processes, while we are primed to reject information – even the very same information – if it comes from some other agent. Sometimes expertise provides a reason to 'pre-authorise' another agent, but often the most forceful motivating reason is that we perceive that the other person 'has values, commitments, and goals that are similar to ours – that is, that in some meaningful way they share our worldview' (Niker et al., forthcoming). So, another nudge-style technique is to select mouthpieces for arguments intentionally so as to increase the likelihood that some subset of people will take notice.

Consider the case in the UK, for instance, in which Marcus Rashford – a top Premier League footballer at Manchester United – played a key role in forcing the government to U-turn on its decision not to provide food vouchers to vulnerable children over the summer months. By sharing his story of how his family relied on free school meals when he was growing up, Rashford opened more people's eyes to the reality and extent of child poverty in the UK. Within a short period of time, his campaign had made it politically unviable for the government to continue with its policy, meaning that around 1.3 million children benefited through the COVID Summer Food Fund in 2020.[8] Despite the fact that many others were campaigning for the same result, including education leaders, teachers' unions and the Labour Party, on the basis of well-established scientific evidence, this outcome would have been much less likely if it weren't for Marcus Rashford's intervention.[9]

Rashford's involvement, in itself, may not count as an epistemic nudge; his campaign was so effective because of how starkly it challenged a narrative within Conservative politics that 'poor people are poor because they are lazy'. But perhaps part of why the campaign was so effective at rallying popular support, in addition to Rashford providing a voice for marginalised people within society, was because certain people paid attention to the issue of child poverty *because* Rashford was talking about it. We can also easily imagine that some individuals, in an effort to bolster support for the policy U-turn, may have engaged in epistemic nudging by discussing or sharing Rashford's campaign with specific others *on the basis* of a judgement that his advocacy would make it more likely that their existing beliefs would be challenged or altered – and that this might, in turn, mobilise them to some political action, such as signing a petition to the government.

Both kinds of nudge work by influencing the credibility a person accords to relevant information – in these cases, information relating to the need to maintain or improve some aspect of the existing social net. The advantage of nudge-based salience-raising measures, relative to others discussed in the previous section, is that they are designed to avoid (or at least be less susceptible to producing) backfire effects, given the ways they address themselves to features of a person's existing worldview. But, by virtue of this, they raise some ethical concerns. Some worry, for instance, that these kinds of persuasive techniques are disrespectful because they attempt to manipulate whether and how a person engages with certain information.

There are different ways of cashing out this concern. On the first, critics claim that epistemic nudges 'take advantage of non-rational features of our nature (such as our reliance on . . . the salience of options) to produce their effects' (Levy 2017: 498). Nudges are problematic, according to this line of argument, to the extent that they bypass our capacities for responding to reasons (see e.g. Blumenthal-Barby and Burroughs 2012). But we can respond by claiming that epistemic nudges – at least those that work by adjusting salience – do not bypass our capacities for responding to reasons; rather, they *add* something to the deliberative process, namely the sense that something is important (Noggle 2018: 166). This addition often serves to activate – not bypass – our capacities for responding to reasons. And the reasons we are responding to are, in a relevant sense, our own reasons.

But even if one accepts this, they may still think there is something disrespectful going on because these persuasive techniques are epistemically paternalistic. A practice is epistemically paternalistic when it involves 'interfering with someone's cognitive activities – primarily, with the conduct of their inquiries – with the aim of improving their epistemic position, but without their consent' (McKenna 2020; also see Ahlstrom-Vij 2013). We think there is an interesting discussion to be had over whether epistemic nudges (as a category) are epistemically paternalistic or not and, if they are, how this affects their moral permissibility. We recognise that there is some interference with a person's freedom to conduct their inquiries in the way they see fit, as critics worry about, in the epistemic nudges we've outlined. What is less clear is that they are motivated or justified by the aim of making those interfered with epistemically better off. In the examples given above, some sort of epistemic shift might occur as a result of the nudge, but this need not make the person epistemically better off in any real sense. The nudges are performed for the sake of harnessing additional popular support for socially just policies. If they happen to make someone epistemically better off, in terms of holding more true beliefs (about what justice requires) for instance, this is a happy by-product. This diffuses, to some extent at least, the worry about epistemic paternalism.

Conclusion

After offering a partial philosophical explanation of why crises can induce rational optimism, based in the epistemic function that crises can play, we've discussed some ways in which individual citizens might seek to persuade others of the lessons of the COVID-19 crisis. We've focused our attention on a range of salience-raising measures and have argued that direct attempts to change people's minds, despite being uncontroversial ethically speaking, need to negotiate the empirical worry raised by backfire effects. Indirect measures like epistemic nudging, then, may offer a more effective way for private citizens to help certain people see the various insights that crises can make salient. We've diffused ethical concerns with epistemic nudges, but a practical worry remains.

In short, one might still reasonably question their ultimate value: how can nudging a few other people towards the light really make much of a difference; particularly if fundamental institutional change is required? We don't wish to overemphasise what we think epistemic nudges can do. But, at least in democratic regimes, we don't think that their value should be underestimated either. In particular, even reaching a relatively small proportion of people through epistemic nudges might prove to be significant in reaching tipping-point thresholds for supporting socially just policies. In this way, it is possible that epistemic nudges might serve as one means to securing the fundamental institutional changes that are required for bringing about a more just society.[10]

Suggestions for further reading

- If you haven't read it yet, Arundhati Roy's short essay 'The pandemic is a portal' (in her *Azadi: Freedom. Fascism. Fiction.* and also published in *The Financial Times* on 4 April 2020) is well worth reading.

- For more on backfire effects and the possibility that certain kinds of nudges might offer an option for increasing responsiveness to genuine evidence, see Neil Levy's short article in *Journal of Medical Ethics* (43: 495–500) entitled 'Nudges in a post-truth world'.

- If you're interested to learn more about the idea of transformative experiences, then you can read L.A. Paul's book *Transformative Experience* (Oxford: Oxford University Press, 2014).

Notes

1. Which, in countries like the United States, often means losing medical insurance too.

2. For example, in 1863 President Abraham Lincoln decided to suspend the right of habeas corpus in response to the American Civil War.

3. For discussion of these questions, see Keeler (1993), Birkland (2006), Klein (2007) and Boin, 't Hart and McConnell. (2009).

4. It is possible that updating her worldview in this way may be productive of other changes in Zoe's social outlook more generally, for example by highlighting tensions with other views she holds; but it need not be in order to count as an instance of the phenomenon we're interested in here.

5. See https://www.buildbackbetteruk.org/start-organising and a video that seeks to get across the main points of the campaign via an analogy, which revolves around the question: 'What would you do if your house fell down?' (https://vimeo.com/426904398).

6. This definition captures the spirit of Richard Thaler and Cass Sunstein's original definition in *Nudge* (2009), while shedding certain aspects of their characterisation which are not essential to the practice of nudging. For example, Thaler and Sunstein conceive of nudges as a public policy intervention addressed to a general population and undertaken by policymakers as 'choice architects'; epistemic nudges, however, need not have any of these features and so can be used by anyone at the level of individual interaction (Smith 2021).

7. The insight at the heart of the technique, though, is not a recent one. In 1669, Blaise Pascal wrote in his *Pensées*: 'It is necessary to have regard to the person whom we wish to persuade ... what principles he acknowledges ... and then observe in the thing in question what affinity it has with the acknowledges principles' (cited in Feinberg and Willer 2019).

8. See: https://www.gov.uk/guidance/covid-summer-food-fund.

9. What is particularly important about this example is that Rashford is a representative of a group of marginalised knowers. Leonie Smith and Alfred Archer suggest that 'it is likely that hearing such stories *from* privileged speakers

without input from the epistemically marginalised themselves may further epistemically objectify marginalised knowers as things to be talked about rather than to' (2020: 792).

10. We thank Katharina Bauer, Aveek Bhattacharya, Anca Gheaus, Julia Hermann, Leonie Smith and Adam Swift, as well as audiences at the University of Stirling's departmental philosophy seminar and Modern Research Group for helpful discussion of the ideas in this chapter.

Bibliography

Ahlstrom-Vij, C. (2013), *Epistemic Paternalism: A Defence*, Basingstoke: Palgrave Macmillan.

Birkland, T.A. (2006), *Lessons of Disaster: Policy Change After Catastrophic Events*, Washington DC: Georgetown University Press.

Blumenthal-Barby, J.S. and H. Burroughs (2012), 'Seeking better health care outcomes: the ethics of using the "nudge"', *The American Journal of Bioethics*, 12 (2): 1–10.

Boin, A., P. 't Hart and A. McConnell (2009), 'Crisis exploitation: political and policy impacts of framing contests', *Journal of European Public Policy*, 16 (1): 81–106.

Brownlee, K. (2012), *Conscience and Conviction: The Case for Civil Disobedience*, Oxford: Oxford University Press.

Feinberg, M. and R. Willer (2019), 'Moral reframing: a technique for effective and persuasive communication across political divides', *Social and Personality Psychology Compass*, 13 (12): e12501.

Keeler, J.T.S. (1993), 'Opening the window for reform: mandates, crises, and extraordinary policy-making', *Comparative Political Studies*, 25 (1): 433–86.

Klein, N. (2007), *The Shock Doctrine: The Rise of Disaster Capitalism*, London: Penguin.

Levy, N. (2017), 'Nudges in a post-truth world', *Journal of Medical Ethics*, 43: 495–500.

McKenna, R. (2020), 'Persuasion and epistemic paternalism', in G. Axtell and A. Bernal (eds), *Epistemic Paternalism: Conceptions, Justifications, and Implications*, London: Rowman & Littlefield.

Niker, F. (2018), 'Policy-led virtue-cultivation: can we nudge citizens towards developing virtues?' in T. Harrison and D. Walker (eds), *The Theory and Practice of Virtue Education*, London: Routledge: 153–67.

Niker, F., G. Felsen, S.K. Nagel et al. (forthcoming), 'Autonomy, evidence-responsiveness, and the ethics of influence', in M. Blitz and C. Bublitz (eds), *Neuroscience and the Future of Freedom of Thought*, London: Palgrave Macmillan.

Noggle, R. (2018), 'Manipulation, salience, and nudges', *Bioethics*, 32: 164–70.

Nyhan, B. and J. Reifler (2010), 'When corrections fail: the persistence of political misperceptions', *Political Behavior*, 32: 303–30.

Nyhan, B. and J. Reifler (2015), 'Does correcting myths about the flu vaccine work? An experimental evaluation of the effects of corrective information', *Vaccine*, 33: 459–64.

Paul, L.A. (2014), *Transformative Experience*, Oxford: Oxford University Press.

Peter, C. and T. Koch (2016), 'When debunking scientific myths fails (and when it does not): the backfire effect in the context of journalistic coverage and immediate judgments as prevention strategy', *Science Communication*, 38: 3–25.

Roy, A. (2020), 'The pandemic is a portal', in A. Roy, *Azadi: Freedom. Fascism. Fiction.*, London: Penguin: 203–14.

Smith, Leonie (2021), 'Epistemic exclusion and epistemic self-defence: collective and individual responsibilities, rights and harm', PhD dissertation, University of Manchester.

Smith, L. and A. Archer (2020), 'Epistemic injustice and the attention economy', *Ethical Theory and Moral Practice*, 23: 777–95.

Smith, Zadie (2020), 'The American exception', in Z. Smith, *Imitations: Six Essays*, London: Penguin: 11–16.

Thaler, R. and C. Sunstein (2009), *Nudge: Improving Decisions about Health, Wealth and Happiness*, London: Penguin.

Williams, B. (2010), 'Making sense of humanity', in B. Williams, *Making Sense of Humanity: And Other Philosophical Papers 1982–1993*, Cambridge: Cambridge University Press: 79–89.

CHAPTER 18
LIVING THROUGH THE PANDEMIC: AN EXPERIMENT IN EGALITARIAN LIVING FOR THE MIDDLE CLASSES?
Anca Gheaus

Introduction

A philosopher once famously asked, 'If you're an egalitarian, how come you're so rich?' (Cohen 1989). The honest answer – at least if coming from someone genuinely committed to living in an equal society – is often: 'Because my will is too weak to divest myself of unfair privilege.' There is a motivational gap, for many of us, between what we think justice would require of us and what we are able to make ourselves do: most notably, what we are able to give up in terms of personal comfort, resources, and ultimately flourishing, in order to make possible a more just world. Just as we are struggling with the crisis, one that has worsened many kinds of inequalities, some of us also have had – by force – the opportunity to experience lifestyles that are much closer to what our lives would look like if we lived in a better world. I will explain this interesting aspect of the middle-class experience during the crisis, and speculate on the ways in which it might help with closing the motivational gap. I contend that the experiment in living that has been imposed on people around the world by the lockdowns may contain a valuable lesson: it can help the more privileged amongst us to imagine everyday life in an egalitarian society.

For better and for worse, well-off people have spent several months leading much quieter and less consumption-driven lives than we used to before the pandemic, lives in which personal relations have unavoidably taken a more central stage. I outline a few thoughts about the ways in which life during the COVID-19 pandemic could, for some of us, be like time-travelling to a possible just world in the future. I don't know whether such lessons will ultimately prove at all effective for transitioning to such a world. Yet, if better futures need to be imagined before being enacted, these lessons may at least increase the chances of improving the world.

The motivational gap

Like many other philosophers, I assume that a just society would be a lot more egalitarian than ours.[1] In a nutshell, it would provide everybody with the same opportunities to lead flourishing lives (see e.g. Rawls 2001). Outcomes would be more equal, with inequalities usually only tolerated if they benefit everybody. In addition, some inequality of outcomes would be permitted if it reflected certain individual preferences: for instance, some might wish to work shorter hours and earn less money. Work would be rewarded in proportion to how burdensome it is. In this kind of world people would relate to each other as equals – they would all have an equal voice, enjoy the same basic social respect, and nobody would be marginalised, stigmatised or oppressed (Young 1990). Children's rights would be protected (Brighouse and Swift 2014; Clayton 2006). Individuals and states alike would recognise that care is crucial for all of us at some stages of our lives, and institutions would provide it as a matter of justice (Kittay 1999). Thus, care-givers would get due support, and people would be taught early in life relationship skills, including the art of negotiating personal and public conflicts peacefully (Lynch, Baker and Lyons 2009; Gheaus 2018; Brownlee 2020). Not least, each generation would give the same weight to the interests of people that are still to come as it gives to its contemporaries (Gosseries and Meyer 2009).

This kind of world cannot come about if well-off people continue to live in the ways they did before the pandemic. To have a more equal society, the middle classes (and, of course, the very rich!) need to change our lifestyles significantly. Indeed, this is the reason why supporters and critics of egalitarianism alike worry that there is a grave inconsistency – maybe even hypocrisy – in endorsing egalitarian values without changing the way we live (see Cohen 1989 for an entertaining explanation of this). Such change is difficult, for several reasons, not all of which have to do with the motivational gap; for instance, many of us may fail to appreciate how bad the *status quo* is.[2] But most significant is the inability to make the necessary changes to our lifestyles. First, we find it hard to imagine what it would mean to live differently – how hard (or easy) that would prove to be; without this kind of understanding we may overestimate the hardship involved, and so be too scared to even try. Second, we are creatures of habit, which means that it is difficult for us to change routines, even if we thought that new routines would be morally better and sustainable, once acquired. Finally, we don't believe that those around us, the people with whom we have social relations, could also possibly make the same changes to a sufficient extent (Macleod 2019 explores most of these reasons). Without collective change, only very marginal improvements are possible, and most of us may feel that significant individual sacrifices in lifestyle are overly demanding for such minimal gains.

But now some of the unchosen hardships that the current crisis has imposed on middle classes worldwide can help overcome these hurdles. Those who might have been oblivious to the injustices of the world had yet another demonstration of the arbitrary inequalities in privilege that allowed the luckiest to shelter from the worst without losing jobs or livelihoods while others were left with no choice but to continue to work, and risk their and their loved ones' health. The sudden shock of the COVID-19 crisis has enlivened the imagination by presenting us with a new and unexpected daily reality. We have had a first-hand taste of a life with less consumption which, as I shall soon explain, has some advantages for individual flourishing alongside the obvious downsides. Most of all, it is now perhaps easier to imagine as feasible – that is, as involving bearable burdens – some of the changes that would be required to create and maintain egalitarianism. For some of us the shock has also dislocated our habits, at least temporarily. Finally, this has been a collective experience. Politicians told us that we have all been 'in this together', and to some extent this is true (although the differentials in privilege also mean that we haven't at all been in it together when it comes to sharing most of the costs!). In the best-case scenario, the shared nature of the experience should be a catalyst of collective action.

A dystopian lesson

Before elaborating on how the experience of recent months can serve as a model for life in a just world, a few words about experiences from which we can learn what we *don't* want our society to be. First, the central slogan of the lockdown has been 'social distancing', and trying to comply with it takes a great toll on most people's emotional well-being and sometimes on their mental health. Some, seeing the dangers early on, tried to correct the slogan to merely require *physical* distancing, stressing the importance of reaching out to each other (Aminnejad and Alikhani 2020). They knew how bad loneliness can be for people – so bad that a just society would be one of egalitarian sociability and inclusion, not of social isolation. Increasingly, philosophers argue that part of what justice requires is to give everybody the education necessary for, and plenty of occasions to form and cultivate, good personal relationships (Brighouse and Swift 2014; Gheaus 2018). The social disconnection endured by many over the pandemic has hopefully made evident the unfair hardship suffered by those regularly condemned to loneliness. These groups include elderly people who lack mobility and younger ones who never had the opportunity to acquire social skills. Unfortunately, loneliness hasn't been a rare occurrence in recent decades; instead, scholars talk about an 'epidemic' of loneliness, causing long-term and deep misery to people from all walks of life (Brownlee 2020). Now more of us have a better sense of how it must feel, which may lead to us having more empathy at the interpersonal level and taking loneliness more seriously at the level of policy.

Second, isolation has revealed just how much we rely on day-care centres, kindergartens, schools and after-school clubs for bringing up children. It also revealed the value of having many adults and institutions contribute to the rearing of each child. Sharing child-rearing responsibilities is good not merely for the convenience of the adults but, first and foremost, for the safety and well-being of children. Put in terms of rights, children have a right to access multiple sources of care. This concern has recently drawn attention to the reasons we always had to oppose, for instance, home schooling (O'Donnell 2020). Urgent public health risks probably meant that children's (and their families' and teachers') well-being required isolation at home, with the unintended consequence of *de facto* monopoly of parental power over children. And, sadly, it has been reported that the power has already been abused (Grant 2020). But a just society would be one of more communal child-rearing (Gheaus 2020), not of home schooling and the seclusion of children. Mandated social distancing and the quarantining of children in their (usually nuclear) families are, possibly, the impositions that hit middle-class people the hardest. In these respects, the world since March 2020 has been dystopian.

Blueprint for a utopia

Nonetheless, other difficulties that we have had to accept overnight might model what it would be like to live in an egalitarian world. First, for a long stretch of time many people had to forgo paid domestic services and had to do their own housekeeping, in order to minimise social contact. In addition, and for the same reason, parents had no choice but to spend significantly more hours minding and educating their children, who could not attend schools *in situ*. In a world in which everybody earned more or less the same income, it would make more economic sense to do one's own laundry, cleaning and so on, and there would be a lot less reliance on nannies. If these services were paid as well as other types of work, there would be no financial gain to be had by paying others to do one's household chores in order for one to be free to work longer outside one's home. Families, then, would be unlikely to outsource homemaking and childminding to anywhere near the levels that were common before the COVID-19 crisis. Indeed, in this respect home economics and family-making would look more like Scandinavian societies in the 1970s, at the height of their egalitarianism, than the vastly unequal societies in which the rich employ the poor to clean their homes, cook their meals and take charge of the repetitive tasks involved in bringing up their children. The lockdowns made it dangerous to rely on others' domestic help; in an egalitarian world it would be extraordinarily expensive to do so, since there wouldn't be anybody forced to perform this kind of labour for modest pay – let alone for a pittance, as is usually the case today.

Next, and related, we have been seeing a steep curbing of consumption levels with respect to a wide range of goods.[3] In general, people living in an egalitarian society would not be able to consume anything close to what the well-off were doing before COVID-19: everybody would have roughly the same economic resources, which means that today's well-off would command much less purchasing power than they currently do. In particular, travel, and especially flying, would be far less common. This is not only because middle-class incomes would fall, but also because taxes on fuel would reflect the full environmental cost of pollution and resource depletion. We would also shop and throw away less for the same reasons. We would have to learn – or perhaps relearn – how to enjoy a more local and non-consumerist life. These sacrifices in consumption would serve intra-generational justice aims, because global wealth redistribution couldn't happen without lowering the existing consumption standards of the middle classes. And, even more obviously, they would be necessary in order to achieve ecological sustainability for the sake of intergenerational justice.

Further, if the world was just, care work would be properly rewarded (Okin 1989). Today, those who care for others, the vast majority of whom are women, are some of the worst-off members of our societies: they are at high risk of poverty, especially in old age, often economically dependent on abusive spouses and also lacking in power and status since care work is vastly devalued. Care work cannot be valued properly unless most of us come to appreciate the skills that it requires to be done well, as well as its hardships. (Perhaps many men are already aware of the hardships, which explains why they are so keen to avoid care work. However, if one takes at face value homemakers' complaints, many other people casually assume that stay-at-home carers 'don't work'.) In addition, as generations of feminists have explained, this kind of work remains socially devalued partly because it is part of the unseen 'women's work'. The most promising way to elevate its status would be to have men doing a larger share of it (Gornick and Meyers 2003), in order both to appreciate its true value and difficulty and to break the connection between gender and caregiving. Over the past few months, men in heterosexual couples who struggled to work from home couldn't escape the tough realities of homemaking and child-rearing; they didn't have anywhere else to go! Alas, this doesn't necessarily mean that they were doing more of these tasks themselves; but, at the very least, they could not fail to notice the essential role of care work in enabling everything else to function.

Next, people have presumably experienced an increased awareness of what is going on around the world, and in particular the suffering and death of fellow human beings. Many of us experienced a heightened interest in political debate and a renewed recognition of how each individual's well-being depends on everybody else's. Awareness of others' needs and our interdependencies are themselves necessary – though, unfortunately, not sufficient – for the kind of solidarity needed to sustain any egalitarian ethos. Such awareness may be a motivational key to bringing about collective action that is itself a precondition of much-needed change.

The silver linings

The egalitarian-minded can therefore see the coronavirus lockdowns as a rehearsal for experiencing some aspects of everyday life in a more just society: local lives and, more generally, lower consumption, with fairly distributed hands-on responsibility for one's household and for those family members who need support. The lockdowns have also given us warnings about the importance of preventing loneliness and ensuring that all children have some non-parental sources of care. But these months were not all about practising the *restrictions* that we would have to accept for the sake of justice;

they have also gifted us with an opportunity to appreciate its attractions. This was our chance to experience, first hand, the pleasures of a quieter and less polluted world. And indeed, several cities started to transform themselves in ways that can preserve some of these gains, using the lockdown to finally enlarge their pedestrian areas and cycle routes, in attempts to restrict pollution after the pandemic. The lucky among us enjoyed the luxury of additional time to pay more attention to other people. Indeed, perhaps one of the most important benefits of living in an egalitarian world is that everybody would have access to the preconditions of enjoying personal relationships and, in particular, relationships with one's children (Brighouse and Swift 2014). These preconditions range from mundane practices, such as common meals, to the more reflective ones, such as an appreciation of our need of each other. On the same note, the lockdowns should have helped us to prepare for future peaceful long-term cohabitation. In years to come, it will be so much easier to guide our children in their choice of a spouse with just one question: 'Would you be all right locked down in a quarantine with that person?'

Conclusion

There are two keys in which a reader may be inclined to interpret the considerations put forward in this chapter. One, the more optimistic, suggests that during lockdowns some of us may have learned that, all things considered, life in an egalitarian society could be better not only morally but also prudentially. If more time for oneself and one's near and dear, less pollution and a gentler pace of life are a greater gain than fewer opportunities to travel and consume are a loss, perhaps it would be more rational to continue lockdown lifestyles. I would not go that far. Such comparisons of value are notoriously difficult to make: who can tell whether relationships or the unencumbered exploration of the world – for instance – is more important to human flourishing; other, perhaps, than each individual for oneself? (And we will differ greatly in our assessments.) But a more modest claim is very plausible: I speculate that the experience of the lockdown has proved, to some of us, that a more local life, conducted with more modest means, could be bearable and, in some ways, even sweet. At least sufficiently so to make it possible for us to summon the will to change, and thus to allow an escape from the charge with which I started: 'If you are an egalitarian, how come you're so rich?'[4]

Suggestions for further reading

- Cohen, G.A. (1989), *If You're an Egalitarian How Come You're So Rich?*, Oxford: Oxford University Press.
- Gheaus, A. (2020), 'Child-rearing with minimal domination: a republican account', *Political Studies*, Online First, doi: 10.1177/0032321720906768.
- Lynch, K., J. Baker and M. Lyons (2009), *Affective Equality: Love, Care and Injustice*, London: Palgrave Macmillan.

Notes

1. Even egalitarian philosophers disagree about the exact details of a just society; the picture that I sketch here glosses over such disagreements. Today's most prominent version of egalitarianism is to be found in the work of John Rawls.

2. Other chapters in this volume engage closely with this issue. See e.g. chapters by Matthew Adams and Fay Niker, and by Adam Swift.

3. This was particularly true of early pandemic days, before online consumption has soared, as Julia Hermann has correctly remarked to me.

4. I am grateful to Matthew Adams, Katharina Bauer, Aveek Bhattacharya, Julia Hermann, Fay Niker and Adam Swift for useful feedback on this essay.

References

Aminnejad, R. and R. Alikhani (2020), 'Physical distancing or social distancing: that is the question', *Canadian Journal of Anesthesia*, 67: 1457–8.

Cohen, G.A. (1989), *If You're an Egalitarian How Come You're So Rich?*, Oxford: Oxford University Press.

Brighouse, H. and A. Swift (2014), *Family Values: The Ethics of Parent–Child Relationships*, Princeton: Princeton University Press.

Brownlee, K. (2020), *Being Sure of Each Other: An Essay on Social Rights and Freedoms*, Oxford: Oxford University Press.

Clayton, M. (2006), *Justice and Legitimacy in Upbringing*, Oxford: Oxford University Press.

Gheaus, A. (2018) 'Personal relationship goods', *Stanford Encyclopedia of Philosophy*. Available online: https://plato.stanford.edu/entries/personal-relationship-goods/ (accessed 9 November 2020).

Gheaus, A. (2020), 'Child-rearing with minimal domination: a republican account', *Political Studies*, Online First, doi: 10.1177/0032321720906768.

Gornick, J.C. and M.K. Meyers (2003), *Families That Work: Policies for Reconciling Parenthood and Employment*, New York: Russel Sage Foundation.

Gosseries, A. and L.H. Meyer (2009), *Intergenerational Justice*, Oxford: Oxford University Press.

Grant, H. (2020), '"Many girls have been cut": how global school closures left children at risk', *The Guardian*, 1 June, Available online: https://www.theguardian.com/global-development/2020/jun/01/many-girls-have-been-cut-how-coronavirus-global-school-closures-left-children-at-risk (accessed 9 November 2020).

Kittay, E. (1999), *Love's Labor: Essays on Women, Equality, and Dependency*, New York: Routledge.

Lynch, K., J. Baker, and M. Lyons (2009), *Affective Equality: Love, Care and Injustice*, London: Palgrave Macmillan.

Macleod, C. (2019), 'Diagnosing the "burdens" of the rich egalitarian: how capitalism nurtures pleonexia', paper delivered at workshop 'The Legacy of G.A. Cohen: Ten Years On', Centre for Moral and Political Philosophy, The Hebrew University of Jerusalem, 10 December.

O'Donnell, E. (2020), 'The risks of homeschooling', *Harvard Magazine*, May/June 2020. Available online: https://harvardmagazine.com/2020/05/right-now-risks-homeschooling (accessed 9 November 2020).

Okin, S.M. (1989), *Justice, Gender and the Family*, New York: Basic Books.

Rawls, J. (2001), *Justice as Fairness: A Restatement*, Cambridge, MA.: Harvard University Press.

Young, I. M. (1990), *Justice and the Politics of Difference*, Princeton: Princeton University Press.

CHAPTER 19

CORONAVIRUS AND CLIMATE CHANGE: WHAT CAN THE FORMER TEACH US ABOUT THE LATTER?

Julia Hermann, Katharina Bauer and Christian Baatz

Introduction

In an opinion piece for the *New York Times*, Meehan Crist calls the coronavirus pandemic 'an inflection point for that *other* global crisis, the slower one with even higher stakes, which remains the backdrop against which modernity now plays out' (Crist 2020). Looking at the current pandemic in relation to climate change doesn't just demonstrate the inadequacy of the human reaction to climate change. It also shows that measures fostering low-carbon societies are more feasible than is often assumed. There are important differences between the current pandemic and climate change, but there are also surprising similarities. And to make things a bit more complicated, the differences and the similarities are closely related. We identify some significant similarities and differences, and explain how they give us reasons for despair as well as for hope. We conclude by reflecting on what lessons can be learned from experiences of the current pandemic and by making three concrete suggestions for a more adequate response to the climate crisis.

Notable differences and surprising similarities

There are of course significant differences between the climate crisis and the COVID-19 crisis. The first relates to *speed and time frame*: the climate crisis has developed over centuries rather than years or months and will require mitigative action beyond 2100, given that man-made CO_2 can affect the earth's climate for thousands of years. In contrast, there is a reasonable chance that in the foreseeable future a vaccination will allow us to overcome most of the harms and risks connected to coronavirus and prevent a similar outbreak of this particular virus (SARS-CoV-2).[1]

The second difference relates to the *political response*: although the climate crisis has the higher stakes, it is the current pandemic that prompted drastic political measures, at least in most countries. A number of factors can explain the different reactions, some of which point us to further differences between the two crises. One reason why the pandemic has seen a stronger response, and the third difference we would like to mention, is the *real or perceived proximity of the threats* posed by COVID-19 as compared to climate change. We contend that threats related to the latter are often felt more distantly and deemed less relevant in the following ways:

First, for many citizens and decision-makers, especially in the Global North, climate change is *spatially remote*. It will affect others living elsewhere. This may be partly a misconception, but in general climate change hits the Global South much earlier and harder than the North and has a higher impact on poor and marginalised people, wherever they live (Field et al. 2015: 35–94). In contrast, most people face the risk of getting COVID-19 themselves and have close relatives or friends for whom an infection would be particularly dangerous. Second, climate change is *temporally remote* since serious impacts are projected for the future. A middle-aged Scandinavian has good reasons not to be terribly frightened about climate change, though this may not hold for, say, Southern European or sub-Saharan farmers. Still, climate change threats are much less imminent than a virus you could contract tomorrow. And even if climate change is close, its threats are often not fully appreciated. This is because, third, its risks are rather *abstract*. For example, heatwaves are usually not perceived as scary and lethal – though they can be – and linking any given heatwave to climate change requires complex attribution research (Hulme 2014).[2] In contrast, contracting a dangerous, flu-like illness is something most people can imagine and are frightened of. These three differences make global and intergenerational 'buck-passing' (Gardiner 2011: 160–4) much more tempting in the case of climate change than in that of the pandemic.

An explanation for why our response to climate change is so inadequate comes from the field of evolutionary moral psychology. Humans developed dispositions to react with strong emotions such as fear, outrage or shame to immediate events or threats, such as a member from another tribe attacking them with a stone. Since climate change is perceived as a distant and abstract threat, it does not trigger a strong emotional response (Hopster 2020: 208; see also Marshall 2014: 55–7). Relatedly, people hardly notice slow processes such as climate change and thus do not exhibit strong emotional reactions to them. Unlike the coronavirus crisis, the climate crisis lacks abruptness (see

Hopster 2020: 208; Marshall 2014: 48). This is probably the reason why, until recently, it was not perceived by the majority of people as a crisis in the way the pandemic immediately was. The term 'climate change', unlike 'climate crisis', suggests a slow, gradual process. However, as school strikes, Extinction Rebellion actions and similar movements across the world show, 'climate change *can* trigger a strong emotional response and *can* be regarded as an urgent crisis, even motivating millions of protesters to mass the streets' (Hopster 2020: 208). Likewise, developing countries are condemning international inaction on climate change with increasingly emotional accusations during climate negotiations.

So, despite obvious differences, there are also surprising similarities between the two crises – four of which we would like to highlight. The first concerns what Stephen Gardiner calls *skewed vulnerabilities* within the context of climate change (Gardiner 2006: 402). In essence, this is the idea that those who are most vulnerable to the effects of climate change are the countries and people who have emitted the least historically and whose emission levels continue to be relatively low. We can see a similar feature in the COVID-19 crisis: while the mobility of the world's middle- and upper-class people played an important role in spreading the virus around the world, the poor and marginalised are disproportionately affected everywhere. For them, social distancing is much more difficult (if not impossible), healthcare provision is much worse (or close to non-existent), and there is no safety net. A case in point are *favelas*, densely populated informal settlements of the poor, in Brazil (Watson 2020).

Second, in both cases, *early warnings were ignored, dismissed or even suppressed*. In 2012, a report issued by the German government concluded that the healthcare system could easily be overwhelmed by a viral pandemic (Deutscher Bundestag 2013). However, the study's authors claim that political decision-makers were not really interested in their results and were unwilling to take action (Gerster 2020). Likewise, warnings at the beginning of the COVID-19 outbreak were not taken seriously, were dismissed or were suppressed (e.g. in China, Iran, Europe, the USA, Brazil and Turkey). Powerful politicians such as Donald Trump and Jair Bolsonaro trivialised the virus and ridiculed those who articulated the warnings. Of course, ignorance, dismissal and suppression endured much longer in the case of the climate crisis than in the case of the current pandemic (Mulvey and Shulman 2015).

The third similarity is the *time lag* between cause (infections/emissions) and effect (serious illness/climatic impacts). This time lag can in part explain why many governments implemented COVID-19 countermeasures reluctantly, only acting seriously when it was (almost) too late. Again, the scales are different: the temporal distance between cause and effect is much bigger in the case of climate change, but in both cases there is a time lag that is detrimental to an adequate response.

Fourth, reasonable response measures to climate change may, just like responses to COVID-19, turn out to be *less burdensome than originally thought*. The virologist Christian Drosten recently said that the general lockdown implemented by the German government in March 2020 (based on his advice, among others) was probably not required to sufficiently limit the spread of the virus. As in Japan, more specific measures might have proved similarly effective, such as wearing masks in all public places, limiting the number of participants at private festivities and more focused testing and quarantining to prevent transmission clusters (Drosten 2020). Hence, the more we learn about COVID-19, the more we can fine tune the initial blunt response. Perhaps, then, with more experience, COVID-19 countermeasures will be inconvenient rather than ruinous for most people. This would make them similar to climate policies. Although people (claim to) perceive, say, higher gas prices or vegetarian days in public canteens as a serious threat, these measures are merely inconvenient, requiring people to change their habits, rather than limiting their freedom unduly.[3]

Between hope and despair

Times of crisis are times of uncertainty and incalculable risk. They evoke fears and can lead to despair, but they also give reason to hope that people will learn from the crisis and come out stronger on the other side. Our assessment of both crises oscillates between hope and despair.

In the first instance, though the various lockdowns have led to lower emissions in the short run, coronavirus could turn out to be 'a disaster for the climate' in the long run (Crist 2020). As history shows, emissions tend to 'roar back', as was the case in the aftermath of the financial crisis in 2008 and the oil shocks of the 1970s (Barboza 2020). The virus could have several negative impacts on the climate: it could undermine the resolve of governments and industries to cut emissions (Barboza 2020); the expected global recession could hinder the shift to clean energy; and it is likely to slow international action as climate gatherings and summits are being postponed (Crist 2020). In Europe, some airline companies have pushed for a delay in emissions-cutting policies, given the financial losses they suffered due to public health measures. The Brazilian government even abused the COVID-19 crisis to permit the destruction of large areas of the rainforest (Novacic 2020). Last but not least, deep disagreement over the pandemic response may have increased polarisation in many societies. The more citizens distrust their government, scientists and other institutions, the more difficult it will be to implement far-reaching climate policies.

Yet there are also grounds for hope. Some governments clearly demonstrated their ability to solve problems, to protect citizens and quickly support businesses, hopefully reducing disenchantment with politics. And when people realised the threat posed by COVID-19, they often listened to experts instead of populists. Furthermore, the fact that some rather drastic changes in human behaviour are now taking place might make it easier to conceive of radical changes to resist climate change. 'Things that were supposed to be unstoppable stopped, and things that were supposed to be impossible ... have already happened' (Solnit 2020). We have experienced what it is like if business meetings and conferences take place online, and holidays are not spent far away (see Gheaus, this volume). More sustainable alternatives to the pre-pandemic Western way of life are taking shape. During lockdown people could notice an improvement in their natural environment (e.g. clearer canals in Venice, cleaner air in China and Italy, and so forth), which might motivate them to demand stronger efforts in moving towards low-pollution, low-carbon mobility systems, and to adapt their own lifestyle accordingly. 'Maybe', wonders Crist (2020), 'among the relatively wealthy, jumping on a plane for a weekend away or for a destination wedding will come to seem unthinkable.'

During the first months of the crisis, we witnessed a certain optimism. Many authors expressed the hope that the pandemic would bring about valuable changes: an increase in solidarity, greater awareness of the consequences of certain behaviours, such as frequent flying or daily commuting, greater appreciation of important but overlooked professions and so on. We were surprised how things that had been taken for granted or regarded as indisputable suddenly changed, and how quickly some rather radical and uncomfortable political decisions were taken. And we wanted to see this situation as *the* chance to get rid of the attitudes and forms of behaviour that sustain socio-economic and intergenerational injustices. In this spirit, in April 2020 the American writer and activist Rebeca Solnit described the times of the current crisis 'as akin to a spring thaw: it's as if the pack ice has broken up, the water starts flowing again and boats can move through places they could not during winter' (Solnit 2020). Breaking the ice of the *status quo* of negative behavioural patterns can allow for positive change. Maybe the coronavirus crisis, with its new spirit of change, solidarity and creative solutions, can teach us a lesson about hope.[4] Good examples are the Argentinian grassroots social movement Barrios de Pie, delivering fresh meals to quarantined seniors across the country, and 'commoning' initiatives in Naples, Italy, advocating the transfer of private goods into common goods to facilitate local self-government and aid initiatives (de Tullio and Lijster, forthcoming). Yet, even in such hopeful examples despair lurks as local communities and social networks have to fill the void of missing healthcare and a lack of interest and political leadership (Ortega and Orsini 2020). In regions where institutional support is insufficient it is not only trustworthy social initiatives that are taking over. And in some places, criminal organisations have jumped into the power vacuum, for example by imposing curfews on the residents of Brazilian *favelas* (Eisele 2020).

Furthermore, apart from hope and fear, anger and the ascription of guilt to the main polluters are strong and important motivating forces for climate activists – in particular in the Global South (Kleres and Wettergren 2017), and these emotions are also motivating movements that react to the structural injustices (in particular in health systems) that become painfully visible during the COVID-19 crisis. The reinforcement of such strong emotional motivations by the coincidence of the two crises could generate an increased sense of urgency, which may be a catalyst for change.

It is tempting to see the COVID-19 crisis as a historic moment – an opportunity to break with undesirable, environmentally harmful habits of consumption, unsustainable economies and structural injustices. We should not overestimate the likelihood of such positive outcomes, though. Despite the fact that many parts of the world are currently being hit by a second wave and the numbers of people infected are rapidly going up again, and although life can hardly be described as returning to 'normal', there is a high risk that the momentum will pass and our hopes will be disappointed. So far, promising initiatives and the awareness that we might be able and willing to change our lifestyles are just a good start. Furthermore, we should not be so occupied by our hope to change the world and use the crisis as an opportunity that we lose sight of the actual problems of those who directly suffer from the consequences of the pandemic.

The reactions to the pandemic show that change is not easy. Human beings are creatures of habit. As quickly as they came about, some of the positive impulses for change in reaction to the acuteness of the pandemic have faded again. This rather gives reason to despair about a positive learning curve for coping with the complex challenges of climate change, especially since they require much more far-reaching structural changes. When measures to control the virus were gradually loosened, most things went back to the pre-pandemic mode: planes started flying and traffic jams during rush hour became part of everyday life again. Still, at least a certain number of people and businesses are rethinking their behaviour. They learned to appreciate holidays in their home countries, realised that long-distance flights are inefficient and superfluous for short business trips, and discovered that working from home is more effective than expected.[5] Reducing traffic alone will contribute relatively little to decarbonisation. But fractures in habits and well-established business cultures might be an important step towards a deeper cultural change and breaking free from fossil-fuel-dependent structures.

Referring to the ways in which states are now trying to revive their economies, Crist (2020) claims that '[o]ur response to this health crisis will shape the climate crisis for decades to come'. If the strategies for leading countries out of economic recession are not developed with the climate crisis in mind, this will have disastrous consequences. Perhaps the coronavirus crisis has contributed, at least for a moment, to making us drastically aware of the possibility of a global catastrophic scenario that shows us the fragility of our habitual way of life – and of life as such. What can be done to prevent people from returning to normal, missing the opportunity provided by the pandemic? What can we do to use the motivational power of hope instead of falling back into despair and fatalism?

Conclusion

All things considered, we are cautiously optimistic that the things we have learned from the global pandemic can help us to better address the climate crisis. The answer to the question 'What can coronavirus teach us about climate change?' depends on when the question is asked. A few years from now, the lessons that we can draw from the pandemic will be different from those that we can draw now. It is admittedly still very early for the attempt to spell these out. Furthermore, our own perception of both crises is limited to a privileged Western perspective and does not cover the diversity of challenges within the two crises. However, given the high stakes and the portentous connection between the pandemic and the climate crisis, it seems worthwhile to sketch some potential lessons and concrete suggestions.

One lesson that could be learned from the experiences of the pandemic is how important it is to take scientific findings seriously and make transparent decisions based on both shared values and up-to-date, accurate information. Following this model was much more successful in protecting citizens from illness and death than a populist approach prioritising protecting business as usual. It seems worthwhile to try to motivate citizens and their representatives to follow this model also when it comes to climate change policymaking.

Another, related lesson could be that new, unfamiliar policies and the changes in habits, routines and cultures that these may require are less burdensome and easier to adapt to than previously thought. A green tax reform, shifting the tax burden from labour to (greenhouse gas-intensive) energy, will make some cherished activities less affordable but will also open up new avenues for both businesses and consumers. More expensive meat/dairy products and the introduction of veggie/vegan days might make people realise that climate-friendly food can be quite tasty as well. Reduced travel frees up time to relax or do other valued things. With the experience of modest COVID-19 countermeasures fresh in their minds, people might be less reluctant to accept such changes.

With regard to individual behaviour, at least for a particular privileged group with a certain lifestyle, it holds true that 'people all over the world are learning from the coronavirus pandemic that we cannot take our lifestyles for granted' (European Environmental Bureau 2020). And it turns out that changing this lifestyle is not necessarily a purely negative experience. Changes in individual behaviour patterns will not be very effective on their own, though. By way of 'behavioural contagion', such changes at the individual level would have to extend to the larger structures by which our lives are shaped. There is an endless debate about the relative roles of individuals and institutions in combating climate change. Is the influence of individuals insignificant, or do we tend to underestimate the relevance of individual emitters and the power of consumers (Fragnière 2016)? Combating global warming requires both: individual behaviour change and institutional change. The two are inseparably related, and while changes at the individual level could never be sufficient, they are necessary for changes at the institutional level (Schwenkenbecher 2014). However, the capitalist global economy depends on growth, including growth in consumption. Behavioural change towards a decrease in consumption would be at odds with this system. A rising awareness of the possibility of change at the individual level during the current crisis must be accompanied by the insight that this change can only become sustainable if it is combined with a reformed economic system. Hopes for economic change may be facilitated through the experience of the current crisis, varying from implementing rather modest reforms like the Green New Deal (e.g. EEB 2020) to degrowth visions (e.g. Kallis et al. 2018). There is no agreement on what kind of changes would be most reasonable, but in any case it is necessary to switch to consumption patterns involving lower and ultimately net-zero greenhouse gas emissions.

The coronavirus crisis is changing our perception of what is possible, both in a negative and in a positive sense. Politicians are willing to listen to scientific experts and impose drastic measures that limit personal freedom; citizens are willing to accept those measures and change their behaviour significantly. Now it's time to realise that climate change is an even greater threat, and to start responding to it appropriately. We want to conclude with three concrete suggestions for how the experience of the current COVID-19 crisis can be used to improve the human reaction to global warming.

One suggestion is to use the structures, the strength and creative potential of grassroots movements that were newly founded during the COVID-19 crisis or that have intensified their work during this period to achieve concrete sustainability goals at the local level, for example by enforcing structures of circular economy.[6]

Another suggestion is to develop possible future scenarios based upon the temporary changes in behaviour and perception that we have witnessed in the past months, and to encourage a public discussion of those scenarios.[7] Citizens and scientists should create such scenarios together, which should include concrete predictions and illustrations of economical and societal drawbacks of the climate crisis that will affect us all.[8]

Finally, arts-based and/or multisensorial approaches can allow for contextualising and condensing abstract topics, thereby providing a more comprehensive cognitive and intuitive understanding of complex phenomena (Heinrichs 2018). Arts projects can prompt emotional reactions to concrete effects of climate change (see e.g. Eliasson 2014). A problem with such projects is that they often do not reach a sufficiently large and diverse audience. Particular efforts should be made to expand the reach of relevant arts projects, for instance by providing the opportunity to experience art through social media, by keeping entrance fees for exhibitions low, or by exhibiting and performing art in central public places.

Suggestions for further reading

- Gardiner, S.M. (2011), *A Perfect Moral Storm: The Ethical Tragedy of Climate Change*, New York: Oxford University Press.

- Hopster, J. (2020), 'Shall we adapt? Evolutionary ethics and climate change', in J. Hermann, J. Hopster, W.F. Kalf and M. Klenk (eds), *Philosophy in the Age of Science: Inquiries into Philosophical Progress, Method and Societal Relevance*, London: Rowman & Littlefield: 195–213.

- Meyer, L.H. and M. de Araujo (2020), 'The COVID-19 pandemic and climate change: why have responses been so different?', *E-International Relations*, 20 April 2020.

- Solnit, R. (2016), *Hope in the Dark: Untold Histories, Wild Possibilities*, Edinburgh and London: Canongate.

- Thompson, A. (2010), 'Radical hope for living well in a warmer world', *Journal of Agricultural and Environmental Ethics*, 23 (34): 43–59.

Notes

1. But note that new threats from similar and other, so far unknown viruses might emerge.

2. However, see the weather attribution project (World Weather Attribution, n.d.), which tries to present the complexities of attribution research in an accessible manner.

3. For the poor, higher gas prices are a serious issue, but one that can be addressed within a greenhouse gas price scheme (Baranzini et al. 2017).

4. This could even be a lesson in radical hope in terms of the courage to imagine what has been unimaginable, and completely reinventing one's culture and lifestyle in view of devastation (Lear 2006; Thompson 2010). Radical hope can be an important force to motivate activism and creative initiatives.

5. At the time of writing it still remains to be seen what the effects of the second wave and the new series of local and national lockdowns will be.

6. See Blériot 2020; see also Borealis Group 2020. In April 2020 the city of Amsterdam launched the next step towards becoming the first circular city based on the 'Doughnut Model', explicitly arguing that this is not only a reaction to the climate crisis, but also a COVID-19 response (City of Amsterdam 2020).

7. A first step in this direction is the project 'Will the world never be the same?', where people all over the world were asked to write a 'post-corona letter', in which they describe what the post-corona world should look like, according to them (University of Twente 2020). Letters like the following could serve as inputs for the kinds of scenarios we have in mind: https://www.utwente.nl/en/bms/ehealth/research/story-lab/post-corona-letters/Letters/English/2050.pdf.

8. Here we are thinking of starting citizen science initiatives with the aim of giving citizens an active role in the creation and the discussion of such scenarios. Citizen science projects are becoming more and more common in a broad range of fields. They are valued for their empowering and democratising effects, among others. See e.g. Vayena and Tasioulas 2015; Wiggins and Wilbanks 2019.

References

Baranzini, A., J.C.J.M. van den Bergh, S. Carattini, et al. (2017), 'Carbon pricing in climate policy: seven reasons, complementary instruments, and political economy considerations', *Wiley Interdisciplinary Reviews: Climate Change*, 8 (4): e462.

Barboza, T. (2020), 'Coronavirus shutdowns are lowering greenhouse gas emissions; history shows they'll roar back', *Los Angeles Times*, 19 March.

Blériot, J. (2020), 'The Covid-19 recovery requires a resilient circular economy', Ellen MacArthur Foundation, 7 May. Available online: https://medium.com/circulatenews/the-covid-19-recovery-requires-a-resilient-circular-economy-e385a3690037 (accessed 26 October 2020).

Borealis Group (2020), 'A solution to build back better after the Covid-19: the circular economy'. Available online: https://www.borealisgroup.com/news/a-solution-to-build-back-better-after-the-covid-19-the-circular-economy (accessed 20 October 2020).

City of Amsterdam (2020), *Policy: Circular Economy*. Available online: https://www.amsterdam.nl/en/policy/sustainability/circular-economy/ (accessed 20 October 2020).

Crist, M. (2020), 'What the coronavirus means for climate change', *The New York Times*, 27 March.

Deutscher Bundestag (2013), *Bericht zur Risikoanalyse im Bevölkerungsschutz 2012*, Berlin: H. Heenemann.

Drosten, C. (2020), 'Zweite Corona-Welle: ein Plan für den Herbst', *Die Zeit*, 5 August. Available online: https://www.zeit.de/2020/33/corona-zweite-welle-eindaemmung-massnahmen-christian-drosten/komplettansicht (accessed 20 October 2020).

Eisele, I. (2020), 'Brazil's favelas forced to fight coronavirus alone', *DW*, 2 July. Available online: https://www.dw.com/en/brazils-favelas-forced-to-fight-coronavirus-alone/a-54031886 (accessed 20 October 2020).

Eliasson, O. (2014), *Ice Watch, 2014*. Available online: https://olafureliasson.net/archive/artwork/WEK109190/ice-watch (accessed 20 October 2020).

European Environmental Bureau (EEB) (2020), *Turning Fear Into Hope: Corona Crisis Measures to Help Build a Better Future*, Brussels: EEB. Available at: https://eeb.org/library/turning-fear-into-hope-corona-crisis-measures-to-help-build-a-better-future/ (accessed 31 August 2020).

Field, C.B., V.R. Barros, K.J. Mach et al. (eds) (2015), *Climate Change 2014: Impacts, Adaptation, and Vulnerability. Part A: Global and Sectoral Aspects. Working*

Group II Contribution to the IPCC Fifth Assessment Report, Cambridge and New York: Cambridge University Press.

Fragnière, A. (2016), 'Climate change and individual duties', *Wiley Interdisciplinary Reviews: Climate Change*, 7 (6): 798–814.

Gardiner, S.M. (2006), 'A perfect moral storm: climate change, intergenerational ethics and the problem of moral corruption', *Environmental Values*, 15 (3): 397–413.

Gardiner, S.M. (2011), *A Perfect Moral Storm: The Ethical Tragedy of Climate Change*, New York: Oxford University Press.

Gerster, L. (2020), 'Der Bericht, den keiner las', *Frankfurter Allgemeine Zeitung*, 5 April. Available online: https://www.faz.net/aktuell/politik/inland/virus-pandemie-szenario-keiner-las-den-bericht-von-2012-16712045.html (accessed 23 October 2020).

Heinrichs, H. (2018), 'Sustainability science with Ozzy Osbourne, Julia Roberts and Ai Weiwei: the potential of arts-based research for sustainable development', *GAIA – Ecological Perspectives for Science and Society*, 27 (1): 132–7.

Hopster, J. (2020), 'Shall we adapt? Evolutionary ethics and climate change', in J. Hermann, J. Hopster, W.F. Kalf et al. (eds), *Philosophy in the Age of Science: Inquiries into Philosophical Progress, Method and Societal Relevance*, London and New York: Rowman & Littlefield: 195–213.

Hulme, M. (2014), 'Attributing weather extremes to "climate change": a review', *Progress in Physical Geography: Earth and Environment*, 38 (4): 499–511.

Kallis, G., V.S. Kostakis, B. Lange et al. (2018), 'Research on degrowth', *Annual Review of Environment and Resources*, 43 (1): 291–316.

Kleres, J. and A. Wettergren (2017), 'Fear, hope, anger, and guilt in climate activism', *Social Movement Studies*, 16(5): 507–19.

Lear, J. (2006), *Radical Hope: Ethics in the Face of Cultural Devastation*, Cambridge, MA and London: Harvard University Press.

Marshall, G. (2014), *Don't Even Think About It: Why Our Brains are Wired to Ignore Climate Change*, London: Bloomsbury Academic.

Mulvey, K. and S. Shulman (2015), *The Climate Deception Dossiers: Internal Fossil Fuel Industry Memos Reveal Decades of Corporate Disinformation*, Cambridge, MA: Union of Concerned Scientists. Available online: https://www.ucsusa.org/resources/climate-deception-dossiers (accessed 26 October 2020).

Novacic, I. (2020), 'Coronavirus in Brazil is fueling another crisis: destruction of the Amazon rainforest', *CBS News*, 5 May. Available online: https://www.cbsnews.com/news/coronavirus-brazil-amazon-rainforest-destruction/ (accessed 20 October 2020).

Ortega, F. and M. Orsini (2020), 'Governing COVID-19 without government in Brazil: ignorance, neoliberal authoritarianism, and the collapse of public health leadership', *Global Public Health*, 15 (9): 1257–77.

Schwenkenbecher, A. (2014), 'Is there an obligation to reduce one's individual carbon footprint?', *Critical Review of International Social and Political Philosophy*, 17 (2): 168–88.

Solnit, R. (2020), '"The impossible has already happened": what coronavirus can teach us about hope', *The Guardian*, 7 April. Available online: https://www.

theguardian.com/world/2020/apr/07/what-coronavirus-can-teach-us-about-hope-rebecca-solnit (accessed 20 October 2020).

Thompson, A. (2010), 'Radical hope for living well in a warmer world', *Journal of Agricultural and Environmental Ethics*, 23 (34): 43–59.

de Tullio, M. F. and T. Lijster (forthcoming), 'Commoning against the coronacrisis', *Law, Culture, and the Humanities*.

University of Twente (2020), *Post-Corona Letters*. Available online: https://www.utwente.nl/en/bms/ehealth/research/story-lab/post-corona-letters/ (accessed 20 October 2020).

Vayena, E. and J. Tasioulas (2015), '"We the scientists": a human right to citizen science', *Philosophy & Technology*, 28: 479–85.

Watson, K. (2020), 'Coronavirus: Brazil's favela residents organise to stop the spread', *BBC News*, 2 April. Available online: https://www.bbc.com/news/world-latin-america-52137165 (accessed 26 October 2020)

Wiggins, A. and J. Wilbanks (2019), 'The rise of citizen science in health and biomedical research', *The American Journal of Bioethics*, 19 (8): 3–14.

World Weather Attribution (n.d.). Available online: https://www.worldweatherattribution.org/ (accessed: 26 October 2020).

CHAPTER 20
PANDEMIC AS POLITICAL THEORY
Adam Swift

COVID-19 as a kind of natural experiment

Political theorists sometimes use thought experiments. Some are abstract. Rawls's 'original position' represents people simply as free and equal; they are behind a veil of ignorance that denies them knowledge of a kind that might bias them in their choice of principles of justice to regulate society.[1] Others, like the (in)famous 'trolley problems', are specific. Would you switch the points on the runaway train if you knew that the result would be to save ten people but kill five? What about intentionally sacrificing just one very heavy person to stop the train altogether?[2] Some theorists don't like this kind of thing, but defenders claim that constructing imaginary scenarios is an effective way of revealing our intuitions and honing the principles that underlie, or should underlie, our judgements about real-world situations.[3]

The pandemic might have been a thought experiment (rather as it might have been a disaster movie). 'Imagine a new deadly virus has suddenly appeared in the world. It is highly infectious and can be carried without people knowing they've got it. It doesn't affect all people equally: how likely people are to get it, and how bad it is for them if they do, is affected by their age, sex, ethnicity, health status, economic situation ...' This is the kind of dramatic scenario that might be used to explore a wide range of normative considerations: how to balance the interests of young and old; how to weigh economic and health considerations; how to distribute risks between rich and poor; what limits on people's freedom of movement and association may justifiably be imposed on them to reduce risks to others; how to make morally responsible political decisions in conditions of urgency and uncertainty; and so on.

The pandemic is not, alas, a thought experiment. But we could think of it as a kind of natural experiment. That term is used in various ways (Titiunik 2020) but I mean by it simply something that just happens in the world but yields evidence that helps us test theories and increase our knowledge and understanding. It is an experiment without an experimenter. So conceived, we can ask what we have learned from the pandemic. Sometimes natural experiments generate genuinely new insights: new observations lead to new theories and new true beliefs about the world. I don't want to claim that the pandemic has taught us *nothing*. Many have been surprised by the extent to which citizens of liberal democracies have been willing to comply with serious restrictions on their freedom of movement and of association. Like those subject to more authoritarian regimes, they have shown themselves capable of the discipline needed to solve collection action problems, at least for a while, and at least in the face of a serious and widespread threat to life. But for all the unprecedented experiences and sense of changing possibilities that have undoubtedly been part of the story, most of what the pandemic has thrown up counts, for me, as confirmation of what many already knew: *we live in societies where people are subject to unjust laws made in unjust ways.* That hardly qualifies as new knowledge, so it is hard to conceive this as a genuinely epistemic gain. Rather, the pandemic has provided more vivid evidence of that claim. It has starkly revealed how bad things really are.

At school, chemistry lessons sometimes consisted of what we called 'experiments' but were really 'demonstrations': seeing chemicals react to produce a different-coloured compound wasn't exactly generating new knowledge but it did teach us something. I see the pandemic as 'demonstrating' some truths about the way we do politics. In laying bare the nature of politics – and its pathologies – we can hope that the pandemic will yield educative benefits. Whether people will learn the lessons is another matter, and whether they will in fact be motivated to act on them even if they do is different again. We know enough about the self-serving processes by which people form their beliefs, and about the challenges facing individuals who need to act collectively to pursue shared goals in situations where many of them do not feel personally at risk, to doubt that even clear evidence about how bad things are will prompt sustained attempts to make them better. Still, those lessons are worth setting out clearly.

Unjust decisions unjustly made

Politics is really quite simple. At least it is the way I propose to understand it, as concerned with the state and its laws. There are more expansive approaches – perhaps there is politics wherever there is power – but my narrow definition allows us to focus on some key points. The state is a coercive apparatus. It will resort to physical force to get people to do things: things they may not want to do, things they may think they shouldn't do, and things they may very well think they shouldn't have to do. It does this by making laws and requiring compliance with them. Disobey, and the state's agents – police, courts, prison warders – will try to make you. Politics, then, is essentially the process by which some people decide the rules and force others to follow them.[4]

From a normative perspective – concerned with moral issues about how human beings are permitted or required to treat one another – there are three big questions we can ask about all this. First, and most fundamentally, is this kind of coercion justifiable even in principle? Could it *ever* be permissible for some people to decide the rules and set up an apparatus to impose them on others? Though I think the pandemic could be used to argue against anarchism, I'm not going to make that case here; I'm simply going to assume that the answer is 'yes'. Second, there is the issue of *procedures*: assuming that a rule-making, compliance-enforcing institution could in principle be justified, how should the rules be made? Which ways of deciding what people should be forced to do are, or would be, just or legitimate (see Cruft, this volume)? Third, there is the matter of *content*: bracketing the issue of who should get to choose the rules, what rules should they choose? Which coercively imposed arrangements give people justice – that is, distribute benefits and burdens justly between them – while leaving them free to do those things they should be free to do?

In my view the pandemic has starkly exposed injustice in both the content of the political decisions with which we are expected to comply and the procedures by which those decisions are taken. Unlike the innocent defendant mistakenly convicted after a fair trial, those on the wrong end of unjust policies are wronged twice over. Here I'm going to focus only on matters of content. To address procedures would involve me in discussion of all sorts of defects in the way we do politics, such as politicians' lack of honesty and openness in their communications with the citizens they are elected to serve, their refusal to accept responsibility when things go wrong, and their unwillingness to set aside self-interest, partisan gain and personal friendships when deciding policies, who to put in positions of authority, or which companies should be awarded contracts spending public money.[5] Merely listing those desiderata might suggest to readers the kind of thing that might be said about the injustice of our current political procedures, and about how they have been demonstrated by the COVID-19 crisis. But I don't have the space to do more than offer these hints in that direction and so I will confine myself to unjust decisions, rather than the unjust ways in which they are taken.

To claim that the pandemic has starkly revealed injustice is not to say that it has systematically increased its level. The symptoms of an illness can become clearer without any corresponding increase in its virulence. It has *always* been the case that some people make decisions that determine how well others' lives go – from how long they live to how much free time they have – and those decisions were *already* unjust, both procedurally and in terms of their content. My point is not that the pandemic has made things worse, though it has certainly exacerbated some existing inequalities (Blundell et al. 2020). It's rather that the pandemic has revealed how bad they are.

Highlighting and exacerbating injustice

'The pandemic' might be regarded as an entirely natural – perhaps biological – phenomenon. What we are talking about, on that view, is a new virus which reproduces itself in human beings, and impacts on their health, to differing extents depending on their age, sex, ethnicity, disability, prior health conditions and so on. Some people get it and others don't, some die from it while others experience no symptoms at all, and so on, because they differ physically or physiologically. One might think that while it's *unfair* that some people are more likely to suffer illness, or die early, than others – and that kind of unfairness has indeed always been with us – it's not *unjust*. Nobody has wronged anybody. It's simply the luck of the biological draw.

There are two problems with this way of thinking about things. First, even if the virus and its immediate impact on people's health were simply 'natural' phenomena, how we *respond* to them is clearly subject to normative evaluation – and is surely a matter of justice. We can simply leave victims of the virus to suffer the costs of their bad luck or we can seek to mitigate its impact on them. The obvious way to do the latter is by devoting collective resources to medical care, but there are many other ways in which policy decisions can affect the impact of people's health on their overall well-being, such as decisions about how much income support they get if they are too ill to work. Societies differ greatly both in how they choose to distribute medical care and in how well they provide in other ways for those who suffer ill health. People disagree a lot about what justice requires in these matters, but policies that respond to health conditions are social decisions that can surely be judged to be less or more just, even if the incidence of the conditions themselves can't.

But, and this is the second point, social arrangements – and hence policy decisions – also make a huge difference both to who gets and doesn't get the virus in the first place, and to how badly they suffer, strictly in health terms, if they do. It is common to talk about 'the social determinants of health', and medical sociologists have produced swathes of research documenting the extent to which people's health status itself is influenced by social factors (see e.g. Marmot and Wilkinson 2005). So when, two paragraphs back, I talked about the effect of the virus depending partly on people's 'prior health conditions', I was sneaking into my list of supposedly 'natural' causes a category that already reflects social arrangements. It is well known, for example, that being obese increases the risk of death if one contracts COVID-19 (Wadman 2020), but it is also widely agreed that, in Western countries, obesity is strongly associated with poverty (Bentley, Ormerod and Ruck 2018). Similarly, when I listed 'ethnicity' under the same heading, I was inviting the thought that that members of different ethnic groups might differ in relevant ways as a matter of basic physiology. In fact, however, any contribution of such factors to the explanation of inequalities in COVID-19 death rates, for example, is trivial. People with non-white skin are more likely to die than their white fellow citizens because they are more likely to be poor, more likely to suffer from other health problems (like obesity itself) that themselves have social influences, more likely to work in high-risk settings, more likely to live in overcrowded housing, and so on (Bentley 2020; Platt and Warwick 2020). The distribution of ethnic groups across income levels or health, employment and household statuses is not a fact about the natural world. Nor is the fact that people living in poverty are more likely to be obese. Nor, indeed, is the very fact that poverty exists at all in wealthy countries.

Social arrangements make a difference to how the virus affects people's health: how likely people are to get it and how badly their health will be affected if they do. And they make a difference to how people's health affects their overall well-being – how much the quality of their life as a whole depends on how ill or well they are. These arrangements result from policy decisions, and both social arrangements and the policy decisions that generate them can be evaluated as less or more just. In other contexts I would address carefully the question of how exactly to make such judgements – inequalities aren't necessarily unjust; policies that permit inequalities aren't either – but here I am simply going to assert that both the arrangements and the policies are unjust (see Swift 2019, parts 1 and 5 for a more cautious discussion). They do not properly weigh the interests of those affected by the policies, they do not distribute justly the benefits and burdens that result from the policies, they do not strike the right balance between holding individuals responsible for their lifestyle choices and sharing in a solidaristic way the risk of bad health outcomes. *All this was always true.* The social gradient in health was there all along. In the UK, indeed, recent policy decisions taken in the name of 'austerity' had caused that gradient to steepen well before the pandemic came along, just as – by lowering the 'safety net' – they had also increased the overall suffering of all those who get ill (Dorling 2018). What's new is only that the virus has upped the stakes and increased the effects of the injustice.

But this is only the beginning of the story. In narrowly treating 'the pandemic' as a virus that affects people's health, I've said nothing yet about the steps that states have taken to combat it. The policy responses to the pandemic – lockdowns, social distancing measures, income replacement schemes and so on – have affected everybody, whether or not they have suffered any ill effects of the virus itself. They have not, however, affected everybody equally. Those on low incomes have been harder hit than those on high incomes in *every* way: in addition to their higher health risk, they are more likely to lose their jobs, less likely to be able to work from home, more likely to be locked down in smaller spaces and so on. To be clear, those worse affected by the policy response are not always those worse affected by the virus itself. For example, men are more likely than women to get and die from the virus, but the interaction between the closure of schools and nurseries and traditional gender roles means that women have been harder hit than men by the measures taken to control it. Similarly, middle-aged and older people are more vulnerable to the pandemic, while it is the young who have suffered most from states' attempts to manage it. Like the impact of the virus itself, the overall effect of the policy response has been to highlight and exacerbate existing unjust inequalities.

The intergenerational issue is perhaps the most interesting (see Yarrow, this volume). Put simply, many of the elderly, whose interests in health and longevity are being protected by the sacrifices of younger people, have lived through better times than look likely to be enjoyed by those doing the sacrificing. The inequality between those born at different times in what we might think of as 'expected lifetime well-being' was already there before COVID-19 came along. Young people might – and did – already complain that their parents' and grandparents' generations had enjoyed levels of well-being that would no longer be available, while destroying the planet in the process. Their sense of injustice will presumably be all the greater when they realise that, while relatively unlikely to suffer badly from the virus itself, they will be the worst affected by the economic impact of the lockdown and social distancing, to say nothing of its effects on their mental health.

Compared to that complex case, the way in which the policy response to COVID-19 has exacerbated class inequalities – roughly, inequalities between those with different levels of education, in different kinds of job, and with different levels of income and wealth – is obvious and straightforward. While people with a university degree, and on higher incomes, have generally been able to stay at home, stay safe and get paid, the worse-paid, less-educated are much more likely to have risked their lives (if essential workers) or their livelihoods (if not). Longer-term, the shift to working, communicating and socialising online all favour the more educated, just as the move to e-learning works better for their children. Even without class-related inequalities in the quality and quantity of online teaching that schools provide, better-off parents are better able to help their children take advantage of it. Here, clearly, we see an exacerbation of unjust inequalities that have been there all along.

Education policy in England provides a great example of how the policy response to the pandemic has exposed pre-existing inequalities. The lockdown meant that students were not able to sit the exams that they would normally have taken at sixteen (GCSEs) and eighteen (A levels). Instead, teachers were required to say what grades their students would have got; indeed they were required to rank them individually. Going by teachers' predictions, however, would have led to considerable grade inflation, so the government's Office of Qualifications and Examinations Regulation (Ofqual) ran them through an algorithm designed to bring the (otherwise anomalous) 2020 results into line with earlier years. It did this by adjusting the predictions in light of schools' previous results, so that, in effect, the grades of students in 2020 would depend not on their own efforts and achievements alone, but on the results attained by those who had gone before them. As is well known, there is an association between the class composition of a school and its results – children from more advantaged backgrounds tend to do better – and it is widely accepted that the inequalities in exam results, and resulting inequalities in opportunities, are unjust. The algorithm, then, was building that very injustice into the grading system, and laying bare the extent to which children's opportunities are socially determined. As one commentator put it, Ofqual tested the algorithm for various biases 'and found that it was broadly speaking fair, in the sense that it accurately reflected the injustices inherent in the system' (Taylor 2020: 10).[6] In the end, there was such a public outcry that the government backed down and agreed to treat teachers' predictions as authoritative, though to my mind it was striking that many people objected more to the very idea that individuals' results should depend on others' than to the fact, nakedly exposed by the algorithm, that they reflect social circumstances.

Conclusion: business as usual

For all the shocking changes it has brought to our lives, the pandemic has plainly demonstrated, and in vivid terms, something about our political business as usual. It has brought to the surface injustice in the procedures by which political decisions are made: politicians 'spin', massage statistics and, increasingly, lie; they seek personal and partisan advantage rather than the common good; they give jobs and contracts to cronies. And – the topic I have focused on here – it has exposed injustice in the political decisions that are made by those procedures. As far as the latter are concerned, some specific effects may indeed have been starker than they were before – some unjust inequalities have been exacerbated, for example – but the underlying story is nothing new.

I said at the beginning that political theorists like to use thought experiments. Those experiments have their limitations, educationally speaking. After all, they happen only in the realm of thought, and are in any case read only by a tiny minority of the population. Certainly, there's little sign of their effectiveness in challenging injustice in the real world. Indeed, the dissemination of Rawls's 'original position' was famously accompanied by political changes in the wrong direction as far as his conception of social justice was concerned (Scheffler 1992). Faced with this evidence about the inefficacy of her usual method, one could imagine a crazed theorist deciding to get her message across by doing something people couldn't fail to notice: releasing a deadly virus into the world. That would not be an experiment, strictly speaking; more of a demonstration. Her aim would not be to generate new knowledge but simply to illustrate her claims, and to demonstrate them in terms so stark that they would be hard to deny. But just as she was about to put her plan into action, the world came along and supplied exactly the thing devised by her warped mind ...

One big difference between political theorists and normal people is that the former are quick, and indeed eager, to imagine ways of doing things different from our own, while the latter tend to be more fatalistic.[7] It's not that most people disagree that current arrangements are unjust, it's more that they don't see much point in going on about it, since they don't see things changing any time soon. All teachers of courses on social justice will be familiar with the 'But it's not going to happen, is it?' student response. By disrupting normality, while simultaneously laying bare the injustice which we might otherwise simply accept as given, might the pandemic do what all our books and articles couldn't? I'm not optimistic. After all, business as usual resumed soon after the near collapse of the global economy in 2008, with the policy response of 'austerity' unjustly imposing the greatest costs on those both least responsible for the crisis and least able to bear them. Still, viewed as a lesson in politics – as a wake-up call alerting us to how bad things have got and as evidence that big changes are possible – we can at least hope that it will be more effective, educationally speaking, than political theorists have been.[8]

Suggestions for further reading

- Dorling, D. (2018), *Peak Inequality: Britain's Ticking Time Bomb*, Bristol: Policy Press, especially section 6.

- Marmot, M. and R. Wilkinson (eds) (2005), *Social Determinants of Health*, Oxford: Oxford University Press.

- Swift, A. (2019) *Political Philosophy: A Beginners' Guide for Students and Politicians*, London: Polity Press.

Notes

1. The seminal text is Rawls (1971, revised edition 1999), but the easiest way into his theory as a whole is Rawls (2001).

2. The *locus classicus* is Thomson (1976).

3. For an accessible introduction to the issues, see Brownlee and Stemplowska (2017).

4. Here I draw on Swift (2019).

5. On the last of these, see Geoghegan (2020).

6. Even by that standard, the algorithm wasn't entirely fair. For good statistical reasons, the algorithm made smaller adjustments to teachers' predictions where class sizes were smaller. Since smaller classes are more common at private schools – itself part of the explanation of their better exam results – the results of children at private schools were less likely to be downgraded.

7. I owe this formulation of the thought to a conversation with Stuart White (somewhere around 2006).

8. I am grateful to Matthew Adams, Katharina Bauer, Anca Gheaus, Julia Hermann and the two editors of this volume for very helpful suggestions in the writing of this piece.

References

Bentley, G.R. (2020), 'Don't blame the BAME: ethnic and structural inequalities in susceptibilities to COVID-19', *American Journal of Human Biology*, 32 (5): e23478.

Bentley, R.A., P. Ormerod and D.J. Ruck (2018), 'Recent origin and evolution of obesity-income correlation across the United States', *Palgrave Communications*, 4 (146): https://doi.org/10.1057/s41599-018-0201-x.

Blundell, R., M. Costa Dias, R. Joyce et al. (2020), *COVID-19 and Inequalities.* London: The Institute for Fiscal Studies.

Brownlee, K. and Z. Stemplowska (2017), 'Thought experiments', in A. Blau (ed), *Methods in Analytical Political Theory*, Cambridge: Cambridge University Press.

Dorling, D. (2018), *Peak Inequality: Britain's Ticking Time Bomb*, Bristol: Policy Press.

Geoghegan, P. (2020), 'Cronyism and clientilism', *London Review of Books*, 42 (21), 5 November: 9–12. Available online: https://www.lrb.co.uk/the-paper/v42/n21/peter-geoghegan/cronyism-and-clientelism (accessed 9 November 2020).

Marmot, M. and R. Wilkinson (eds) (2005), *Social Determinants of Health*, Oxford: Oxford University Press.

Platt, L. and R. Warwick (2020), *Are Some Ethnic Groups More Vulnerable to COVID-19 Than Others?* London: The Institute for Fiscal Studies.

Rawls, J. (1971), *A Theory of Justice*, Oxford: Blackwell.

Rawls, J. (1999), *A Theory of Justice*, revised edition, Oxford: Oxford University Press.

Rawls, J. (2001), *Justice as Fairness: A Restatement*, Cambridge, M.A.: Harvard University Press.

Scheffler, S. (1992), 'Responsibility, reactive attitudes, and liberalism in philosophy and politics', *Philosophy and Public Affairs*, 21 (4): 299–323.

Swift, A. (2019) *Political Philosophy: A Beginners' Guide for Students and Politicians*, London: Polity Press.

Taylor, P. (2020), 'Short cuts: Ofqual and the algorithm', *London Review of Books*, 42 (17), 10 September. Available online: https://www.lrb.co.uk/the-paper/v42/n17/paul-taylor/short-cuts (accessed 9 November 2020).

Thomson, J.J. (1976), 'Killing, letting die, and the trolley problem', *The Monist*, 59 (2), 204–17.

Titiunik, R. (2020), 'Natural experiments'. Available online: https://arxiv.org/pdf/2002.00202.pdf (accessed 9 November 2020).

Wadman, M. (2020), 'Why obesity worsens COVID-19', *Science*, 369 (6509): 1280–1.

INDEX

Note: Figures are given in *italics* and tables in **bold**.

Index

Index

face coverings 205, 209
   see also mask-wearing
fairness 38
false content
   dissemination 169–70
   engaging with 173
familial coercion, voting 145–6
favelas 245, 248
Feinberg, Matthew 226
Ferguson, Neil 199
Ferracioli, Luara 128
financialisation, housing 78–9
Finland 63
flat-shares 124
food voucher campaign 227
Fourth Industrial Revolution 104n.2
Fragoso, Katarina Pitasse 5
framing, salience-raising measures 226–7
Fraser, Nancy 100
fraudulent voting 140, 143–4
free choice principle 138–41, 143
freedom of speech 167–76
Fuller, Lon L. 179
functionings 15, 19–21
   risks to 16–17, 19
future scenarios, behavioural change 251

Gardiner, Stephen 245
gas price rises 246, 252n.3
Gates, Bill 167
gatherings 155, 157
gender roles, injustices 262
gender vulnerabilities 49
genuine opportunities 15–17
Gerber, A. 141
Germany 245
global warming *see* climate change
Goldman, A.I. 194
'good' policies from 'bad' sources 118–19
'good reasons' condition, policy 111
Goodin, R. 98
Gordon, Linda 100
Gostin, L.O. 192
government-appointed experts 195
government measures
   housing adequacy 61, 63–4
   social connections 159
   social norms 130

government–state terminology 188n.4
grandstanding 206, 215n.3
grassroots movements 248, 251

habits 234–5, 248–50
Hacker, Jacob 87, 91
harms
   benefiting from 114–15, 117
   children's vulnerability 44–5, 48
   lockdown measures 130, 133n.1
   misinformation 167–8
   mitigating 193
   moralised baseline 120n.13
   relevant alternatives 116–17
   school closures 115–16
   state non-transparency 181
hate crime 168
hate speech 170, 171–2
health
   secure functioning 20–1
   social determinants 14–15, 261–2
health insurance 19
health risks
   election attendance 143
   intergenerational justice 72
Herington, J. 192–3
Hispanic Americans 19
Hollstein, Tanja 147
home working 161
homelessness 55, 59–60, 63, 65n.2, 222
Honig, Bonnie 159
hope
   climate change and 246–9
   grounds for 220–3
   in renewal 219
hospital resources 29–30, 34
household model 126–7
households, living alone 123–35
houseshares 124, 131
housing
   as corrosive disadvantage 21
   financialisation 78–9
housing adequacy 55–67
   criteria 57
   definition 56
   young people 74
Howard, Jeffrey 193, 206
human rights 56–7, 125
Hume, David 119n.3, 120n.6, 194

Index

Index